ATTINGHAM
THE FIRST
FORTY YEARS
1952 to 1991

Attingham Park, Shropshire, by George Steuart, 1783–5, home of The
Attingham Summer School, 1952–1983.

GEOFFREY BEARD

ATTINGHAM

THE FIRST
FORTY YEARS
1952 to 1991

THE ATTINGHAM TRUST
FOR THE STUDY OF
THE COUNTRY HOUSE IN BRITAIN
1991

This study is published with the
assistance of a bequest from the Estate of
MARY SEILER
Attingham 1960

and support from
JOHN LEWIS
Attingham 1981

First published 1991
© 1991 The Attingham Trust
for the Study of the Country House in Britain
and Geoffrey Beard

Filmset in Palatino
10½ on 12 point
Printed by
W. S. Maney & Son Ltd
Hudson Road, Leeds

CONTENTS

Foreword
    By John Lewis, *Chairman, The Attingham Trust*   PAGE vii

Author's Acknowledgements   ix

I.   The First Five Years: 1952 to 1956   1

II.   Years to consolidate: 1956 to 1962   17

III.   The American Connection Strengthens:
       1962 to 1970   25

IV.   Changes at Attingham Park: 1970 to 1975   44

V.   Attingham, A Changing Order: 1975 to 1979   65

VI.   Attingham, New Challenges: 1980 to 1985   80

VII.   Strength on Strength: 1985 to 1991   113

Appendix
       The Attingham Summer School *Alumni*,
       1952 to 1991   172

Index   209

FOREWORD

IN ITS FORTIETH YEAR, which happily also marks the thirtieth anniversary of the foundation of the American Friends, 'Attingham' is fortunate in having as its biographer its present Director, Dr Geoffrey Beard. *The First Forty Years*, which he has written, not only captures the unique ethos of the Summer School, but also provides a history of the Trust.

All who have, in whatever capacity, attended a Summer School and a Third, Special or Study Week, are now able to refresh their memories of a very special interlude in their lives and of those who have made, and continue to make, Attingham exceptional. But perhaps most importantly, this book sets the stage for 'Attingham' in the future. I commend it, warmly, to all *alumni*.

London, August 1991

John Lewis
Att. '81
CHAIRMAN
THE ATTINGHAM TRUST

AUTHOR'S ACKNOWLEDGEMENTS

IT WOULD BE POSSIBLE, given the full content of its archives in London and New York, to write an overwhelmingly exhaustive account of the first forty years' activity of the Attingham Summer School and its offshoots. That would, however, be beyond the economic framework which is possible in 1991. Even with the generous help (noted below), which I acknowledge warmly, only so much is possible. Nevertheless, I feel I have been able to give a full recital of all the main events and personalities in the Trust's forty years of activity, from its founding in 1952 to the conclusion of its Fortieth Summer School in July 1991.

My work has been eased by the care taken to organize the American Friends' archives by Bill Woolfenden (Att. '59) and for the hospitality afforded me at the Archives of American Art Office in New York (where they were housed) while I consulted them. Helen Lowenthal's files were passed on to me at her illness by her niece, Julia Boyd (Att. '71). My colleague, the Trust's Secretary and Assistant to the Director, Annabel Westman (Att. '77), loaned me her meticulously arranged files, and answered many questions. Sybil Bruel, Executive Secretary to the American Friends of Attingham, made many enquiries on my behalf, and the text was typed, with her customary efficiency, by Maureen Barton. Considerable help in production and distribution has been given by Linda Hind, Mills B. Lane (Att. '88) and Graham Maney.

After thought and consultation I decided to include an Appendix of the names only of those who had attended the Summer School. I have made frequent reference to the 'Met Museum' for the Metropolitan Museum of Art in New York. The abbreviation (Att. '79) in parentheses, following a name, indicates the year of attendance on the Summer School. I have not done this for attendance on the Third, Special or Study Weeks. Other abbreviations in use are: APVA (Association for Preservation of Virginia Antiquities); SPLIA (Society for Preservation of Long Island Antiquities); and SPNEA (Society for Preservation of New England Antiquities). An Index, compiled by Barbara Hird, is included.

Several persons provided poems, photographs or drawings but in this respect I would thank, especially, Jim Abbott (Att. '91), Kent Brinkley (Att. '89), Sybil Bruel, Jay Cantor (Att. '71), Tony Frederick (Att. '89), Will Gwilliam (Att. '89), Ralph Harvard (Att. '86), Nancy Hirst (Att. '79), and Bob Kennedy (Att. '63). The complete typescript was read by Helena Hayward, long associated with the Trust's work as its second Director (and now its Consultant Director), by John Lewis, as my Chairman, and by Annabel Westman, as Assistant to the Director.

Some parts relating to the American Friends' finances were read by Isabel Benham (Att. '54). Needless to say, while this help was invaluable, all conclusions are my sole responsibility and I should be grateful for any correction of what is written. Mistakes will have been inevitable in drawing an impression from an incomplete archive written, often, by many long since dead. To captious critics, however, I offer, as Dr Johnson did, one reminder: 'In this work, when it shall be found that much is omitted, let it not be forgotten that much likewise is performed'.

BATH, JULY 1991   GEOFFREY BEARD

I · THE FIRST FIVE YEARS
1952 to 1956

IN THE SPRING of 1951 Helen Lowenthal, then on the staff of the Victoria and Albert Museum, set out on one of her frequent lecture tours to America. Apart from the many speaking engagements, one of her social appointments was to have tea at Dumbarton Oaks in Washington with Mr and Mrs Robert Woods Bliss. They had set up in their great house the 'Institute for Byzantine Studies' (now administered by Harvard University), with Mrs Bliss also noted for her great and abiding interest in England. She had long admired its country houses and landscaped parks, and had considerable knowledge of the relevant literature through building up her very important 'Garden Library'. She and her husband were charter members of the then recently created American National Trust. They found the English National Trust, then well over sixty years old, with all the extraordinary things it had to offer, a most congenial topic of conversation. Mrs Bliss said:

> What a pity that more Americans, especially those who are connected with museums, universities and architectural schools, could not have some sort of organized course and tour planned to introduce them to houses of architectural interest, their gardens and their great collections of pictures, furniture, porcelain and silver.

As Lydia Bond Powel (Att. '52), Keeper of the American Wing at the Metropolitan Museum in New York, wrote in 1961, in a speech about the first ten years of 'Attingham':

> The suggestion could not have fallen in more receptive ears. The Bliss flame ignited the Lowenthal timber into a brisk conflagration by the time the latter reached my house in New York.

Much encouraged by Lydia Powel's enthusiasm Helen settled down on her return to England to prepare a detailed memorandum on educational activities in connection with National Trust properties. She sent it to the Deputy Secretary, Joshua (later Sir Joshua) Rowley, who was to conduct all the early 'Attingham' correspondence on behalf of the National Trust's Secretary, Jack Rathbone. Rowley wrote to Helen on 1 August 1951 about the three main points she had raised: a visit by three or four members of the American National Trust, organized tours for schoolteachers, women's garden clubs and similar organizations, and a summer school. He noted:

> The last of your three points was the question of a summer school which we decided should be held at Attingham. Everybody here thinks this is

an excellent plan, and I have written to George Trevelyan to ask him what he thinks . . .

George (later Sir George), who was Warden of the Shropshire Adult College based at Attingham, wrote to Rowley on 11 August about 'the possible course for American students of architecture'. He was enthusiastic:

> definitely this is of interest and it would be well worth considering the possibilities of holding it here . . . It would be worth considering Miss Lowenthal's suggestion during August . . .

Rowley then suggested Helen should see George Trevelyan and they finally met at the Victoria and Albert Museum at '1 o'clock on Thursday, September 27, 1951'. Rowley noted in a letter to Helen of 12 October that he was glad she 'had got on so well' with Trevelyan. By 15 November Rowley was telling Helen that Mr Harold Nicolson 'will very gladly lend (his) name as sponsor for the American Summer School. It is a very excellent idea and I hope it is a success'. The Curwen Press, then one of England's best printers, had been contacted and on 26 November 1951 a leaflet printed by them was issued by the National Trust. As it was the formal announcement of what was intended for the summer of 1952 the title page and text are given in facsimile (page 3). The National Trust assumed the overall responsibility for distributing the prospectus to a great number of universities and friends in America. George Trevelyan was 'to supervise tutorial work' and whilst the leaflet had, regrettably perhaps, no mention of Helen, she was busy behind the scenes. She recorded in an address to the Summer School at West Dean on 10 July 1986 — which was repeated in 1987 and issued subsequently as a tape-cassette — how she had motored up to Attingham to see George, early in 1952:

> So we got into a motor car and we drove all the way from London to Shropshire in pouring rain in February and there was George Trevelyan in bed in a Jaeger dressing gown with 'flu! And George Trevelyan (anyone else would have waved us away) even in a state of 'flu was excited about the idea of another course . . . we had tea with George and thought about catching 'flu and George there and then said: 'Oh, the easiest thing in the world, we will have a Summer School, we'll produce a brochure! — which we did, and we sent it out to America, where it excited not the slightest interest!

Correspondence is perhaps the better guide to the exact sequence of events. On 8 January 1952 George had undertaken, in his letter to Rathbone:

> to arrange the running of the conference for the first fortnight at Attingham and over the Derbyshire weekend. The final week will be in London, and I understand from my discussion with Miss Lowenthal and Mr Rowley yesterday that this will be their concern and not our responsibility.

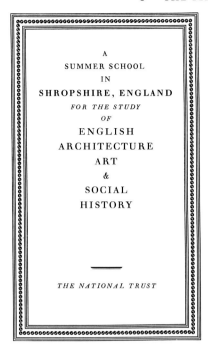

A

SUMMER SCHOOL

IN

SHROPSHIRE, ENGLAND

FOR THE STUDY

OF

ENGLISH

ARCHITECTURE

ART

&

SOCIAL

HISTORY

———

THE NATIONAL TRUST

The 1951 leaflet announcing the formation of the Summer School in 1952, printed by The Curwen Press.

A SUMMER SCHOOL IN SHROPSHIRE, ENGLAND
FOR THE STUDY OF ENGLISH
ARCHITECTURE, ART AND SOCIAL HISTORY

IT is planned to hold a three weeks' summer school from 10 July 1952 at Attingham Park, Shropshire. This course is sponsored jointly by the National Trust and the Education Committee of the Shropshire County Council, who run this fine eighteenth-century mansion as an Adult Education College.

The aim of the course is to introduce American students and teachers working in the Fine Arts to a closer knowledge of the great houses of England from the Middle Ages to the nineteenth century, and to provide opportunities for studying the growth of the great country houses and their place in English history. Shropshire is an excellent centre. Apart from the interest of Attingham Park itself, it will be possible to visit such great houses as Chatsworth, Hardwick, Kedleston and Haddon in the Derbyshire area, Blenheim Palace, Oxford and the neighbourhood of Stratford on Avon and Bath.

Sponsors of this course include Mr. Harold Nicolson, a member of the Executive Committee of the National Trust; Professor Anthony Blunt, Keeper of the King's Pictures and Director of the Courtauld Institute; Professor Pevsner (of Cambridge University); Professors Wittkower (of London University) and Geoffrey Webb, Secretary to the Royal Commission on Historical Monuments. The course will be a serious one and it is hoped that it will rank for recognition by those

American Universities co-operating. Mr. Trevelyan, the Warden of the Shropshire Adult College at Attingham, will himself supervise tutorial work, a library will be available and there will be a number of resident tutors. If desired, a written examination can be set.

Full costs for keep and tuition will be 150 dollars. It is hoped that this sum will cover the cost of visits undertaken during the course, but it may be necessary to charge a small extra fee if costs continue to rise.

A minimum membership fee of two dollars for the National Trust will be required also.

Places are limited to 60 and applications, with a 50-dollar deposit, should be sent to Mr. George Trevelyan, Attingham Park, Salop, by 15 February.

26 November 1951

But how was American interest focused, with the formation of the 'American Friends' in 1962 still some ten years away? There is no doubt that Lydia Bond Powel was invaluable in persuading friends and museum contacts. Letters on file from the Directors of various University Colleges of Education — Frank Seiberling, jun., at Ohio State, was typical — leaflets sent to various architectural schools, to Henry-Russell Hitchcock at Smith College, the United States Information Service, Fred Rath, Director of the National Council for Historic Sites and Buildings, the English architectural historian, Marcus Whiffen (who was asked to tutor but was soon to leave to work in America) — all these and many more were pressed to help. Photographs of Attingham were sent to Mrs Powel and she announced the course at the annual meetings of the American National Trust and the Society of Architectural Historians. Many of her friends were ready to sign up. The University of Michigan, Department of Fine Arts, even announced through its Chairman, George H. Forsyth, jun., that they would 'grant credit to any student of ours who completes the course successfully'. It is worth charting out some of those whom Mrs Powel and others had recruited. They were the first Attingham Class of '52, due to meet in England from 10 to 31 July. The full list of twenty-two American names is given at the end of this account, and also appears in the *Alumni Directory* issued by the American Friends in 1984. John N. Graham II was Curator of Collections at Colonial Williamsburg and Charles and Florence Mont-gomery were well into distinguished careers at the Henry Francis du Pont Museum at Winterthur. Professor James Van Derpool was Librarian of the superb Avery Architectural Library at Columbia University and (as noted) Lydia Bond Powel was Keeper of the American Wing at the Metropolitan Museum. H. F. Koeper led the School of Architecture at the University of Minnesota, Hardinge Scholle was at the American National Trust, Miss Barbara Snow at *Antiques Magazine* and Frank Sommer, then Professor of Sociology at the University of Delaware, later became the Du Pont Museum Librarian. The antiques trade was represented by the distinguished dealer, David Stockwell (accompanied by Mrs Stockwell), and 'National Monu-ments' by Lydia's cousin, Mrs (Hope) K. Hare Powel, Regent of Mount Vernon for five years and a previous Board member for eleven. The architect Edward Maverick, eventual donor of a scholarship, was then based in New York as was another architect, Daniel Hopping (then with Rudolph Associates). Mrs de Morinni, teaching French in many colleges, Ernest Lo Nano and Hanley Henoch completed the New York representa-tion of nine persons.

To this American group of twenty-two was added Inge 'Lucy' Antonsen from Copenhagen and a number of English members (Miss W. Graham-Samuel, Mrs D. M. Dyson, Mrs S. Adams, Miss N. Powell, Miss N. Paterson, Miss R. M. Jacobs and Mr A. Bower). What happened to all thirty of them when they arrived at Attingham Park itself? Lady Berwick was in residence, and Helen Lowenthal and George and Helen Trevelyan

Lydia Bond Powel (left) and Lucy Antonsen, members of the Class of 1952.

Part of the 1952 Programme cover, first of forty to come.

NATIONAL TRUST SUMMER SCHOOL

on

THE GREAT HOUSES

of

ENGLAND

At Attingham Park, Shrewsbury

were eager to greet the first Class and start the programme. The opening address was given by the Earl of Rosse, with sponsors of the course being Harold Nicolson, Anthony Blunt, Geoffrey Webb, and Professors Pevsner and Wittkower. The last four, with Francis Watson and John Summerson, were to become frequent lecturers from 1953 onwards. The fees by present standards and for such 'quality' were modest. A terse note records: 'Pevsner, Webb, Wittkower, Blunt, 10 guineas'.

Each day the intrepid group went off, accoutred for the weather, to Shrewsbury, Ludlow and their environs, on a week later for a Derbyshire weekend, back to Attingham and then leaving for London on 23 July, with overnight stops at Stratford-upon-Avon and at Balliol College, Oxford. A formal dinner saw the National Trust represented by Lord Esher, the Secretary, J. F. W. Rathbone, the Deputy Secretary, Joshua Rowley and the Historic Buildings Secretary, Robin Fedden. On Sunday 13 July the Boyd Neel Orchestra had given a concert 'held in connection with the Summer School on The Great Houses of England' playing music by Mozart, Bach, Boccherini, Haydn and Schubert. It was this mixture of scholarship and relaxation — ever an 'Attingham' requirement — that Helen and George were to excel at providing. The programme of houses to be visited had been arranged sensibly to cover 'Fortified Medieval Manor Houses' (Stokesay: Haddon); 'The Castle' (Chirk); Tudor (Pitchford, Hardwick; Hatfield); Inigo Jones (Queen's House, Greenwich); seventeenth century (Ham House, Chatsworth); Vanbrugh and English Baroque (Blenheim Palace, Melbourne); Palladianism (Chiswick House); Adam reaction to Palladianism (Hatchlands, Kedleston, Syon). Naturally it was not (and never will be) possible to visit the houses in chronological sequence as can be done in a lecture. But there was enough to excite and to exhaust.

So what of a typical day or two's programme? Friday, 18 July 1952 heralded the weekend move to Derbyshire.

Friday　　To Hardwick via Melbourne. Coffee in Lichfield. Melbourne Sandwich lunch. 2.30 Hardwick. On to Bakewell. Tea 5.00. 7.30 Dinner at *The Peacock*.

Saturday　10.30 Chatsworth, guided by Francis Thompson and Tom Wragg. 1.0 Lunch at *The Rutland Arms* (6s.). 2.45 Haddon Hall (Lord John Manners). 5.0 Tea at *The Peacock*. Tissington and Dovedale; drinks at *Peveril of the Peaks*.

Sunday　　Chatsworth: Park. 12.30 lunch. *The Rutland Arms*. Afternoon. Kedleston (Dowager Viscountess Scarsdale). House: Park: Church. 4.30 Back towards Attingham, with tea in Derby. 8.30 Attingham.

So whilst the army, in the British style, marched 'on its stomach' with more hotel meals, coffees and teas than was perhaps good for the figure, it was all affordable: lunch 3s. to 6s. and tea at 1s. 6d.

Finally the move south to London with visits to Hatfield, Cliveden, Apsley House, Hatchlands, Knole, Penshurst, with a visit and lunch at the

House of Commons, by river to Greenwich and dinner at the seventeenth-century George Inn at Southwark, one of the few remaining galleried inns in London.

It was predictable that the course would excite and the letters flowed in, some almost immediately, as Mrs Hare Powel sailed home on the S.S. *Ile de France*. 'I want you to know', she wrote to Helen, 'how much I appreciated your many kindnesses and constant courtesies, far more than merited but believe me deeply appreciated'. And similar messages from Ed Maverick, Dan Hopping and others, bubbling away with their meetings as 'Jim Van Derpool showed his excellent slides', Barbara Snow wrote it up for *Antiques Magazine*: 'We have all talked about our wonderful summer so much I feel sure you can count on a great crowd from here in '53.' Helen, indefatigably, had gone off on an August trip to Italy, but not before she had done what the Attingham staff has always done — bed only when the day's thank-you letters have been written, and back came the replies, from Lady Berwick and six other owners, from Francis Thompson, the Chatsworth Librarian, all dazed that the Americans had said that 'I had added to their enjoyment and your kindness at also telling me I did'. Francis Thompson enthused:

> Yesterday I heard from dear old Miss Webb, the Dowager Duchess's maid — 'Webby' as she is to us — that the Duchess and Webby herself liked them all very much. My only regret is that besides the enchanting young Duchess you did not see the equally enchanting young Duke . . .

Subsequent generations of Attingham class members have been able many times to see and thank 'Debo' Duchess, one of Attingham's most active patrons, for all the kindnesses long shown at Chatsworth, and then also at Hardwick, home of Evelyn, Duchess of Devonshire from 1908 to 1956.

At the end of 1952 it was time to take stock of the first venture and Joshua Rowley wrote on 25 November to Lydia Powel. Almost single-handedly she had recruited the 1952 Class. Rowley raised three points with her: (a) the cost, (b) the size of the course, and (c) its composition as to Americans and Europeans. In her important reply of 15 December Lydia answered as follows: as to cost, she felt the first 'intake' could afford the 150 dollars but as 200 dollars was envisaged for 1953 junior-curatorial assistants, who were already applying, they would find it difficult. 'Perhaps', she wrote:

> it would be possible to have two categories, as it were, for seniors and juniors . . . but I think the course would lose its value if too many financially able amateur sightseers were admitted. I feel strongly that the professional approach directed to people of similar backgrounds and professional interests has made the course valuable. I should be very sorry if it slipped into something that was more social than professional in its membership.

Lydia wrote on, precisely. She would welcome certain economies, especially in food. She was alarmed that 'as Americans we should be indulged in

England simply because our conditions at home happen to be different. I hope very much that it will be possible to have some European students also'. Finally she thought one coach was preferable to two, that the numbers, thirty, were about right: 'More than that would have been difficult to handle, both in the houses we visited and at Attingham. Two bus loads descending seems too much like a char-a-banc party.' She further indicated this agreed with her consultation with Messrs Van Derpool, Hopping, Henoch and Maverick in New York and her cousin Mrs Hare Powel.

Joshua Rowley replied on 19 December agreeing with what Lydia had written, 'particularly that we want a professional rather than a social

Lady Berwick at Attingham Park, c. 1962.

atmosphere about the course', and promising to limit the 1953 increase above 150 dollars to the minimum.

One of the 1952 lectures had been given by the historian Dennis Brogan, and he had been unusually sharp on the origins of the Berwicks, and yet perhaps had forgotten that Lady Berwick was on the front row. It is reported, I am not sure how reliably, that at the conclusion someone asked Lady Berwick if she had enjoyed the talk: 'I didn't hear too much of it and what I did I didn't take to', she said, with feeling. Small wonder that when Joshua Rowley wrote on 19 December 1952 to Lydia Powel he should put an exclamation mark at the end of his comment about the forthcoming 1953 programme:

> We have got more or less the same lecturers as last year, including John Summerson, but excluding, you will be surprised to hear, Dennis Brogan!

Later still in 1952, Joshua Rowley, mindful of the need for an important opening address for the second Class of '53 (arranged for 8 to 23 July at Attingham), wrote to Vita Sackville-West at Sissinghurst Castle. Her reply is not on file but a note by George says 'Sackville-West will come for love'; without fee. But alas, it was not finally to be and the Duke of Wellington came instead. Magisterially it was all set out again. Paddington trains met on 8 July, 9 to 16 July at Attingham and then visits (17 to 28 July) through Derbyshire, the Cotswolds, Bath, Salisbury, arriving in London on 29 July. Five shillings a day per student was allowed for entrance fees, and much was packed in, including many lunches and teas.

> July 22   To Cirencester via Kelmscott, Lechlade, Fairford, Cirencester Park (lunch in Park: see house), Nether Lippiatt, Bibury.

Something of the administrative background is gained from the correspondence files. On 1 July 1953 Helen wrote to the Editor of the *Times Educational Supplement* detailing the success of the 1952 Summer School:

> This is the combined venture of the Shropshire Education Committee through the Warden of Attingham Park (George Trevelyan) and the National Trust, for whom I originally planned the venture with Mr. Rowley of the Trust.

She continued:

> This year's students have been recruited by the enthusiasm of last year's, without any advertising on our part ... The cost to the Americans is high since there is no subsidy (we charge £18 per week) and the expenses of touring are considerable.

Similar letters went to the architectural press, the *Daily Telegraph*, *Country Life*, Nigel Nicolson at *The Spectator*, *The Sphere*, the *Illustrated London News* and the *Manchester Guardian* (who were asked to send a reporter to cover the Duke of Wellington's opening address).

There were social obligations to be catered for too. Hugo Burrow, Curator of the Holburne of Menstrie Museum at Bath, was much occupied with that section of the programme:

> I have spoken to Lady N—, she says that the 26th being a Sunday, would not suit, as she has no servants on that day in the week and would like to lay on eats and drinks. However, if she can present her grand-daughter on the 16th instead of the 24th she will be freer as to dates; but will not hear from the Ld. Chamberlain until after the Coronation.

Among the 1953 students was Barbara Wriston, who was asked, and who, in her careful analytical way, provided good criticism of various aspects of the programme. She had, of course, thoroughly enjoyed it.

Accommodation
Barbara thinks the accommodation at Attingham is perfectly adequate though a little austere for people who arrive straight from Claridge's. She also thinks that the number of bathrooms, which obviously cannot

Sir George Trevelyan helping to serve the Class of 1953 at Attingham Park.

be increased, might be allotted more successfully between men and women. She was surprised to find no soap and on a stay of 10 days 2 towels were allowed: the first was kept for 9 days and the other issued 24 hours before they left.

As for 'General Remarks', ever the plea:

> We do not allow enough time for instance for people to change travellers' cheques, wash their clothes and write letters. As there appeared to be a party every night this is hardly surprising. There should be very few entertainments (when everyone is tired) in the evening.

Barbara further suggested that an inclusive charge of 200 dollars seemed possible but that rough details of the following year's programme should reach America by the end of October. She mentioned the use of an extremely simple lecture on the lines of '500 Years of English History', to lay emphasis on the influence of English architecture and decoration in America in the seventeenth and eighteenth centuries and to explore the connections between the country house and literature of the eighteenth and nineteenth centuries. Finally, she noted seven organizations who should be made to do some propaganda work. It was a first-rate start to the continuing system of members submitting reports, and as Rowley noted to Helen: 'This is quite enough to go on with.' And there was always such a lot to do. A fragmentary record in Helen's hand notes the various things she had to attend to, over five days:

10th	Summerson arriving
11–15	Reyner Banham helping
12th	Dr (Christopher) White to be met
14–15	Francis Watson and wife
15	Goodhart-Rendel; — Lady Berwick

Also, any scribe can see the present difficulty of knowing precisely who attended when. Beyond the firm lists of 'full-time students' there were often at least five part-time and two attending just for one or two lectures, staying the night and leaving — 'Mr X, Miss Y', devotees of Attingham's many other programmes which were the products of George's fertile mind, now recorded only in his great red scrap-books, kept in his house at Hawkesbury.

The response to the first two Summer Schools held at Attingham encouraged the National Trust and the Shropshire County Council Education Committee, who were responsible for the Adult College, to offer a further course in 1954. The Earl Spencer was to give the introductory address on 'The Social and Historical Significance of the Country House' on Friday 9 July. All those coming from London had caught the 11.10 a.m. from Paddington and were met at Shrewsbury Station at 3 p.m. The four addresses the course was to be based at, were, Attingham, *The Peacock* at Rowsley in Derbyshire, *The King's Arms*, Chipping Campden and (21–29) *The Francis Hotel* at Bath. And again the panoply of names, but unless one follows the file rather than the printed programme (now no longer by the superb, but comparatively expensive Curwen Press, but by Walker's of Shrewsbury) it would not be known that John Summerson lectured instead of Nikolaus Pevsner on 10 and 11 July. He was supported by Reyner Banham talking on 'Vanbrugh' (perhaps he never did so again!), by Dr Margaret Whinney on 'Inigo Jones' and by Francis Watson on 'English Villas and Venetian Decorators'. On 17 July the group left for Derbyshire for the obligatory visits to Chatsworth, Haddon, Kedleston and Melbourne, travelling on via Aynhoe Park and Hidcote Gardens to arrive in Bath for dinner.

The tour of Bath was conducted by its then leading architectural historian, Walter Ison, and, after a memorable visit to Prior Park, the 8 p.m. lecture on 'Eighteenth-Century English Furniture' was given by Ralph Edwards, the Keeper of Furniture and Woodwork at the Victoria and Albert Museum. The great second edition of his *Dictionary of English Furniture*, in its three maroon volumes, was almost off the press as he spoke.

Each year's Attingham had many members whose name or service to the curatorial and allied professions became subsequently notable. It is always invidious to mention names (which is why we do it). Abbot Lowell Cummings (SPNEA and Yale) was there, with Charles Wall of Mount Vernon in 1953, Isabel Benham, important to Attingham's financial help in America in later years, in 1954, and of course, in each of the first five years, 1952 to 1956, Lydia Bond Powel. Miss Van Der Toorn and Dr C. H. De Jonge, both of The Hague, were welcome Continental visitors in 1954. Lady Trevelyan, George's mother, and Barbara Robertson, from Combe Hay Manor at Bath, were casual attenders at various parts of the full programme.

Almost as the 1954 Class was about to assemble, Helen and George were thinking of where to go in 1955. One worry was that George felt that as Attingham itself was financed by Shropshire ratepayers that they were excluded from the house for ten days in the middle of the summer. He felt 'Attingham' as a School might have to find another centre and Joshua Rowley asked George Howard about houses near York offering the right facilities. What was certain is that York was to be an important venue for the fourth Class of 1955 (8 to 29 July).

In a letter sent to all American members of the Classes '52 to '54 in November 1954 (and copied to Helen), Fred Rath (Att. '54), Director of the National Trust for Historic Preservation in Washington, wrote:

> It was in Chipping Campden that a group of us (Henry Flynt, Bill Pierson, Russell Plimpton, Walter Densmore and I) agreed that 'Something Should be Done'. We thought we might make a concerted effort to aid and abet the promotion of the course in the States . . . To simplify matters and to give a small bit of cohesion, we ought to have a name. No one has come up with anything brilliant yet. AA, standing for Attinghamites Anonymous, was suggested by a whilom devotee of the Mytton and the Mermaid but not seriously. Suppose we remain nameless until you suggest and decide what it shall be . . .

Fred indicated they could circulate 2,000 brochures about the 1955 School, that he understood its cost to be $200 — 'still a very great bargain', the number of places, thirty-five, 'with some reserved for students from Europe and the Commonwealth' and that 'prospective students are being instructed to send their applications to me at this office together with a note of their qualifications and special interests'. 'It is specifically noted however', he continued:

> that final selection of candidates will be made by the Directors of the Summer School, not by you or me or the American National Trust. What we shall try to do if possible is to have every applicant meet a former student, who will submit a statement to be sent with the application to England . . . I think you will want to know that several of us are trying seriously to promote some $750 scholarships for the course . . . to cover basic transportation and School expenses . . .

He concluded: 'probably no one of us could do the whole job alone. But if a majority of us are inclined to work together informally, it could be fun and the results should be good.'

Whatever attractions York promised for the future, the course opened as usual at Attingham. Sacheverell Sitwell had promised to give the opening address, Pevsner was due to deal with the 'Medieval and Tudor House' in one lecture and 'The Elizabethan House' in another. The last was a morning lecture with the evening given over to a pianoforte recital by Kathleen Long. Helen herself, as she did in so many years, lectured on 'The English Garden', and the careful rhythm was maintained by Margaret Whinney, John Lowe (on 'Interiors 1640–1820', in two lectures) and

Professor Ellis Waterhouse on 'The English Collectors'. One marvels at the consistent high standards of scholarship such lectures could be expected to offer, and there was no diminution in quality in York. John Summerson on 'Robert Adam' (as Curator of the Soane Museum, who better?), Laurence Whistler on 'Vanbrugh' and Dr Bill Singleton on 'Lord Burlington' and, later, 'John Carr'.

At Harewood the party was greeted by the late Princess Royal and the tour of York Minster was conducted by the Dean, Eric Milner-White, a noted collector. As for the composition of the Brains Trust about 'The Place

Helen Lowenthal and George Trevelyan, co-founders of The Attingham Summer School, *c.* 1956.

of the Historic House Today', none better than George Howard from Castle Howard, Christopher Hussey of *Country Life*, Robin Fedden from the National Trust, Bill Singleton of the York Institute of Architectural Study, and the Planning Officer for the North Riding (John Vincent). Small wonder that at the final evening party at the Treasurer's House in York on 28 July 1955 the programme laconically announced 'Bus back about 10, if required'.

As for the members, they included Professor Marion Ross from the Architectural School, University of Oregon, Charles Sawyer from the Division of Arts at Yale, Jim Parker from the Metropolitan Museum, the

Deputy Director of the Kunst Industrial Museum in Oslo (G. Kavli), the Assistant Secretary to the Historic Buildings Council (Elizabeth Hall), O. J. Weaver, an Assistant Inspector of Ancient Monuments, and Prinz Franz zu Sayn-Wittgenstein, Head of the Denkmalamt in Munich.

Lydia Powel summarized the respective personalities of Helen and George in these early years in her 1961 paper previously referred to.

> The explanation of the Drang Nach, Attingham and its value to us all is not far to seek. First there is this beautiful house and all those connected with it: who do so much to make it what it is. Lady Berwick's and Lady Trevelyan's gracious hospitality — Sir George's boundless energy, kindness and tact without which we would not function at all . . . [And Helen] she who from the beginning has dreamed up the programme, persuaded eminent lecturers to come to Attingham and to go on tour with us. In the midst of a busy professional career at the Victoria and Albert, she somehow finds time to write the scholarly notes we receive with our itineraries, answer endless letters, worry about finances and soothe ruffled temperaments, etc., – etc. But I warn you that if you are too tardy about getting into the 'bus at the appointed time, if you are inconsiderate with your photography, or in any way behave like a spoiled child — you'll get your knuckles rapped and probably serve you right. Just remember she chasteneth whom she loves and that without her vision and back-breaking hard work we would have had no summer school at all . . .

Let me conclude this first section of Attingham's story with a note about finances. Ever important, they have given rise across the years to many difficulties and misunderstandings. Certainly the seeds of the latter were sown at an early point due to the involvement of a 'College' maintained by a local authority, Shropshire County Council. The case of Attingham Park itself was an involved one in that it depended for its financial existence on an endowment from a Shropshire businessman, grants from neighbouring Local Authorities and Universities, and a grant from the Shropshire Education vote. It was a Trust and the terms of its deed were that the project should be directed towards the benefit of Shropshire generally and of people within the area administered by the contributing authorities. The Trustees or Governors had therefore tacitly varied their interpretation of the Trust deed in allowing the Summer School to take place at the Hall. What they could not do, they maintained, was to bear any of the expenditure incurred by the School. Joshua Rowley had first written to George Trevelyan on 20 March 1952 to imply that he understood 'Attingham to be financially responsible for the time the students spent there and in Derbyshire' and that the cost of the London days would involve a transfer to the National Trust of received fees. From the outset the National Trust, whilst willing to lend its name to the enterprise of a Summer School, could not underwrite it or undertake administrative work. After a year or two the Trust made a modest nominal claim for financial help with administration, but waived this in order that the accruing balance could be used to improve future Schools or award a scholarship or two. As late as 1969 financial matters were still giving trouble and necessitate re-examination later in this account. What was the basic problem?

The School, whilst guaranteed by the Shropshire Education Committee, had all its finances (including profit or loss) within the control of the Governors of the Adult College at Attingham. The first Class of 1952 was run at a small loss, but from 1953 to 1955 a modest balance was obtained for the Adult College of £57 in 1953, £93 in 1954 to none in 1955, although The National Trust received £49. In 1956 a balance of £242 was achieved from which The National Trust was offered £50 by the College, with an offer of £25 in 1957. Rather than disperse the balance which was slowly accruing,

Line drawing Hardwick Hall, Derbyshire, west front 1598; drawing by Will Gwilliam (Att. '88).

Joshua Rowley, through The National Trust Assistant Secretary, Christopher Wall, suggested that the balance be kept 'in hand for improving future summer schools'. Scholarships were of course in mind, but when in December 1958 a request for £200 was made to the Adult College for these purposes (being the accrued balances and observation of the fact that the 1958 School showed a balance of £440) it was refused as 'a positive change in the agreed policy for running this summer school'. The matter was not resolved finally until 1970, when after lengthy negotiations with Shropshire County Council (in which the new Attingham Chairman, Tony Galliers-Pratt, in succession to John Tillotson, played an important role), the Summer School Council took full responsibility for the financing of its now well established annual event. Throughout this period Helen (as in so many subsequent years, and followed, generously, by Helena Hayward) took hardly anything — in 1952 she had an expense account 'of up to £30' and '£20 for the time expended'. All of this, wrote Rowley, 'will have to come out of the fees paid by students in the same way as your tutorial fee will do: in other words it will not come from National Trust funds . . .'.

The Atcham Lodge (*c*. 1807) to Attingham Park. John Nash's version of a triumphal arch entrance to Repton's parkland. Used by each Attingham Class, 1952–83.

Photograph: Andrew Arrol. (Att. '78).

II · YEARS TO CONSOLIDATE
1956 to 1962

AS THE EYE flits down the lists of the members of a Class, the often still-folded letters in Helen's files (kept, all too spasmodically, but exuding her enormous energy and multifarious friendships), personal choice must intervene on historical objectivity. The 1956 Class list included not only the names of Ernest Hillman, jun. (to become the first President of the American Friends in 1962), of faithful Lydia Powel, but of two more members of the Metropolitan Museum staff — Clare Le Corbeiller (then Clare Eames) and Edith A. Standen. For over thirty-five years Clare and Edith, distinguished in their own specialities, have also lent distinction to Attingham with their selfless dedication to its aims. As for Edith's final poem, with its cleverly cadenced lines to Noel Coward's *The Stately Homes of England*, why not look it up in the American Friends' Autumn *Newsletter* No. 13 for 1990? There was Helen's life-long friend Mrs Olivia Coan, Dr Graf Kalnein from Baden in Germany, Professor Hope Gladding from Berkeley, Gertrude Howe (Metropolitan Museum) and Russell Plimpton from the Minneapolis Institute of Art.

The same harmonious type of grouping was there in 1957 too, with Faith Dennis and Carl Dauterman from the Metropolitan — Faith was in the 'Department of Renaissance and Modern Art' (as it was 1957) and Carl was Associate Curator of Decorative Arts — Marvin Schwartz, then at the Brooklyn Museum, Isabelle Miller (Curator of the Museum of the City of New York), Harry Grier from the Frick Collection (to be the American Friends' first Secretary), Charles Nagel, Director of the St Louis Museum, Missouri, and Willard Duncan from Colonial Williamsburg. They joined up with their other colleagues and with Dr Blauensteiner from Vienna and the Viscountess Bridgman from the family long seated at Weston Hall in Shropshire.

For the first time in 'Attingham's' short history the 1956 Class went north, in its third week, to Scotland, indeed as far north as Aberdeen. Already Newby, Bramham, Harewood and majestic Fountains Abbey had been seen in Yorkshire and now, vastly different in elevation, Melrose, Lennoxlove, Hopetoun and the castellated severity of Mellerstain, by William Adam and (later) his son Robert. Schomberg Scott, beloved architect, Colin McWilliam, the Edinburgh architectural historian, and Ian G. Lindsay talked about it all; teas were eaten at Kinross, Crathes and Brechin (eaten everywhere, in fact) and at the end of the School, a £3,000 exercise, overall, there was a modest balance, 'being income in excess of expenditure', of £254. The Shropshire Adult College took $^{10}/_{17}$, presumably

The *Mytton and Mermaid* Hotel, opposite the gates of Attingham Park,
where generations of Class members imbibed and then walked 'home'
across the park.

the number of days it was involved (£120), The National Trust for Scotland
£84, and £50 was put to the credit of The National Trust, raising its 'balance'
to the heady total of £254.

Financial statements can help by their precision. John Hayward
travelled up from London by 'sleeper' train accompanied by his wife
Helena. John was Assistant Keeper of the Metalwork Department at the
Victoria and Albert Museum, and an internationally recognized expert on
silver, arms and armour. The supper at the great rambling seventeenth-
century The Binns, Linlithgow, needed extra staff (£4), and 'Drinks,
Edinburgh, Cider etc' (£3) and 'Drinks, Edinburgh, Sherry etc' (£18) leave
one wondering who got what. 'Nay Toddy' as the Scots might justly say,
but seasoned visitors to the 'Mytton and Mermaid' at Attingham's very
gates probably needed no hints. As Edith Standen had written in her
superb 1956 poem:

> And though it's a mile to the nearest pub
> and the rain has made us damp,
> We'll tramp through the stately homes of England.

And tramp they did, as they have done across another thirty-five years,
occasionally even carrying unborn children. Attingham directors should
perhaps correlate the inducement rate of the great stairs at, say, Hardwick
to their lack of midwifery experience.

I said that financial statements can help with precision: equally they can lead to speculation. The 1957 statement — the School visited Northamptonshire and again Scotland — has, under 'Expenditure in England': 'entrance fees to houses £60 6s. 6d.' and 'cost of wines and soft drinks £87 12s. 9d.'

Due to the geographical scatter of the great houses in Norfolk it has never been an easy county for Attingham to visit. 1958, 1966, 1973, 1981 might seem regular enough; and its most distinguished historian, R. W. Ketton-Cremer from Felbrigg, set off the 1958 School on 4 July with a talk on 'Country House Life in the Eighteenth Century'. But there was much to do before the wide landscaped painterly stretches of Norfolk could greet tired eyes and tireder feet. Again the resounding names as lecturers, Sir John Summerson, Alec Clifton-Taylor, Professor Ellis Waterhouse, Sir Francis Watson. I have been fortunate to hear all four lecture, years later, of course, and they were consummate performers at a difficult art. But in 1958 Summerson spoke on 'Lord Burlington', Alec Clifton-Taylor on 'Vanbrugh' and Francis Watson on 'William Kent Furniture'. Helen and George mixed such lectures with a poetry recital by George Hagan, and a concert by the Oxford Bach Choir at St Chad's in Shrewsbury. Like its high ethereal fading notes the tension mounted and subsided. A tour of old half-timbered Shrewsbury one day, arriving at Henry Holland's classical Berrington Hall on another and, by 19 July, a fortnight after the start, the Elizabethan Gothic silhouette of Burghley and the drive on to Norwich through Wisbech and King's Lynn.

All those who love England's version of Palladianism find what they need in Norfolk. Raynham, supremely Houghton and Holkham, the eighteenth-century dressings over seventeenth-century interiors at Felbrigg, majestic Blickling with its 1620 Long Gallery, and then, quietly, a sherry party at Regency Sheringham with its Repton landscape. And all too soon the picnic lunch at Wyatt's Heveningham and the slow return to London via Cambridge 'where the party will dine at the Garden House Hotel'. An overnight stay and only then London and the final baroque touch: '7.0 p.m. Depart for Greenwich from Westminster Pier'.

If it was Scotland for the first time in 1956, it was, more adventurously, Ireland in 1959. But first there was the usual assembly on the first Friday of July at Attingham with the opening 'keynote' address by Dr A. L. Rowse on 'Court and Country in English History'. Then the considered architectural approach, chronologically, from the 'Medieval House' to the 'Age of Adam' by the experienced team of Summerson, Pevsner and Clifton-Taylor. On 12 July the Earl of Rosse prepared the way with a foretaste of goodies to come with a lecture on 'Eighteenth-Century Ireland'.

Melbourne, Kedleston, Chatsworth, Hardwick and Haddon in three days and across to the north-west for the departure on the afternoon flight from Liverpool to Dublin and Trinity Hall Hostel. Perhaps it is a proof of fortitude amongst Attingham members that they had a lecture at 9 p.m.

Kedleston Hall, Derbyshire, *c.* 1760, visited almost annually from
1952; drawing by Will Gwilliam (Att. '88).

that same night from Maurice Craig. And what a wonderful programme
had been planned with the help of Attingham's patron, Desmond
Guinness. Excellent stuccoes to see at Kilmainham, the Rotunda Hospital
and 20 Dominick Street, the great Charlemont Casino by Sir William
Chambers (not then, of course, restored to its present splendour). Here the
President of Ireland received the group. Malahide Castle, Castletown,
Leixlip, Carton, Beaulieu, Slane Castle, Powerscourt and Russborough,
with Sir Alfred Beit's fabled collections. Not neglected was a visit to the
Guinness Brewery and to the studio of the *haute couture* designer, Sybil
Connolly. Hospitality, as one might expect in the ancestral country for
many Americans, was lavish, with 'entrances to houses' accounting for
only £25 in an expenditure of some £700. 'The way had of course been
carefully prepared, not only by Lord Rosse, Maurice Craig and Desmond
Guinness, but by an exploratory trip undertaken by Helen and Christopher
Wall: it was possible to do this for £30 each.'

Meanwhile, The American Association of Museums told Helen that it
felt it could advise the American National Trust in the selection of curatorial
staff, particularly younger people, to attend the School. This might have
been slightly begging the question as there was no mean crowd already

involved. The applications, when complete, were forwarded to the Directors of the School by the 'American sponsors'. In 1959 these sponsors were, at the Metropolitan Museum, Lydia Bond Powel and Edith Standen; Bertram Little (then Director of SPNEA); Barbara Wriston (then at the Boston Museum of Fine Arts); James Van Derpool (Avery Library); Charles Sawyer (University of Michigan); Hope Gladding (formerly University of California); Russell Plimpton (formerly Director, the Minneapolis Institute of Fine Arts); William Pierson (Williams College); Charles Wall (Mount Vernon); William Hutton (Toledo Museum); Charles Nagel (St Louis Museum), and Harry Grier at the Frick Collection. With such expertise in choosing, no wonder that each School's American members were a remarkable group. What could they expect in the way of accommodation at Attingham? The 1959 Joining Instructions said:

> There are only a very limited number of single rooms but it should not be necessary to ask more than three to share the large cubicled rooms, so all will have ample space. The beds are very comfortable. There are no private bathrooms at Attingham.

As the autumn of 1959 came, the Attingham 'Committee', with the active secretarial help of Christopher Wall, started to consider again the School's relationship to the Adult College. Some focus had been given to this during the summer in that an architectural guide prepared for the use of the Summer School by Walter Ison failed to attract financial support from the Shropshire County Council. The informal committee running the Summer School had also been anxious for some time to devise a plan which would enable them to offer scholarships and to build up a contingency fund for extraordinary expenditure. The Education Secretary to the County Council, Martin Wilson, had offered to recommend to the College Governors that in 1960 two scholarships should be offered, one to an American. If the financial results of the 1960 School allowed they might also consider a grant towards the Ison guide. However, Wilson pointed out on 5 February 1960 that 'Attingham has to make its financial way just like other independent or voluntary institutions'. It was suggested that Wilson meet the Committee's new Chairman, John Tillotson, and the affair flickered on uneasily.

Such matters could not be allowed, however, to affect the School itself. Tillotson made good suggestions for the Northamptonshire week in 1960. Attingham came first and, as a variation to normal policy, Derbyshire last. After all, the area could offer not only attendance at a Shakespeare play at Stratford-upon-Avon, but dreamy Compton Wynyates, Vanbrugh's Kimbolton, Drayton, Deene, Hawksmoor's Easton Neston, Chicheley (with madrigals after dinner), Boughton and Milton. As Tillotson had written to Helen in September 1959:

> There are overwhelming riches in Northamptonshire and it is going to be a most difficult task to make our selection . . . Lord Spencer and Sir Gyles Isham will advise on that point.

The School was to base at Northamptonshire County Council's Residential Centre for Adult Education, Knuston Hall, south of Northampton.

As for the members, there were some repeat names — faithfully, Lydia Bond Powel, Edward Maverick, Mrs Earle Kress Williams, Hanley Henoch, Louisa Biddle, Sarah Mortimer and Margaret Valk. And joining them, John Sweeney from Winterthur, Otto and Margaret Wittmann from Toledo, David Rust, then doing his doctorate, Chloë Hamilton from Oberlin's Art Museum, Murphy Smith, Librarian of Manuscripts in the Library of the Philadelphia Philosophical Society, and Margaret Stearns, Assistant Curator of Costumes at the Museum of the City of New York. Some only came for the Northamptonshire section (Jimmy Biddle and Lydia Powel, for example) and they there joined some of the lecturers (such as Hugo Burrow and Alec Clifton-Taylor), Lady Trevelyan, Dr and Mrs Lawson Stote (who were so generous over many years with teas in their garden at Swan Hill Court House in Shrewsbury) and, of course, Helen, George, John Tillotson and Christopher Wall. Carsten Hopstock came in from the Norsk Folkemuseum and Contessa Loredana Da Schio from Italy.

The fees of six distinguished lecturers at £110 seem sparse by 1991 standards. It was possible to award two scholarships at a cost of £95, to go to the theatre in Stratford at £1 each and to skim above costs by a mere £100 or so. Solvent, just, to which perhaps the cost per student, per day, at Attingham of £2 10s., undoubtedly contributed.

Swan Hill Court, Shrewsbury, home of Dr and Mrs Lawson Stote, and their daughter Sally. The Stotes generously gave tea to Attingham members over several years.

When the 1961 school opened on 5 July, it was with Lydia Powel's summary of ten years of activity, previously quoted. Two new lecturers to join the established team of Pevsner, Summerson and Clifton-Taylor were John Cushion, a consummate ceramics historian from the Victoria and Albert Museum, and Erna Auerbach, the specialist in Elizabethan portraiture and miniatures. Visually too, apart from the houses, a floodlit performance of *Macbeth* at Ludlow Castle. Before the party left Attingham for Derbyshire and Buckinghamshire Lady Berwick gave a sherry party and there was a 'farewell dinner'.

All members in an Attingham class are important. All this account can do, repeatedly, is to isolate some names who, for various reasons, have remained important to the Trust's activities in New York and London. Catherine Bohlen, in whose name a scholarship is still awarded, joined the distinguished historian, Edith Standen from the 'Met', and, at the onset of important events in Attingham's history (the American Friends were founded in 1962), Phelps Warren and John and Elayne Varian. Their vital role is discussed elsewhere in these pages. As far as I can establish the group was joined by the first Canadians, Elaine Dodge from Nova Scotia and Mrs K. Ryder from New Brunswick, Edwin Boone (whom the 1984 Attingham *Directory* refers to as 'dilettante: retired'), and many others about whom the record is more or less silent.

When the group assembled at Missenden Abbey in Buckinghamshire it was for a busy programme, centring on visits, over two days, to Windsor Castle and then Eton College, Oxford, Chiswick, Osterley, Strawberry Hill, Waddesdon and Claydon: rich fare indeed. Oliver Millar, then Deputy Surveyor of the Queen's Pictures, together with Robin Mackworth-Young, the Royal Librarian, escorted the party through Windsor, and on the second day Francis Watson (not then appointed as Surveyor of the Queen's Works of Art) gave further tours. Almost nineteen packed days with everything in for forty people at a little over a total of £3,000. Additionally three scholarships worth £140 were awarded.

The years of consolidation, the first ten years to 1961, perhaps had their greatest recognition in what the School has always been about. Lydia Bond Powel again:

> To begin with I venture to say that the majority of those in the U.S. who are engaged in Restoration and Preservation today are *alumni* of Attingham — through them the British National Trust has extended its influence and experience to Williamsburg, Mount Vernon, Winterthur, Deerfield and to Museum directors and curators without number. Architects, designers, decorators, collectors and the lay public, who support the Preservation Movement, have profited immeasurably from what they have learned in England.

By 1962 the basic cost of the Summer School had crept to $275, but the applications came steadily in to Hardinge Scholle in Washington and Edith Standen in New York. Then the applications were forwarded by the distinguished American sponsors (of which a list was previously given) to George and Helen in England. The 1962 Class, after Attingham and Derbyshire, was going down into Wiltshire to stay at Philipps (or Dinton) House, near Salisbury. The house had been built in the neo-Grecian style by Sir Jeffry Wyattville in 1813–16 for a branch of the Wyndham family. From here visits were made to Longleat, to the splendid triangular-plan house of Longford Castle, Montacute, then but sparingly furnished, majestic Wilton and the sylvan reaches of Henry Hoare's Stourhead. Lydia Powel joined Edward Maverick, Edith Standen, Margaret Stearns and the architectural historian, Professor Caroll Meeks, and forty-two other eager class members. But 1962 was important for another reason, with far-reaching implications — the founding of the 'American Friends of Attingham Inc' in New York.

John Hayward, Helen Williams and Professor Nikolaus Pevsner at Attingham Park for the 1962 Summer School.

III · THE AMERICAN CONNECTION STRENGTHENS
1962 to 1970

WHEN PHELPS WARREN, of whom more presently, and John and Elayne Varian attended the Class of 1961 — the tenth anniversary year of the Summer School — there was much talk about its importance in some parts of American cultural life. Elayne Varian, as Phelps Warren recorded on many later occasions, 'initiated' the American Friends of Attingham in 1962. 'and her husband John, being a lawyer, set up the organization, incorporating it in the State of New York'. Whilst therefore formed in June 1962, it was not until 3 April 1963 that the Varians turned the 'Corporation' over to a group of *alumni* in the New York area. These became the Members of the Corporation, and in essence, the governing body of the Friends. It was their duty to elect the 'Directors', who in turn elected the officers, and decided the broad matters of policy.

On 20 November 1963, writing out of his office, Lewis, MacDonald and Varian at 425 Park Avenue, John Varian filed Form 1023 for charitable exemption. Donations of money or property were to be used to help selected qualified United States residents:

> to attend educational institutions in the United States and in England . . . particular attention being given to the special summer school course given at Attingham Park in England . . .

Obviously the group was concerned to spread information, enrol students and raise sufficient funds to help them attend 'Attingham'. The worthy 'educational, non-profit organization' was now in existence, with 'all officers and directors serving without remuneration'. Who were they?

The first President was Ernest Hillman, jun., with John Varian acting as Treasurer and Harry Grier as Honorary Secretary. Funds were of course as yet few — the 1962 Financial Statements shows:

Operating Contributions	$275
Contributions	575
Cumulating for Scholarships	300

But with events such as the 'Benefit' in November 1963 — 'An Attingham Afternoon' with Harry Grier and Edith Standen showing slides of their English 'adventures' — the 1963 budget had increased materially:

Operating	$293.95
Contributions	1712.31
Checking	2056.26
Cumulating for Scholarships	1260.

It was stated, and needed no undue stressing, that funds for the operation of scholarships:

> were originally received almost entirely from *alumni* of the courses . . . but as the Corporation's activities have become known, other organizations have contributed funds . . . but over half of the funds each year come in the form of small donations from individuals.

Phelps Warren (1906–85); the historian of Attingham needs every chance to recognize his very important contribution, given over some fifteen years, 1964 to 1979, as the second President of the Friends. His own words, taken from 'Some Historical Notes by the Retiring President, May 15, 1979' are exact:

> I date these notes May 15 . . . because it was on that date, 15 years ago, when I was first elected president of the Attingham Friends.
> Though I attended Attingham in '59 it was not until a year or two later that I became Attingham-involved in this country.

Phelps then talks of Lydia Bond Powel's contribution of single-handedly enrolling the first Class of '52, of his helping her collect Attingham mail and so on in later years, and continues:

> In 1964 I made the giant step from 'errand boy' to president of the Friends, succeeding Ernest Hillman [Att. '56], the first president (1963–4). I have been president since then but for the year 1967–8 when I was writing *Irish Glass* (1970) and the president's office was filled by Mrs. John F. Varian [Elayne, Att. '61], the Friends' co-founder with her lawyer husband.
> The 'Attingham experience' was at work in Mrs. Varian when she persuaded her husband to create the legal entity, American Friends of Attingham, incorporating it in New York State, June 13, 1962. It was a paper-corporation with Varian staff members as incorporators and officers. But on April 3, 1963, former students of Attingham took over at an organization meeting in Mr Varian's Park Avenue office when Ernest Hillman was elected president.
> Administration of the Friends was soon localized in a corner of my living-room but early on it became apparent that professional secretarial skills were required. The late Harry Grier [Att. '57] then second in command at the Frick

Phelps Warren (1906–85), President of The American Friends of Attingham, 1964–79, on the terrace of the House of Commons with Dame Joan Vickers and the Class of 1963.

Collection came to the rescue providing the accomplished services of Mrs Maurice Kahn [Peggy, Att. '68]. The entirely gratuitous Grier-Kahn benefits lasted until the fall of '68 . . .

The remainder of Phelps's summary will be quoted in its correct chronology. What of Phelps himself? Again it is Christopher Monkhouse's written tribute at Phelps's death on 2 February 1985 which is the best record of his business career:

> Beyond the walls of Attingham, Phelps's name will probably best be remembered by the interior design profession as co-founder in 1929 of the distinguished wallpaper firm of Katzenbach and Warren. Part of the success of that firm Phelps always attributed to the fact that it opened its doors for business after Black Thursday, and hence was able to gain the attention of certain clients, who previously would have been totally absorbed by clipping coupons. Of course, Katzenbach and Warren's real attraction lay in the ground it broke by making more readily available some of the great European wallpapers, especially French, along with commissioning designs from contemporary American artists . . .

As well as being a collector of, and the only serious historian of Irish glass (Phelps revised his standard work in 1981), he also collected Dutch and white *faience*. He designed a room at his house at 955 Lexington Avenue to house his collection of glass and ceramics, along with his library and study, dining room and even spare bedroom on occasion. As Monkhouse (Att. '66) noted, taking a leaf from Sir John Soane's house museum at Lincoln's Inn Fields in London:

> Phelps may even have surpassed Soane as the master of compression, made possible by his unwavering respect for classical design and the order it so naturally imposes . . .

So there was a good businessman, with a tidy, cultured mind and an office organization, and Phelps gave his all to Attingham's activity in America. The task was helped just a little by an appreciative notice — 'Attingham is a Magic Word' — in the *New York Herald Tribune* in early November 1962.

In 1964 Phelps set out to James Biddle the purposes of the American Friends. He had Lydia Powel as his Vice-President, Harry Grier as Secretary and John Varian as Treasurer. The Directors were Biddle, Ernest Hillman, Dan Hopping, Edith Standen, Phelps and Lydia.

a) To knit together the Attingham *alumni* family in the United States of America
b) to spread information about the Summer School course
c) to procure qualified students for the Course
d) to offer scholarships when possible for promising American students.

The third week of the 1963 Class was held at Ditchley Park, Oxfordshire, and on 21 July John Tillotson gave a lavish supper party there. It was an appropriate setting, for the great house of Ditchley, designed and built by James Gibbs and Francis Smith and with outstanding Italianate stuccoes, had been newly opened as an Anglo-American Conference Centre. It was a delightful spot from which to visit Blenheim, Rousham, Stowe and Broughton Castle. Many house owners, Masters and Wardens of Oxford colleges, museum curators and distinguished lecturers, such as Sir John Summerson, John and Helena Hayward, Mark Girouard, Alec Clifton-Taylor and Francis Watson, attended the dinner. Phelps Warren came in from New York, with Lydia Powel, and Barbara Wriston (who had now moved to the Art Institute in Chicago). As for the members, John Sweeney (Att. '60) came again, together with Anna Spitzmüller from the Albertina Collection in Vienna, Bob Kennedy (who was to be so helpful in Attingham's administration in New York, and was marked by Helen on her members' list as 'excellent') — but who was it that was 'good but always late!'? — and there were three 'tiresome' and two 'awful' entries. Each Attingham Director does the same and dreads mislaying the list.

The 1964 Summer School brochure, announcing 'the variable last week of the course' to be spent at Bath, was the first on which application forms were to be had from Harry Grier at the Frick Collection. The sponsors, more or less the same as in previous years, had added Phelps himself, Otto Wittman and Barbara Wriston as experienced 'names'. The cost was to be in the region of $320 and 'a limited number of scholarships' were available. Phelps himself was to attend the Bath week of the School, and amongst the many other names, several re-visiting, mention should be made of the eminent Hungarian art-historian (who continues in 1991 to advise on 'selection') Professor, Dr Anna Zador of the Art History Department in the University of Budapest, a long-time friend of Helen's. She was the first, in 1964, of the long succession of 'East' European students, some thirty-four, to whom 'Attingham' was a cutural life-line in the darkest years. To read many of their letters is a poignant experience and anyone involved with 'Attingham' feels proud to have played a part in the rich friendships which have evolved and the help which has been selflessly given and received.

It is possible, looking at the detailed members' list for 1964, to see what good work the new organization had done. The group was filled with professors of architecture, consultants to Park Commissions, Presidents of Boards of Education, curatorial staff from the 'Met' (Clare Vincent, Mrs Wagenvoord) from Newark, Worcester Art Museum, Winterthur, Colonial Williamsburg (Mildred Lanier), with Contessa Da Schio revisiting from the Palladian Centre at Vicenza, Dr Rötter from Vienna's Kunsthistorisches Museum, Dr Allmayer-Beck (also from Vienna), together with the New York architect and subsequent scholarship benefactor, Gerald Watland, Maurice Tomlin from the Victoria and Albert Museum and Clare Janinck from The National Trust for Scotland. Perhaps some note had been taken of a letter to Phelps in December 1963:

> It would be a shame to have Attingham given over to too earnest young professionals. There is so much they do not understand.

But if they had 'got through' the scrutiny of Lydia Powel, Chairman of the 1964 Admissions Committee, they deserved to be there. The 'Tutors and Shepherds' (the last appellation appeared for the first time) were John Cushion, John Hayward, Mrs Parry, Lady Simmons (both working as volunteers in the Victoria and Albert Museum), and from Swan Hill Court (of delightful tea fame) in Shrewsbury, Mrs C. Lawson Stote.

Sir Joshua Rowley, mindful that Phelps had been on the '64 Class, wrote to George Trevelyan of what their friend felt:

> Phelps is sure and I think Helen agrees that there should be no evening lectures, however inconvenient this may be from the programme point of view. If the students have had an interesting day and an active one they simply cannot be expected to listen to lectures at night . . .

It was advice which, whilst sensible, has been long ignored!

Well into 1964 the American Friends' membership stood at about 240 in number. Already mail for eight persons has been returned 'not found', and 101 had joined as a result of an invitation mailed in 1963. The 'Third Week policy' of the School was unchanged; 'of welcoming *alumni*, but to a limited number of places, for the last six days'.

No intending Attingham scholar, signing up at whatever date ahead of the final selection, early or late, could have too much of an idea about the programme soon to become so relevant. Those looking at the brochure for 1965 knew that Scotland was envisaged — but Dumfries, Mellerstain, Hopetoun and The Drum — all by various members of the Adam family — or Kinross and Drumlanrig by the great Baroque masters? And by invitation of The Chairman of The National Trust for Scotland, the Earl of Wemyss and March, the reception on Saturday 17 July was to be at his own Gosford House, with its magnificent marble hall and double staircase. So many Scottish owners were then in residence and met the group that it was almost a royal progress, ending out on the Ayrshire coast at dramatically-sited Culzean Castle.

John Hayward, accompanied by Helena, came to tutor, and met Olga Pulmanova from the National Gallery in Prague, Gerhard Hojer from the Bayerisches Nationalmuseum in Munich, and Alf Boe, Chief Curator at the Kunst Industri Museum in Oslo. With John and Helena's linguistic abilities no one was left unwelcomed, and the active American group banished any lingering hesitancy. J. Stewart Johnson, then at the Newark Museum, was one of five or six curatorial staff, with Lisa Terrace (Koch), then a Research Assistant in the Department of Textiles at the Boston Museum of Fine Arts; Nancy Goyne (Evans) and Helen Belknap of Winterthur; David Keith of the M. H. de Young Museum in San Francisco; the 'Met' Librarian, Emma Papert; and several members of University faculties; the interior design consultant, David Hanks; Patti Foos Whitelaw from Charleston and a large group for the Third Week. These included Mrs Earle Williams, Miss Karpinski from the 'Met' Print Room, the art collector from Cleveland, Mildred

Putnam, Margaret Valk, who had been on the 1955 and 1960 classes, and two Winterthur guides (Elizabeth Sly and Mrs Frank Rowlett). The British students, only able to come to the last week, the 'Scottish' one, were the largest number ever, ten, including the Chatsworth Librarian, Tom Wragg, Desmond FitzGerald (Knight of Glin), Maurice Tomlin, Derek Shrub — the three, then at the Victoria and Albert Museum, had two more colleagues with them, apart from Jane Fawcett (The Victorian Society) and Miss Yvonne Buckley from The National Trust.

Obviously, each year's course put a considerable strain on Helen, busy also with her career in the Education Department of the Victoria and Albert Museum. She had been born in Belfast on 21 June 1904, the eldest daughter of John McCaldin Lowenthal and Elsa Iklé. Her father was a linen merchant (as his father before him). After day school there and at the age of thirteen to the excellent boarding school St Felix, Southwold, Helen went to Bedford College, University of London. She states herself, in a *curriculum vitae* prepared for a visit to Eastern Europe, that she took a degree in English History and Art History. Then 'for sixteen years Education Officer of the Victoria and Albert Museum which entailed building a practically non-existent department' to one which by the early '70s had a large staff and covered a wide field.

During the Second World War Helen had worked in an Intelligence Section of the Foreign Office, and she also did part-time work for Army Education which entailed a prolonged visit to the Middle East. After the war there was rewarding work for the Extra-Mural Department of Cambridge University, where she held the first tutorial post for Art History. She lectured abroad for the British Council at this point and visited Germany, France, Yugoslavia, Czechoslovakia, Hungary and America. At least five tours of America and one of China. As Helen noted, after one American tour, in 1952, the first

Helen Lowenthal at the coach microphone, in the Lake District, Special Week, June 1985.
Photograph: Mary Stirling

one, 'I was instrumental in setting up a Summer School for the study of British Country Houses'.

In 1966 the overall cost of the Summer School was announced at $325 and in April the English 'committee' had an acknowledged chairman in John Tillotson, although as Sir Joshua Rowley told Phelps in June 1966: 'So far the School has thrived with George and Helen doing 99% of the work.' The Third week of the Summer School was to be held in Norfolk from 18 to 25 July, but there was much to do before that at Attingham and in Derbyshire. I confess to a sneaking interest in the Class of '66, for not only did I give my first Attingham lecture thereon (inevitably, at Helen's request, on plasterwork!) but Helen's strictures on some of my poorer slides earned me the long-held friendship of Morrie Heckscher and Chris Monkhouse, both *alumni* with distinguished service to the School and to the 'Friends'. And so many others: Hortense Feldblum, ever-ready to support causes in subsequent years, Sam Dornsife (recently honoured by The Victorian Society), Jim Fitch, Columbia's Architecture Professor, Pauline Metcalf, the design historian, Nancy Richards from Winterthur, Charles Wood III and his then wife Elizabeth, also from Winterthur, and Bill Doneghy, who had spent a long career in US Government service as an architect and construction management engineer, and who was to attend several Third Weeks in later years.

In Norfolk the School had the chance to concentrate on its great houses with the help of the Norwich Castle Museum staff and the kindly assistance of R. W. Ketton-Cremer, of Felbrigg, who had given the opening address in 1958. Mr and Mrs Blofeld welcomed the group to Hoveton House — Mrs Blofeld had attended the School in 1960 — and the Marchioness of Cholmondeley came over from Houghton and was also present at the jolly picnic lunch.

A fortnight or so after the 1966 School had finished Helen wrote to Phelps on 8 August:

> I am in the Trust gang at last. Jack [Rathbone] says I can be part-time Education Officer, or rather Lecture Adviser. Practically no pay, but never mind, it will be such a help to do things through them. Also it will, I believe, assist the School. The Trust is keener on the School than ever . . . I have also got Trenchard Cox to say he will come on the Committee.

It was a frenetic life and some members of the Class had worried that Helen was so tired and consequently sometimes inclined to be short-tempered and 'explosive'. It was a characteristic Helen 'fault', as anyone who has been on the receiving end will know, but she expected high standards. But no friend was ever more loyal and true, and able to feel so sorry and generous after an asperic outburst.

Sir Trenchard Cox, still a Patron, had just retired from his post as Director of the Victoria and Albert Museum. As for the 1966 Class, it was the first year that scholars were asked to present a paper or other material on how the School had helped them. In his letter to *alumni* Phelps also said that 'for the past two years we have been in the fortunate position of having more applicants than the School could accommodate'. In fact John Tillotson thought the Third Week was overcrowded and that so many visitors were defeating the School's main purpose and not being fair to the 'serious student'. Finally Helen wrote the thank-you letters and faithful Ruth Bell, George's secretary at Attingham, tidied up the loose ends of another successful Class, the fifteenth.

In January 1967 Hortense Feldblum wrote to Phelps to say that she wished to help towards a tuition-scholarship in 1967 as it was her feeling, noted on the '66 Class, that:

> we would always benefit from an exchange of ideas from applicants in the fields of architecture and interior design from outside of the U.S. Only two English curators were in our [1966] Group and one young architect from Portugal.

The balance of income over expenditure in 1966 was only £66 and so there was a direct relevance to the suggestion. Accommodation at Attingham was still a seemingly modest £3 10s. a day, with a concern to keep the overall cost as low as possible.

The opening address of the 1967 School was given by the new Committee member, Sir Trenchard Cox, on the subject of 'The Country Houses and the Museums'. With a concern for Attingham's curious classical elevation Dr Paul Norton of the University of Massachusetts spoke on 'George Steuart: Architect of Attingham, new light on his work'. The trend in lectures in the first twenty years of Attingham was towards the history of architecture. In the '70s Helena Hayward, as a noted decorative arts scholar, was to change the emphasis and I have continued that decorative arts trend. But one licks the lips: to hear George Trevelyan on 'The Seeing Eye of Architecture' (I heard him on it but once, alas) was a memorable, lively experience. Also the dry authority of beautifully constructed lectures by John Summerson (on Vanbrugh) and the amazing insights of Pevsner on Medieval and Tudor building.

Whilst July 1967 was certainly not the School's first visit to Mawley Hall, or even the first lecture to the School by Helena Hayward (as she had been working in the early 1960s on her Thomas Johnson book, *The Beginnings of English Rococo* (1963), the subject she chose was always very much in her mind); the alchemy of the School in full action was also there. Fed by dinner at *The Feathers* in Ludlow and a floodlit performance of *Measure for Measure* at Ludlow Castle, a sherry party with Lady Berwick, lectures on Robert Adam and John Nash by Clifford Musgrave and Terence Davis respectively, the enjoyable tea at Swan Hill Court, and then off to Derbyshire. Hard work still, with Tissington, Sutton Scarsdale ruins, Bolsover Castle and Hardwick Hall in one crowded Saturday. Then after three days down to Uplands, near High Wycombe, for the Buckinghamshire week. The dreamy delights of summer-time Oxford with Howard Colvin talking on All Souls and a High Victorian tour led by Peter Howell. But in addition, Blenheim, tea at Ditchley, Haseley Court, Nancy Lancaster's house, Windsor Castle, Eton College, Woburn, Waddesdon, Claydon, and finally, towards London, Syon and Chiswick. Always the theme of finishing on the up-beat: it continues still, as though all should end with baroque horns, kettle-drums and crescendo. As it was, a sherry party, with Sir Trenchard and Lady Cox, was as enjoyable, if quieter.

As for members, I can but pick out names I recognize: Joe Butler from Sleepy Hollow Restorations, Charles Chevalier (to come on many Third Weeks), Jane Shadel from the Corning Glass Museum, Charlton Theus, Bob Kennedy, Olga Pulmanova from Prague, with Mrs Hamran from the Aust-Agder Museet in Norway, and Stanislav Stanicic (called 'Stan-Stan' by the Group) from the Zagreb Museum. The British scholars included Clive Wainwright and Gillian Wilson from the Victoria and Albert Museum.

When Helen reported on the 1967 School she said that 'it had been one of the most successful held, notable for the high grade of students attending'. The accounts for the years showed a profit of £237 and it was agreed that this sum should be put in a holding fund, to be used:

    (a)   towards bursaries for students from Iron Curtain countries, where expedient
    (b)   to meet the cost of printing the notes on houses and their contents
    (c)   to leave a sum of approximately £50 in an emergency account.

Helena Hayward and F. St John Gore (Paintings Adviser to The National Trust) were elected to the Committee. As for the School, it was decided too much was attempted. Lectures should be held in the mornings, with no more than one or two in the evenings, and the number of houses visited should be cut down. Fees for lecturers were increased to £18 for a single lecture and £30 for a double one, where an overnight stop was involved.

Meanwhile, in New York the entirely gratuitous Grier-Kahn secretarial help to Attingham was due to come to an end in the autumn of 1968. After a very short period with Elayne Varian as President (whilst, as noted, Phelps was working on his Irish glass book), Phelps came back into what George described as 'the Attingham circus'. At the 1968 Annual Meeting it was proposed that Robert ('Bob') Luck be elected to succeed Harry Grier as Secretary (Harry was made a Director). It was further decided that rather than move the 'Friends' organization to Washington to be under the auspices of the National Trust, it be located at the American Federation of Arts on E.65th Street, with which Bob Luck was associated as Assistant Director. As Phelps further put it, the Vice-President, Bob Kennedy 'is an anchor man', pulling hard to right the problems arising from a period of difficulty, with everyone from Mrs Varian to Phelps himself too busy. What the Federation could give, and allowed unstintingly, was the devoted participation for some ten years of Anne J. Sharkey. Under Phelps's careful oversight Anne dealt with all the correspondence and the thousand and one things that running the American Friends entailed. She is a loved member of the Attingham *alumni*, and the 'Secretary Emerita'. As for the other officers, Lydia Powel was to be listed henceforth as 'Chairman', John Varian continued as Treasurer, and Jimmy Biddle was 'Consultant for National Trust matters'.

For whatever reason the yellow brochure for the 1968 School was the first to have an extra fold in a larger format to announce 'American

Applications'. These were still being processed by Harry Grier, but he had already resigned in favour of Bob Luck. The 1967 Annual Meeting had also suggested that the list of successful applicants for the Third Week be reviewed prior to notification. This led to a wide date band: '*alumni* selected will be notified as soon as possible after February 15th and not later than March 23, 1968'. The cost of the full Summer School was to be $360 and $140 for the Third Week, based at the new University of York. The Members' List is significantly fuller with the Third Week addition of twenty-one members. For the full course there were Cary and Barbara Carson, then both at Harvard (where Cary was doing his doctorate and Barbara was cataloguing the historic scientific instruments), Margaret Kahn, Harry Grier's Assistant at the Frick Collection, Ferris Megarity, the Promotion Director for B. Altman & Co., Mildred Trimble, Chief of the US Government Color Design Division, and the usual talented groups from leading museums and university architectural schools. One student from Yugoslavia (Dr Vera Kruzio-Uchytil of the Zagreb Museum) and two from the Riksantikvariatet in Oslo represented Continental Europe. The British members included Michael Darby, Anthony Burton and John Hardy from the Victoria and Albert Museum.

For the Third Week Hortense Feldblum, Charles Chevalier, Lydia Powel, Mrs Frelinghuysen, Edward Maverick, Margaret Valk and a few others, along with Phelps Warren, were tutored by John Cushion, Helena Hayward, and George's Deputy Warden at Attingham, Geoffrey Toms, and shepherded by Mary Parry, Lady Simmons and Sheila Lawson Stote. This would seem to have been the first School at which Helena, newly elected to the Committee, and Geoffrey had their roles defined. Both were to give invaluable support to Helen in the succeeding years.

Castle Howard, Yorkshire, *c.* 1710, the south front; drawing by Will Gwilliam (Att. '88).

York, one of Europe's most important medieval cities, had no better exponent than the late Dr Eric Gee (secretary to the Royal Commission on Historical Monuments in York), a knowledgeable and delightful raconteur. One of the delights of being at York too was the chance to do almost everything. There were visits to Castle Howard, Harewood House, Bramham Park, Newby Hall, Fountains Abbey with its great prefatory landscape in John Aislabie's Studley Royal schemes of the late 1720s, Sledmere, Burton Agnes and the delightful Colen Campbell villa of Ebberston. But, equally, a Francis Jackson recital on the York Minster organ, a tour of the Minster with the Surveyor to the Fabric, Sir Bernard Feilden, a National Trust reception at The Treasurer's House. Finally a special reserved compartment on the London train and a farewell party at the Courtauld Institute in Adam's fine interiors in Portman Square — a privilege accorded to Helen (who had studied there) by Sir Anthony Blunt (who had lectured to the School, and whose subsequently complicated life as a spy was then not known to the eager wine-bibbers).

The School had now been in existence for almost fifteen years. The financial arrangements with the Adult College had perhaps always been a little too uneasy. Whilst John Tillotson wrote in October 1968 in good heart to Sir John Winnifrith, the Director-General of The National Trust, the true position was still unclear. Mr Tillotson suggested that from the modest profit made in 1968 a grant should be made to The National Trust 'towards the cost of the adaptation of a room in the pavilion of the Old Hall at

John Cushion, who lectured and tutored on ceramics to successive Schools and Special Weeks from the early 1960s — he was also an affable and invaluable helper to us all.

Hardwick, as a lecture room for the use of school-children and others' if the relevant co-operation of the Ministry of Works and the Local Authority could be obtained.

On 1 November 1968 Phelps sent out his 'Open Letter to All Friends'. He noted that both Helena Hayward and Geoffrey Toms had been on tour with the class, Geoffrey handling administrative detail and Helena tutoring. It is perhaps sensible here to say something of Helena Hayward's career. She has been vital to Attingham's undoubted success.

Helena was the only daughter of Sir Henry Martyn, KCVO, and Lady Martyn. Sir Henry was Surgeon-Apothecary to the Royal Household at Windsor. After school at St George's, Ascot, Helena went to the Sorbonne, to Heidelberg University and spent time in Italy. This explains her superb fluency in French, German and Italian. With her Master's degree behind her she married John Hayward who was to become one of England's most distinguished art-historians. After John's war service he was appointed as a member of the Monuments and Fine Arts branch of the army of occupation in Austria (1945 to 1947) and then for two more years a member of the

Helena Hayward at Ditchley Park, 1988. After helping Helen Lowenthal from 1968 Helena succeeded her as Director, 1976–85. She is now Consultant Director of the Summer School and Joint Director of The Attingham Study Week.

Photograph: Nancy Hirst

Control Commission in Vienna. Busy active years for Helena therefore in Austria, where she studied Austrian baroque frescoes. In 1951 John joined the staff of the Victoria and Albert Museum and she could settle to family life, to rearing her two children and to writing and lecturing.

Helena's first book was a dictionary of antique collecting, an invaluable glossary, which *The Connoisseur* published in 1960. It was, however, her pioneering study of the eighteenth-century carver Thomas Johnson which established her reputation (1963). She built this up with editing *World Furniture* (1969) — it is a matter of regret Helena has no control over the umpteen reissues of that invaluable work — and finally, after editing all John Linnell's drawings (*Furniture History*, v, 1969) her two volume study (with Dr Pat Kirkham) of the eighteenth-century cabinet makers, William and John Linnell (1980).

It was, however, Helena's unrivalled ability as a teacher which was of vital use to Attingham. She lectured at the Victoria and Albert Museum and for six years she taught the silver and furniture subjects (English and European) for the Study Centre for the History of the Fine and Decorative Arts which Erica O'Donnell had founded in 1964. It was also about this time — John's name is in the 1964 Attingham programme — that Helena started to accompany him to the School's venues. Then, as noted in these pages, the help over many years to Helen Lowenthal, with whom she became Co-Director in 1971 and subsequently, in 1976, Director of the Summer School.

The 1969 brochure for the Summer School (with the Third Week to be based at Newton Park, near Bath) was the first to announce applications should be sent to E.65th Street in New York where they would be processed by Anne Sharkey. On the back page the full list of Officers, Directors and Sponsors was set out. With the posts of Chairman (Powel), President (Warren), Vice-President (Kennedy), Secretary (Luck), Treasurer (Varian) and National Trust Consultant (Biddle) remaining unchanged, perhaps it is useful to list the other names. The *Directors* were Carl Dauterman, Curator of Western European Arts at the 'Met'; Barbara Snow Delaney (who had been on the first Class of '52), Special Projects Editor at *Antiques Magazine*; Mrs Frederick Frelinghuysen, First Regent, Gunston Hall; Harry Grier, The Frick Collection; J. Stewart Johnson, Curator of Decorative Arts at the Museum of the City of New York.

Then the *Sponsors*. The architect John Desmond; Hope Gladding, formerly Professor of Decorative Arts at the University of California; Bertram Little (Att. '52), Director of SPNEA; Dr Bill Murtagh, Keeper of the National Register in the National Park Service; Professor Robert Moore, the 'Eng. Lit.' specialist from the University of Minnesota; John Pearce, Curator, National Trust; Charles Sawyer, Director of the University of Michigan Art Museum; John Sweeney, Deputy Director at Winterthur; Jim Van Derpool (Class of '52, formerly Executive Director, Landmarks Preservation Commission); Charles Wall, Resident Director at Mount

Vernon, and Barbara Wriston, Head of Museum Education at the Art
Institute in Chicago.

I have given the lists in full, an indulgence I can enjoy rarely in these
pages, to show the great experience and 'corporate' strength the American
Friends could call on. It is a system they have continued to use, to my mind,
with considerable success.

I am not really sure why the English committee chose to change the
format of the 1969 programme from the usual size (a little above American
paper size, the international A4) to a small 8 by 6½ inch folder. Certainly
easier to carry, but the mixture as before. The opening address on Tuesday

1969 Programme.

1 July (also a change) was given by Lord Boyne, and then George spoke about 'The English Country House'. There were some new lecturers: Pamela Tudor Craig (later Lady Wedgwood), John Newman from the Courtauld Institute, and before the visit to Berrington and Croft, John Summerson's Deputy at the Soane Museum, Dorothy Stroud, talked about Henry Holland.

Everyone was given a copy of Ferris Megarity's article 'The cry of the peacock' (*House Beautiful*, April 1969), about his experiences on the Class of '68:

> For three weeks last July I awoke every morning to the cry of the peacock — there is the beguiling memory of Berrington Hall [visited by the 40th Class of 1991], fragrant with garden-fresh sweet peas in dizzying abundance, and Lady Crawley, its delightful owner, who gave up a Buckingham Palace garden party to regale us with lunch in the buttery — hedgehog pie, strawberries and Devonshire cream — and related the legends of this marvellous Palladian creamy stone house, a work of Henry Holland, and its Capability Brown garden . . .

The 18th Class of 1969 probably hoped for treatment as good, and in terms of observing the guidelines set down in 1967 there were fewer evening lectures. Indeed, from the eleventh day on the 'lectures' were listed as 'optional and informal talks', although as they were by Helena Hayward, John Cushion and Geoffrey Toms they were surely not missed?

The third week moved via Chipping Campden to Bath, and at once it was a mixture of what that city could offer — Roman remains under Georgian façades — and as a good centre. Berkeley Castle, where Edward II was murdered in 1327, Corsham Court, with its superb Chippendale-period furniture, a party at Dyrham, tea at the Senate House in Bristol with members of the School of Architecture, Stonehenge, Wilton, Salisbury Cathedral. Fewer peacocks, perhaps, but enough to excite.

Professor Maynard Mack, the distinguished Yale 'Alexander Pope' scholar, led the 'academics', including Merribell Parsons, Curator of Decorative Arts at Minneapolis, Paul Buchanan, then Director of Architectural Research at Williamsburg, Milo Naeve, then Assistant Director of Collections and Curator of Furniture there, and David Warren, Curator at Bayou Bend. Ferris Megarity arranged for the Senior Interior Designer from Altman's (Mildred Loftus) to come, and there were graduate students, National Parks staff, museum education instructors, including Glenn Thompson, the Director of Education and Training Services for the National Trust in Washington. Lucy Sydnor, a former President of the Women's Council of the Virginia Museum of Fine Arts, led those giving a vast amount of experienced but voluntary help. Hortense Feldblum came in for the Third Week; Ferris Megarity came too, but found, as far as I know, not only peacocks at Dyrham but also a candle-lit house. The 'East European' students, one from Czechoslovakia and two from Yugoslavia, were Dr Anna Masarykova from the National Gallery in Prague, Professor

The Class of 1969 at Attingham Park. On the front row are Helen
Lowenthal (J. Sibley Jennings, with sombrero), Helena Hayward and
Geoffrey Toms. Phelps Warren is third from left, back row.

Desa Diana (Town Museum, Split) and Miss Dubravka Mladinov (Zagreb
Museum).

Helen's report on the 1969 School made its usual incisive, quirky
remarks: 'the lectures (with one exception) were a success' — 'the
Shakespearean performance at Ludlow might possibly be omitted in future
as people catch cold and get very tired'. Also she commented that the
generosity of the Third Week group helped to provide six scholarships on
the American side. Unfortunately, as in 1967, George's health prevented
him taking part in the School in the usual way. This was a great
deprivation, but due to the generous assistance of Clifford Musgrave and
Helena Hayward, with the support of Attingham's Assistant Warden,
Geoffrey Toms, the programme was carried through smoothly and had
made a profit of £750.

In itself this focused minds because the disposition of the profits was
within the final control of the Governors of the Adult College. Both Helen
and Helena Hayward were giving constant thought to the School's future,
and equally Phelps Warren was ever logical in his advice. A few weeks
before the October Council Meeting in London Helena wrote to Phelps.
She could see how the character of the students had fundamentally altered
and that the course had not adapted sufficiently to cater for the fact. Too

Anthony 'Tony' Galliers-Pratt, Chairman of
The Attingham Summer School Trust,
1970–82.

much was being attempted, too many houses visited without adequate preparations. More detailed discussion, including ground-plans of the houses and expert guidance on architectural features, was needed. The bibliography needed improving and the notes on houses expanded. As Helena wrote, 'in the past Helen has done all these things single-handed and without payment — fine, as long as student demands were less exacting'. If finances could be controlled from London more might be accomplished.

Phelps sent careful, helpful replies to Helena and to Helen. He welcomed that Tony Galliers-Pratt was to succeed John Tillotson as Chairman — was glad that John would continue to serve the Committee — but felt the appointment of a Shropshire landowner at this particular time, and moreover one with extensive business and financial experience, was particularly sensible. Phelps thought the Third Week quota of 20 was too much: he advocated a slightly larger main course (36 to 38) and a reduction of the 20 to 12. The reason for the reduction was that 'they make the School too large, and too dependent on the financial input from that to be sensible'. He also worried that Helen was tired from attendance at The

Victorian Society school and, as he said, 'Unless George is very much himself by July 1970, and can really take a vigorous part in the School, it seems to us you should be present at the opening and not arrive late and tired out'. It was good advice, fairly expressed, and Helen was at her dearest, pragmatic best, writing on 14 October, the day after the Council Meeting:

> Justifying the things one has done or left undone are of no interest and since the main purpose of all our hopes is the welfare of the Summer School and its firm establishment for future generations when we are all under the sod, no useful purpose can possibly be served by going over many painful points in your letter. Yesterday we had an excellent meeting of the committee . . .

Let me deal with that in sequence, the meeting of 13 October 1969.

Gathering at Helen's house, it was agreed that the most important matter for the future of the School was setting up an independent financial position. The Shropshire Education Committee would cease to guarantee the School, and that would allow profits, presently under the control of the Attingham Adult College Governors, to be used at the School's discretion. As Secretary, Helen was instructed to set the proposal forward. As a Shropshire landowner with extensive contacts, it was realized that the Chairman-Elect, Tony Galliers-Pratt, would have an important role to play in the expected discussions. For her part Helen, who had not been told of George's illness until within a few weeks of the opening of the 1969 School, guaranteed to be at the 1970 opening.

Financial problems always strain an organization. Without proper control it was understandable that there was a slight tendency to feel 'America' could address the problem. Phelps, in his careful way, had pointed out in September 1969 that five similar courses to Attingham charged less!

I should quote part of Helen's important letter of 14 October 1969 to the Chairman of the Adult College Governors:

> Whilst acknowledging the immense benefits conferred over eighteen years by the association of the School with Attingham Park it was none the less felt that our organization, which has now important commitments on both sides of the Atlantic, should be financially independent. We hope you will understand this when you bear in mind a profit of £750 in 1969 and an exceptional profit of £1553 in 1968.
>
> Owing to the absence of a permanent working fund, we are compelled to face future programmes in a state of financial uncertainty. We feel the time has arrived when we should stand on our own feet, and underwrite any possible loss with the support of the American foundation . . . We very much hope that we may continue to base the School at Attingham Park as we have done, paying a just fee for accommodation and services . . .

On 30 October 1969 the Clerk to the Governors wrote to Helen saying that they 'were prepared to agree to the suggestions of your Committee, in principle' and that they were 'warmly appreciative of the value and high standards of the work of the Summer School'. However, it was felt from the Adult College side that there should be some guarantee of financial solvency 'to safeguard the College's position in any difficulties which may arise in the future'. John Tillotson, in sending copies of the letters to Phelps, felt this was reasonable but that as 'we have no funds at all, the question is are the American Friends of Attingham Inc. prepared to underwrite us?' All Phelps could do was really encourage very fundamental discussions with the College Governors, and Tillotson wrote to them in November. Perhaps Helen felt ready for battle, for the New Year opened with an OBE for her in the Honours List. As she wrote to Phelps on 9 January 1970:

> I had flowers and telegrams so that next to being buried it's been the biggest thing yet. I say obituaries are disappointing to those involved, this is MUCH better!

She further mentioned that George Trevelyan was slowly recovering from his illness, that Pevsner and Summerson would both lecture at the 1970 School, and that 'Helena is marvellously good support and such a fine scholar as well. We are so lucky to have her'.

On 18 January she wrote again to Phelps to inform him that:

> Tony Galliers-Pratt has succeeded John Tillotson as Chairman and is taking up the questions on the continuity in the future. Be assured it will continue to flourish.

IV · CHANGES AT ATTINGHAM PARK
1970 to 1975

AS 1970 OPENED Tony Galliers-Pratt was much involved with contacting the Chief Education Officer for Shropshire, J. W. Henry. Mr Henry wrote to Helen on 27 January 1970 in reply to correspondence arising over the previous two months. Whilst the Governors had agreed 'in principle' to the proposals in Helen's letter, dated the previous 14 October, they felt that:

(a)   With effect from 1970, the Governors and the Summer School Committee agree to share equally the responsibility for the finances of the annual summer school — and that annual credit and debit balances be equally shared or borne by the two parties

(b)   That the work of organisation and administration shall continue to be undertaken by the various parties as at present . . .

(c)   That membership of the Summer School Committee shall continue to include the Warden and/or Deputy Warden of the College.

Subject to the acceptance of these arrangements the Governors were ready to make a payment of £384 as a half-share of the balance on the 1969 course.

The letter went for an answer to Tony Galliers-Pratt, as the new Chairman. He wrote, carefully, on 5 February to Mr Henry to imply that: 'there are certain fundamental differences in view between what you propose and what my Committee believe would be in the best interests of the Summer School'. After outlining the School's gratitude for excellent past co-operation, he stated:

Your proposals, which have come to my committee as somewhat of a surprise . . . are unacceptable. We are prepared to take the full responsibility for the financing of the summer school, and if the £384 which we believe should be paid to us is not forthcoming, then we will make other arrangements to cover us in our first year of independence.

Galliers-Pratt hoped the Shropshire Governors would nevertheless make a gesture of goodwill and pay the money over, indicated that the School would continue to consult with the Attingham Warden and his staff, and concluded:

We shall be appointing an honorary treasurer to draw up the annual accounts and that in respect of the Constitution of the Summer School Committee it should not be 'bound to accept any nominees from whatever source'.

The Clerk replied on 9 February saying that on receipt of the name of an individual appointed by the Summer School, the cheque for £384 would be forthcoming. However, he was cautious about the other 'changes in a well

The 1971 Attingham programme, the first in which the name of 'The National Trust' was replaced.

Attingham Summer School Trust
TWENTIETH ANNUAL SUMMER SCHOOL

Sunday July 4th — Saturday July 24th 1971

THE HISTORIC HOUSES
OF ENGLAND

Chairman: A. M. G. GALLIERS-PRATT
Vice-Chairman: JOHN TILLOTSON
Secretary: MISS H. LOWENTHAL, O.B.E.
Treasurer: G. S. G. TOMS, Deputy Warden, Attingham Park

Members of Council:
JOHN L. CORNFORTH, Architectural Editor, *Country Life*
SIR TRENCHARD COX, C.B.E., late Director, Victoria & Albert Museum, London
DR. KENNETH GARLICK, Keeper of Western Art, Ashmolean Museum, Oxford
R. ST. JOHN GORE, Adviser on Paintings, National Trust
HON. DESMOND GUINNESS, President, Irish Georgian Society, Eire
MRS. HELENA HAYWARD, Editor, *World Furniture*
JOHN HAYWARD, Associate Director, Sotheby's; late Deputy Keeper, Victoria & Albert Museum, London
DR. CLIFFORD MUSGRAVE, O.B.E., late Director, Brighton Pavilion Museum
PROF. SIR NIKOLAUS PEVSNER, O.B.E., University of London
SIR JOHN SUMMERSON, C.B.E., Director, Sir John Soane Museum, London
SIR GEORGE TREVELYAN, Bt., M.A., Warden, Attingham Park, Shropshire

Course Directors:
MISS HELEN LOWENTHAL, O.B.E.
SIR GEORGE TREVELYAN, Bt.

established procedure'. A new committee of unknown status was being proposed and, further, the Attingham Warden or his Deputy had always been closely involved as a committee member.

At the School's Committee Meeting held on 19 May 1970 an agenda item was:

> The establishing of the School and the enlargement of the committee by the appointment of a Treasurer.

Helen's notes on the meeting indicate that the 'name of the Association shall be Attingham Summer School Trust'. While the 1970 School brochure, issued months before, was still the 'Nineteenth Annual National Trust Summer School' the 1971 one was under the new title.

The third week of the 1970 School was to be arranged by Dr Clifford Musgrave at the University of Sussex at Brighton. Commemorating the new connection with the American Federation of Arts, its President, Mrs Alice Kaplan, and Director, Roy Moyer, attended the full course. Meribell Parsons, enthusing about the 1969 Class, was pleased that two of her Trustees, Atherton and Winifred Bean, were able to attend. Barry Greenlaw represented the Department of Collections at Colonial Williamsburg, Jane Giffen (later Nylander), as Curator of Textiles and Ceramics at Old Sturbridge Village, had professional colleagues as experienced as Beatrix Rumford from Williamsburg, Philip Solomon, Curator of Decorative Arts at the Indianapolis Museum, Lynn Springer (later Roberts) on the (usual!) way through St Louis to Kansas to Chicago (or is that mere English hype?), Mark Clark from the Dayton Art Institute, Martha Hackley from the Frick Collection and Joanna Hecht, a cataloguer of Western Art at the 'Met' Museum. Fred Haupt, Director of Public Affairs for the National Trust, came in from Washington. Bill McNaught, later to be President of the American Friends (and now the distinguished Director of the American Museum in Britain at Bath) was still a graduate student, as was the late David Pettigrew, who was at the New York State Historical Association. Always welcome was Phelps Warren who attended part of the first week.

Three Continental students, Mrs Vanda Ladovic, Dr Milada Vilimkova and Dr Stephan Tschudi Madsen, came in from Zagreb, Prague and Oslo respectively. They joined a number of English students, Barbara Roberts (then at the Victoria and Albert Museum and later at the Getty Museum), Desmond Guinness (still a Patron), Avril Hart (Textiles, V & A), Mrs O'Malley (from Helen's erstwhile Education Department there), and in the Third Week twelve *alumni*, including Lydia Powel.

Except to the members of each Class, what they did (in programme terms, I hasten to add) is perhaps of less interest. But can the pulse not be quickened by visits to medieval Stokesay Castle, to seventeenth-century Aston Hall, eighteenth-century Mawley and Kedleston, Regency Oakley Park? Quicken it to a dangerous point with Rousham, Blenheim (led by its historian, the late David Green), Petworth, Parham, Penshurst, Firle, Uppark, Knole, Scotney and Sissinghurst — with a harpsichord concert in the Hall at Knole — and the 'patient' is at fever point. Could they cope with looking at the paintings at the Garrick Club and having a party and supper there?

One of the benefits of the visit of a Norwegian scholar in 1968, Dr Johan Knap, was the invitation to some members involved or on the Classes of '69 and '70 to make a visit to Norway. In 1969 the participants on the five-day visit were Gervase Jackson-Stops, Jane Shadel, David B. Warren and John Hardy. In 1970 Jane Giffen (Nylander), James Waite, David Pettigrew and Beatrix Rumford were able to participate, already having Mrs Madsen as their classmate. An amusing sidelight of the 1970 trip was that the participants thought they were invited for a day longer than was in fact the case, and they had to scramble round and find hotel rooms for the last day they were in Norway.

It will be recalled that the 1970 Class was the first under the Attingham Summer School Trust's auspices. It was therefore particularly unfortunate that at the Council Meeting held in London on 24 November 1970 the Chairman had to report a loss amounting to some £732: 'the first time a loss had been incurred'. When the scale of charges for 1970 had been fixed it had been thought that it would be possible to contain a loss to not more than £100. This had not proved realistic: a brighter aspect was that 50 per cent of the 1969 profit, amounting to £310, would be received. It was nevertheless agreed that the arrangements for 1971 at Attingham Park should go forward but that thought should be given to other venues for future Summer Schools.

This may have been heightened as a thought, however improbable, by the fact that Sir George Trevelyan had announced his retirement as Warden, with 1971 being his 'last School'. Geoffrey Toms, who had been Sir George's Deputy, had been confirmed as Warden. As important to the consideration of the future, particularly the financial outlook, the Chairman informed the meeting that the Trust had been given charity status.

In his new position Geoffrey Toms had set out in a letter to Helen of 10 November 1970 how he felt responsibilities should be divided:

To be undertaken from London:
(1)   All publicity, including the sending of brochures.
(2)   The acceptance of all students.
(3)   All transport except that arranged through Attingham with Vaggs Motors.

To be arranged from Attingham:
(1)   Printing of the final programme, provision of joining instructions, students' lists, room lists, and the preparation of the wallets for students.
(2)   Collection of all outstanding fees.
(3)   Arranging of banking facilities, organisation and issue of invitations to the Attingham party, sale of books and brochures.

Geoffrey suggested provision for more free time, and less time spent on long coach journeys. Finally he enclosed a list of books ordered for the Attingham Library from the £60 presented by the 1969 School to the College.

The changes, which in effect the new Chairman had introduced, merited a larger Council and the names were set out on the larger format white programme for the 20th Annual Summer School of 1971. Of course some members had been elected in earlier years and were still serving — Dr Clifford Musgrave in 1966, Sir Trenchard Cox in 1967 and Kenneth Garlick, F. St John Gore and Helena Hayward in 1969.

Chairman: A. M. G. Galliers-Pratt
Vice-Chairman: John Tillotson

Secretary: Miss H. Lowenthal, OBE
Treasurer: G. S. G. Toms, Deputy Warden, Attingham Park

Members of Council

John L. Cornforth, Architectural Editor, *Country Life*
Sir Trenchard Cox, CBE, late Director, Victoria and Albert Museum, London
Dr Kenneth Garlick, Keeper of Western Art, Ashmolean Museum, Oxford
F. St John Gore, Adviser on Paintings, The National Trust
Hon. Desmond Guinness, President, Irish Georgian Society
Mrs Helena Hayward, Editor, *World Furniture*
John Hayward, Associate Director, Sotheby's; late Deputy Keeper, Victoria and Albert Museum, London
Dr Clifford Musgrave, OBE, late Director, Brighton Pavilion Museum
Prof. Sir Nikolaus Pevsner, OBE, University of London
Sir John Summerson, CBE, Director, Sir John Soane's Museum, London
Sir George Trevelyan, Bt, MA, Warden, Attingham Park, Shropshire

Course Directors

Miss Helen Lowenthal, OBE
Sir George Trevelyan, Bt

As in 1962, the 1971 School was to be at Philipps House, Dinton, a property, like Attingham, of The National Trust. The preparations took note of a proposal made by a 1970 Class member of the assembly of an 'Attingham Slide Library'. Whilst considerable attention was given to this, including a letter about it to *alumni* from Phelps, the logistical difficulties of cataloguing and storage seemed insurmountable, given the scattered locations of *alumni*. However, the programme promised what it had always done — a full bibliography and the use of the 'Attingham' library. Approximately ten students were to be accepted for the Third Week (cost $190 each). Students up to the age of thirty-two were to be charged $395 and for those over thirty-two $450. For the first time George's name was not listed as a Course Director, Helen, Helena and Geoffrey Toms taking the responsibility.

Following the attendance of the President and Director of the American Federation of Arts at the 1970 School it was sensible for Anne Sharkey to attend in 1971. As Executive Assistant to the Federation's Director Anne dealt with all Attingham administrative matters in the United States. Thirty-five other persons came, including another staff member of the Federation (Enid Winslow), seven Professors or Assistant Professors, seven graduate students, two landscape architects, a graphic designer, two Winterthur 'guides' and six curatorial staff. I should make mention of Dick Button's presence as President of Candid Productions. When he was appointed a Director of the American Friends in 1977 — he was then President of the Richmondtown Restoration on Staten Island —

Phelps wrote to Helen: 'We are delighted to have as a director the world's champion figure skater, Olympic winner etc.' I am sure he joined enthusiastically in preparations for the high-spirited 'dramatic' performance given at the end of the School (and repeated at the Lowenthal Scholarship Dinner in New York in January 1990). Special mention might be made of its prime author, Jay Cantor, then a researcher in art and architecture and later on the New York staff of Christie's. I only have space, alas, for the opening choruses.

S. OTERIC Productions Ltd. in association with
THE NATIONAL TRUST for places of Historic Interest
or Natural Beauty
PRESENT
The Atcham Players and the Salopian Chorus in a lively Review of
Attingham Summer School's Trust Twentieth Annual Summer School:
THE HISTORIC HOUSES OF ENGLAND
or
THE SCREW OF THE TERN

The Scene:
Lord Cuthbert Magnum Opus, Bart. of Muche Wedlock welcomes a covey of curious culturephiles and cantankerous claustrophobes to his licentiously crenellated ancestral home.

Opening Chorus:

> It's Attingham, we're here
> We've brought our camera gear
> We've come to see your house
> And meet your lovely spouse
>
> We'll penetrate the hall
> And scale the garden wall
> We'll view your private lair
> We'll be just everywhere.

Kodak Cavalcade with percussion accompaniment

Lord Cuthbert welcomes the brood:

> Consider yourself at home
> And friends of the Aristocracy
> I trust you've all read the book
> If not, come, look at my family tree
>
> Consider yourself at home
> I'm putting you in my agent's care
> Please keep yourselves behind the ropes
> You know the furniture is so rare
>
> Please restrict yourself to our first floor
> The second one is such a mess
> But there are many things of interest
> In our newly created store

Come wander through the sculpture hall
And if you don't like the things you see
Then come along for a cup of tea
Or a post card at 4p

Hurry up, hurry up
Hurry up — save time
Hurry up — save time

When you're racing with the clock
Then you have no time to stop
So just move along and quit this song
Cause we're racing, racing, racing, racing
Racing, racing, racing with the clock.

Only one 'Continental' student attended the 1971 School: Dr Bozenna
Majewska-Maszkowska from The Royal Castle Museum, Warsaw. Among

'Racing, racing, racing with the clock'; towards a 7.40 a.m.
breakfast at Attingham Park. The entrance to the
Great Court.

the British students attending for part of the course was Helen's niece, Julia Raynesford (Boyd) and Nigel Galliers-Pratt, Mr and Mrs Lawson Stote and their daughter Sally (then still serving the famous teas on the lawn to each year's Shrewsbury visit). Twelve *alumni* attended the Third Week only, including the first President of the American Friends, Ernest Hillman, Lynn Springer (Roberts), Berry Tracy, Curator of the American Wing at the 'Met' Museum, Mrs Earle Williams (on her thirteenth visit!) and Dr Bill Murtagh, then serving as a Director of the 'Friends'.

When Phelps analysed the 1971 Class in May 1971 he indicated the average age of the 21 men was 35 years, and of the 15 women, 43 years. There were ten scholars (that is, persons with tuition costs underwritten) — of the ten, seven by the Friends, two by Columbia University School of Architecture and one by the National Society of Interior Design's Educational Foundation.

Perhaps as a sign of a new relationship the Class was welcomed to Attingham not only by Tony Galliers-Pratt but by the Chairman of the College Governors, Sir Philip Magnus-Allcroft, Bt., from Stokesay Court. Three lectures were given by Sir John Summerson, two by Sir Nikolaus

Mawley Hall, Shropshire, *c.* 1730, home of Tony and Angela Galliers-Pratt, and now lived in by their son Rupert and his family. Drawing by Michael Colvin of the east front set in a 'frame' taken from the carving in the Oak Drawing Room.

Pevsner and one by Alec Clifton-Taylor. Then my namesake (but no relative), the late Roy Beard, led the tour of Shrewsbury, a visit was made to see the Chairman's house, Mawley Hall, and to take lunch in the Orangery there — a feature of so many sun-drenched 'Frascati days' of later years, endearing generations of Attingham *alumni* to the Galliers-Pratt family. Then away after only seven days at Attingham (now charging more for accommodation) to Derbyshire — Helen's programme noted: 'Wine and Picnic' at Renishaw with Reresby Sitwell, a friend of the Chairman's, tea at Nostell Priory, and a first visit to the 'V & A of the North', Temple Newsam House, Leeds. Monday 19 July was spent in Salisbury with visits to five houses in the Cathedral Close, the Cathedral, with its soaring 'Constable' spire, a magisterial tour on Wednesday of the landscaped gardens at Stourhead, led by its historian, Kenneth Woodbridge. When the group reached London there was a visit to Lancaster House, finished in 1827 for the 2nd Duke of Sutherland in a sumptuous French style meant to emulate Versailles. This party was led by John Cornforth. After a meeting on the 'Problems of Preservation' held in liaison with the Society for the Preservation of Ancient Buildings, there was a final party and supper at 40 Belgrave Square, Tony and Angela Galliers-Pratt's London home.

Helen wrote, sadly, in early autumn 1971 to Phelps. There was 'no George at Attingham, no Ruth Bell, a new domestic staff. However, I do myself lean to sticking to Attingham if at all possible, since the mystique still persists'. Finances had been low — the Chairman and Helen had made loans in 1970 — but when Geoffrey Toms, as Treasurer, presented the 1971 Accounts there was an excess of Income over Expenditure of £1,083 and at 1 November 1971 there was £883 'Cash in Hand at the Bank', of which £222 was earmarked for the 1972 Scholarship Fund. Money was also being considered in New York. The Kaplan Fund had made a welcome contribution of $500 towards a full scholarship. However, John Varian retired as Treasurer and Clyde Snyder (Att. '67), an investment advisor, succeeded. Harry Grier continued as Scholarship Awards Advisor, and as Phelps noted: 'everyone at the American Federation of Arts office, from Director to mail clerk, extends hospitality'.

On 18 August 1971 Tony Galliers-Pratt had written to Helen and others:

> As you will all know, Sir George Trevelyan is retiring this month as Warden of Attingham Park. Although we are all sad that he is retiring from this position, we are nevertheless glad that Mr Geoffrey Toms, our honorary treasurer, has been appointed as Warden. Naturally this will necessitate Mr Toms retiring as honorary treasurer, although we can continue to look to his support as a member of Council and as one of our Course Directors. He will not, however, in future years be accompanying the Summer School as a Course Director once the School has left Attingham Park. I have therefore, after consultation with members of your Executive Committee, asked Miss Rosemary Lomax-Simpson to assume the position of 'Course Administrator'. . . and I have

approached Mr William Thuillier to assume the duties of honorary treasurer.

William Thuillier worked in an executive capacity for Sotheby's, having completed their twelve-month course before joining the Book Department. Further amendments were the resignation of Clifford Musgrave as an Executive Committee member (remaining a Council member) and the acceptance of the Dowager Countess of Radnor to serve on the Council: she is still a Patron, attending a lecture or two at each year's School.

It was necessary that the School should run without undue financial strain on the strong American relationship. In August 1970 the English committee had agreed to be responsible for the subsidizing of overseas students by fund-raising in Britain. It was also mindful, as was America, of the enormous contribution Sir George Trevelyan had made to the success of the Summer School. Firstly, a note about George himself.

George was born on 5 November 1906, the eldest son of the 3rd Baronet, Sir Charles Trevelyan (1870–1958) and Mary Bell (1881–1966). His uncle was the historian, G. M. Trevelyan. The family home was Wallington in Northumberland, and in 1941 Sir Charles gave the house, principal contents and estate to The National Trust, subject to his life interest. In his early years George was, of course, away at school and university; Sidcot, and at Trinity College, Cambridge. At the age of twenty-three he entered

Sir George Trevelyan, Bt., co-founder of The Attingham Summer School, 1957.

the furniture workshops of Peter van der Waals (1870–1937), a designer craftsman of the generation of Gordon Russell, Ernest Gimson and the Barnsleys. Then a period of immersing himself in the educational methods of F. M. Alexander (1932–36), teaching at Abinger and Gordonstoun and then in 1941 four years' war service at the rank of Captain, with two further years, 1945–47, teaching at the Army College. George will perhaps own that his religious teaching for his Wrekin Trust has been his happiest time. He had founded it in 1971 as an educational charity 'concerned with the spiritual nature of Man and the Universe', and continued to be well involved for over fifteen further years, and with holistic teaching since. But for the Summer School it was his lively, pioneering period as Warden of Attingham (for twenty-six years, 1947–71) which made the vital contribution.

The American Friends gave George a Steuben crystal sculptured block. This was selected, designed and worded by the Attingham Friends' first President, Ernest Hillman, and was inscribed:

Sir George Trevelyan, Bt.,
in fond recollection
1952–1971
His 'American Friends of Attingham'

Additionally, the Friends, at their Annual Meeting in May 1971 agreed to seek funds for a 'Sir George Trevelyan Scholarship'. This was to 'enable a young American man or woman of outstanding qualifications to attend the Attingham Summer School in honor of the retiring co-founder and co-director of the School'. It was intended that the scholar selected should take with him to Attingham to present to Sir George, 'a record of those who have honoured him by donations large or small to his scholarship'. This honour fell to Charles Savage, Curator of Education at the St Louis Art Museum, as 'The Sir George Trevelyan, Bt. 1972 Scholar'.

In England it was decided that the best way to honour George was to arrange a party for him at Wallington. This was to be done at the time of the 1972 School, in the Third Week. Preparations were made for his family to be present, and over 100 other guests.

The brochure announcing the 1972 School was changed from white to beige and the result was at once more attractive. The first eight days were to be at Attingham, the second five days in Derbyshire (staying at Tapton Hall in the University of Sheffield) and the third week in York and Northumberland, staying at the University of Newcastle-upon-Tyne. Costs were edging upwards: students up to the age of 32, $415, over, $470, with the Third Week at $200. It was noted that essential preparation lay in the full use of John Summerson's Pelican History, *Architecture in Britain* and in *Painting in England* by David Piper. Accommodation at Attingham was in 'large partitioned rooms': some of the luggage for the attic rooms went up on ropes in the courtyard, almost like a re-creation of Piranesi's 'Carceri'

The south and north elevations of Attingham Park, showing the pavilions and colonnades and the entrance to the Great Court (see p. 50) with the court walls, up which suitcases were hoisted, externally.

engravings — voids, weights, ropes, bustling figures, laughter, scuds of rain.

Helen's report on the 1972 School noted the presence of thirty-six American students, fifteen for the third week, four British students, Contessa Loredano da Schio (Att. '60) from Italy and, as Helen records, 'one full Iron Curtain scholarship member, Dr George Keleayi, from the Ancient Monuments Department in Budapest'. With the exception of three university undergraduates, all members had professional qualifications or were engaged in supportive preservation activities. Five members came from the National Parks Service, there were full curators from ten museums and eleven graduates. Names?: ever a lucky dip. The restoration architects David Rosenthal and Billie Britz, each distinguished in their busy lives, as was Wendy Cooper, then at the Brooklyn Museum (as their 'Mellon Research Fellow'), Ruth Jackson from the Montreal Museum, Ross Taggart, the Senior Curator and ceramics expert at the Nelson Atkins Gallery in Kansas City, and, as noted, Charles Savage from St Louis.

The Third Week attracted fifteen persons including Charles Chevalier, Hortense Feldblum, Bob Kennedy, Pauline Metcalf, Clyde Snyder and David Hanks. Harry Grier was due to come also but he had been killed in a tragic accident earlier in July; walking to the Frick Collection one morning his lack of peripheral vision caused him to step in front of a truck. As Helen recorded, Harry (Att. '57) 'had been a warm-hearted supporter ever since his first coming to Attingham'.

Eight days were spent at Attingham Park. Sadly, the professional demands on eminent lecturers like Pevsner and Summerson meant that they needed to call a halt. Helena, to whom the lecture programme was now due, had attracted younger lecturers such as John Newman from the Courtauld, Dr David Watkin from Cambridge and the late Colin McWilliam, the Edinburgh architectural historian. The running of the course on tour was much assisted by Rosemary Lomax-Simpson, who helped in all possible ways, as well as supervising running costs. Six days were then spent at Sheffield and the last week divided, with two days in York and four in Newcastle. The highlight of the Northumbrian visit was the party given for Sir George Trevelyan at Wallington.

The early winter of 1972 saw Lady Berwick's sad death from a motor accident at the Attingham gates at the age of eighty-three. Attingham was the hereditary property of her husband, an extremely shy man who had died in 1947. He had made his will in favour of The National Trust with, as James Lees-Milne put it in his obituary in the Trust's *Newsletter*. 'his wife's connivance and assent'. She lived on at Attingham in part of the house for another twenty-five years after her husband's death. She had been brought up in Venice, the daughter of William Hulton, an artist living in a small *palazzo* opposite the church of SS Giovanni e Paolo, and a friend of Sickert and Henry James. Her background was artistic and literary. George Trevelyan wrote in *The Times* (17 November 1972) that: 'Lady Berwick's influence permeated the whole enterprise [of the Adult College] and acted as a bridge between the old traditions, and the new aspirations of the college, in using the country house as a cultural centre for the county and district'. Her annual sherry party or picnic tea for Attingham members are fondly recalled by many *alumni*. She was always beautiful, astringent and extremely distinguished, happy that her beloved home gave pleasure to so many.

In the early 1970s much thought was given to the policy of acceptance of individuals for enrolment. Bertram Little (Att. '53) wrote to Phelps on 28 May 1971 urging that the School should not pass over entirely those who could give financial and volunteer support in favour of electing young professionals and students. There was a balance to be struck and Mr Little questioned whether the selection process could be broadened. All such persons as he had recommended had been turned down by the small Selection Committee centred in New York. He felt that goodwill and 'more importantly, perhaps, actual financial support has been thereby alienated'.

One has to admire the considerable tact and yet persistence which Phelps Warren applied to his Attingham correspondence. He could be very firm and direct but always ended such letters with phrases which suggested that such distasteful things were not unusually lingered over. He welcomed, that for a year's trial, from April 1972, the American Federation of Arts were to permit their Director's Executive Assistant, Anne Sharkey, to be also Attingham's Executive Secretary. As for administration in England, as Helen wrote to Phelps on 2 August 1972:

> Helena is absolutely tremendous and Rosemary the best possible tours organizer we could ever find. The old ones will fade, including me, but the whole will go on . . .

Phelps and Bob Kennedy in New York were aware that, brilliant and charming as Helen could be, she was not a good financial administrator. For many years the profits had gone entirely to the Adult College. But for 1972 William Thuillier showed in his accounts that the School had made a profit of £1,302 on a total income of £8,464. At 31 October 1972 there was £1,946 in the bank.

Not for the only time worries had arisen over the complications which arose in suddenly increasing the numbers attending in the Third Week. It was announced that in 1973 this would not take place. Correspondence ensued — the idea of an 'Attingham B' was put forward as an alternative, but Helen indicated that this would put a very considerable strain on the staff. Finally it was agreed to rescind the decision and to allow the usual *alumni* group to join the School in Norwich.

The 22nd School opened on 3 July 1973 at Attingham with John Julius Norwich (Viscount Norwich) speaking enthusiastically and with great fluency about 'The Role of the Country House'. Helena had continued to introduce newer, younger lecturers, and to give two lectures herself. John

Rosemary Lomax-Simpson, Treasurer
and Administrator, The Attingham
Summer School, 1971–86.

Sibyl McCormac Groff,
Treasurer, The American
Friends, January 1990.

Summerson still dealt with 'Baroque and Palladian Houses' and the
Dowager Countess of Radnor gave a splendid talk on 'The Problems of a
Country House Owner' during her years at Longford Castle, Wiltshire.
This was also the year when one lecturer, due to give two talks, on 'English
Decorative Painting' and 'English Collectors and the Grand Tour', arrived
late. Unwisely, Helen allowed him to make the two lectures into one. The
shadows of departing figures left few except the projectionist, and he had
finally drifted off to sleep. Normally matters were much better arranged. In
Helen's report, much shorter than normal, she instanced the great success
of the Norwich week. Whilst the accommodation at Keswick College was of
reasonable quality, 'though somewhat lacking in sufficient bathrooms and
failing to open the bar' (there is a correlation), it was in a beautiful park. But
there were sixty people and Helen again raised the problems that 'taking on
the older alumni for the third week' raised. A separate week for these was,
she felt, becoming more urgent every year, as the group usually contained
older people 'who do not really like College life'. So on to London, a lovely
party, carefully arranged at Fenton House by Edward Fawcett and
Rosemary Lomax-Simpson. And a final meeting, with John Earl, on
'Legislation for Architectural Preservation', and a tour led by Christopher
Monkhouse (Att. '66) in St James's and the City.

Six scholarships were on offer — in two cases, the Harry Grier
Scholarship and the George Trevelyan one were backed up by fifty per cent
scholarships by the American Friends, who also gave two full scholarships,
with two from the National Society of Interior Designers. The extensive
scholarship and expertise within the auction houses was represented by

Edward Lee Cave, then a Senior Vice-President at Sotheby Parke Bernet. And well away from the Eastern seaboard there was the 'poet' docent from Bayou Bend (Virginia Elverson), the Curator of Collections from the New Orleans Museum (Pam Bardo), an Associate Professor of Textiles from the University of Nebraska (Ruth Skjelver), Dr Carol Macht from the Cincinnati Art Museum, and an architectural history professor from the University of Utah (Peter Goss). Arlene Palmer (Schwind) was already well into her specialist 'glass and ceramics career' at Winterthur, as was Jean Mailey, in charge of the Textile Study Room at the 'Met' Museum. Norway again sent a scholar, Gunnar Hjeld, Assistant Keeper of the Royal Palace Collection in Oslo.

It was the year that Alan Campbell, a long-time supporter and officer, attended the School, with Sibyl McCormac Groff (later to be Treasurer), Kathy Hiesinger from the Philadelphia Museum (as the Harry Grier Memorial Scholar), Barbara Ross Luck from the Abby Aldrich Rockefeller Folk Art Collection at Colonial Williamsburg, David McFadden, then doing his Master's degree at Minnesota (now Cooper-Hewitt Museum), Roger Scharmer, enthusiastically, from Sacramento, with Ellen Goheen from the Nelson-Atkins Museum in Kansas City as the second Trevelyan Scholar. The two East European scholars were Dr Hedvig Szabolsci from Budapest and Dr Irene Grabowska from Cracow. Attending the Third Week only were Anne Sharkey; Lynn Springer (Roberts) (Att. '70); Margaret Stearns (Att. '60), then Vice-President of the American Friends; Patti Foos Whitelaw (Att. '65); Ferris Megarity (Att. '68); Bill Doneghy (Att. '66), Professor Bob Moore (Att. '64), David Rust (Att. '60) and another nine equally worthy *alumni*. From England these included the distinguished historian of sculpture, Liz Wilson, from Sotheby's in London.

In America Bob Kennedy was getting busier in his professional life and had declined further office. His leaving prompted a re-alignment of the secretary's post. Bob Luck too had been busy and Phelps asked Margaret Stearns to replace Kennedy as Vice-President and Alfred Mayor (Att. '59) to become Secretary. A steady programme of visits was arranged to keep *alumni* interested, of the nature of a visit (1970) to Judge Untermeyer's collection and to Fairfield Ct (1973), where Ernest Hillman showed an invited group his handsome new house.

The London Committee had a slightly more onerous problem. William Thuillier resigned as Treasurer in November 1973. Rosemary Lomax-Simpson, already the able Administrator, agreed to take on the Honorary Treasurer's duties also, subject to assistance being given by the auditors. It was decided, at the instigation of Geoffrey Toms and John Hayward, to invite six persons to become patrons, of whom four still serve: the Duke of Grafton, the Duchess of Devonshire, Sir George Trevelyan, Bt., Sir Nikolaus Pevsner, Sir John Summerson and Dr Clifford Musgrave. Finances had improved to about £3,000 in the bank but there was need to be ever careful. It was therefore welcome that Mrs Neal S. Wood (Att. '70) of St

Louis had agreed to finance an East European student for 1974 and a second from Rumania was supported by the East Europe Friendship Centre of the Foreign Office. Mrs Wood was invited to become a Patron.

The brochure for the 23rd School of July 1974 was a bright blue, the colour of a rare hot summer's day with no clouds. It was what every member chosen hoped for. A slight change in the title of the Friends in America had been registered: 'The American Friends of Attingham Inc'. Helen, Helena and Rosemary were happy with it, but were perhaps more concerned in securing new scholarship funding from the Leverhulme Trust. Helen was also muttering about the problems of daily walking her dog 'Hardy' when she was busy with Attingham affairs!

For the first time on the brochure George A. Nelson was listed as Counsel to the American Friends (working out of the office of Finch and Schaefler), and as well as Jimmy Biddle, the Consultant on National Trust matters, a Consultant on Scholarship Awards was given as Professor Jim Fitch (Att. '66) of Columbia University's School of Architecture. Among the long list of Directors and Sponsors it is good to see that the confidence rested in the first Trevelyan scholar, Charles Sawyer (Att. '72) had been returned. He was Director of the University of Michigan Museum of Art and a Sponsor for the Class of '74. Tuition fees keep pace with aspirations. Under the age of 32 $470 was needed, over 32 $525, and the Third Week, in Somerset and Dorset, was to cost $240. An extra day had been added to the course, making twenty-two; eight at Attingham, seven in Derbyshire, based at Sheffield, and six at Dillington House, near to Ilminster. The Third Week group were to lodge at a hotel in Ilminster, on a bed and breakfast basis, partaking all other meals and activities with the group at Dillington, one mile distant. Forde Abbey, Sherborne Castle, Montacute, Melbury, dinner in 'Thomas Hardy's Dorchester' — the panoply of English history could unfold in no better place.

It is impossible for any historian, writing in this case some seventeen years after the Class of '74, to know the 'chemistry' that bound the group together. However, the final poem may indicate a little of the camaraderie:

THANKS FOR THE MEMORY
of the Attingham Summer School, 1974

Thanks for the memory
Of picnics on the lawn,
And bells that rang at dawn,
Of evening talks and morning walks
To view the deer and fawn.
So thank you so much.

And thanks for the memory
Of double crucks and beams,
And passage through the screens;
For miles and miles of naves and aisles
As endless as they seem.
So thank you so much.

The gardens are all awe-inspiring.
Your passion for flowers never tiring.
That Attingham 'flu, now expiring,
From A to Zee
Was allergy.

So thanks for the memory
For all you've done for us
At home and in the bus.
Your stately homes with tea and scones
May be the death of us.
But we thank you so much.

Thanks for the memory
Of dear old Tapton Hall
And rusticated wall;
Those midnight groups with laughs and whoops
We tried to love you all.
So thank you so much.

And thanks for the memory
Of Hardwick in the rain,
Robert Adam ousting Paine,
Of swans in moats and cows and goats,
And hedgerows in the lane.
We thank you so much.

The dinner at Sheffield, impressive!
His Worship, Lord Mayor, expressive!
And if our libations excessive,
You'll understand
'Twas the occasion, grand!

So thanks for the memory
Of Devon in the sun,
And meeting each alum.
With work and grit, and charm and wit,
Thank God! We'll soon be one!
So thank you so much.

> (Virginia Elverson: with due respect to Bob Hope)

By plans laid the year before, Dr Paul Petrescu came from the Institute of Art History in Bucharest. He had written to Helen in April 1974, three months before the School began, not only to list his fourteen scholarly publications on various aspects of folk art but to show the superb qualifications most East Europeans attending Attingham have had: a PhD, and a further degree in law. He was of course older (fifty-three), but looking forward to the 'rare occasion to study the splendid treasures of English architecture'.

In August 1974, with the course hardly out of their aching limbs, Helen, Helena and Rosemary prepared a paper reflecting on 'the aims and composition of the Summer School'. They felt the future held a number of problems, and their solution had to be sought soon. They stated that the School had three related purposes:

> serving as an introduction to the architectural and social history of English country houses and their contents, secondly, with the aid of specialists, it set out to provide some instruction in individual fields of study. Thirdly, it was the intention of the course directors to encourage a positive attitude towards these joint studies which will enable those attending to contribute individually to the knowledge shared by all.

After careful expansion of the themes, which were complementary, the authors made two requests:

> (a)   The future of the school should now receive mature consideration from those associated with it in the U.S.A.
>
> (b)   The selection of students should be done with reference to the aims set forth: that is, students should have sufficient background to enable them to benefit from the course and they should have the ambition to use the three weeks to enlarge their horizons and to contribute to the general sum of knowledge. Thus a number of matters irrelevant to the programme must be dropped: i.e. research into unrelated matters, such as ancestor hunting, antique shopping, holiday sprees of one kind or another (we had one student this year whose overriding interest was folk music!) . . . Those who regard the course purely as a means of convenient personal advancement or as a variety of package tour are not likely to join in useful didactic discussions or advance the cause of historical studies.
>
> (c)   We have now come to the conclusion that third week alumni are of value in manifesting to the whole group *why* they have come back at considerable cost, to live in very modest comfort and follow the strenuous programme with so much appreciation. It can now be stated that younger students are liable to have more problems of the kind that give the organization a lot of extra trouble — health, accommodation, inability to be punctual, grumbles about arrangements in the programme and a constant desire to be somewhere other than where they are! It is the young who now form cliques, pursue their own interests at the expense of others, and not the older members of the last week. In particular, we should welcome those with a truly serious purpose, able to contribute themselves, to question and to discuss, and possibly finding through the teachers at the School, a course of further research.
>
> To conclude, this statement is not intended as a criticism of the social behaviour of those attending the course this year, which, compared with a British group of equivalent age, was excellent. Rather, it is made in the hope that recruitment may be encouraged (a) amongst those with wider experience of the subjects to be studied, and (b) those who are slightly older.

Phelps Warren replied on 13 September 1974 assuring the authors that their comments had received careful attention by his Board. He said that efforts would be made to increase the average age in point of years in the selection of 1975 students — 'and not just by the inclusion of a few gray beards!'

The educational background and professional qualification of applicants for enrolment was, Phelps indicated, more difficult to control:

We can, perhaps, exhort authors of letters of recommendation to be more specific about those for whom they are writing; this past year, on our application form's front page, we included a note to the following effect:

And apropos of letters of recommendation, our Committees like best, letters written by *you*, former Attingham students. Please continue to send us your applicants and arm them with *objective* letters: committees seek *enlightenment* from your letters of recommendation.

Phelps' comments, spreading over three pages, must be summarized. He indicated that the Enrolment Committees would be encouraged to spend even more time reading letters (and 'reading between the lines'), that procedures would be examined, increasing the number of committee men and women. It was further suggested that Rosemary, and Geoffrey Toms, be designated in print as Student Counsellors, giving them authority to 'have a word' with students who did not behave as they should. Previous European (English) travel as a condition for enrolment had both arguments for and against. It was agreed that each case would be judged on its merits.

Finally Phelps, after further words of concern to get it right, concluded amusingly:

I am perfectly ready to concede that some of what we have done over the years might have been done better, done more, or perhaps have been better left undone, but at this stage of the game, now, to invite our 'mature consideration' is certainly baffling. What gives, dear ladies, what gives?

I am sure it would be tactless for any historian to decide whether the Class of '75 was any more mature than those which had gone before! Certainly Nick Pappas, until recently the Colonial Williamsburg Foundation Architect, was a splendid choice, along with Phillip Johnston (now Director of the Carnegie Museum of Art at Pittsburgh), Professor Lawrence Ray, Dick Slavin (then at Olana, now Schumacher's Archivist), Ruth Ziegler from Sotheby's, Helen D. Hamilton (later to be Secretary to the Friends), the interior designers, Eloise 'Missy' Childs and Tracy Griswold, Bob Mackay, Director of the Society for the Preservation of Long Island Antiquities, two librarians at Avery and Winterthur (Eleanor Thompson and Deborah Waters) and two or three PhD candidates. The Hungarian scholar was Ilona Sharmany (later Ilona Parsons), and in England, Rosalind ('Ros') Savill (The Wallace Collection) and Phillis Rogers (later Curator of the Palace of Westminster). And certainly the Third Week had all the best names, Hortense Feldblum, Amy Gristede, Sibyl McCormac Groff, John Larson, Ferris Megarity, Lynn Springer Roberts, David Rust, Anne Sharkey, Clyde Snyder, Margaret Stearns and Mrs Neal Wood. I'm sure the others, not mentioned, were equally welcome and equally distinguished.

West Dean Garden and Church

West Dean Church, Sussex, soon to be visited by the class of 1977, and
familiar to each class since the move in 1984 for the first week to West Dean
College; drawing by Will Gwilliam (Att. '88).

V · ATTINGHAM, A CHANGING ORDER
1975 to 1979

PERHAPS THE CLOUD on the horizon in 1975 was less 'people' than 'place'. On 23 July 1975 Jack Boles, Director-General of The National Trust, wrote to Phelps. Attingham as an Adult College was likely to close on 30 November. He hoped, however, the School could stay at Attingham, and this of course proved possible for 1975. The Third Week of the course was to be in Scotland. Leaving Sheffield on 5 July the journey took in the scenic beauties of the Lake District with a halt at Levens Hall. Here everyone could delight in the great topiary garden before journeying north to Ayr where the group was joined by those attending for the Third Week. The delights of the west coast of Scotland included visits to Culzean Castle and Brodick. Then there was the journey east for a five-night stay in Edinburgh. From here the School could radiate, visiting the most important houses in the area, including Mellerstain and Hopetoun, and Bowhill with its famous collection of paintings and furniture. The final party was undertaken by combining with the Edinburgh branch of the National Association of Decorative and Fine Art Societies (of which body Helen was a founder-member and subsequent Vice-President). This took place at Newliston. The tuition rates were $525 (under thirty years) and $575 for those over. The Third Week cost was $300.

Between the Summer School's American Committee and that of The Victorian Society there an arrangement grew up to pass on names of those not enrolled for Attingham. For several years Ruth Emery (Att. '61) acted as a liaison in this important chore and many well qualified persons benefited from the second, albeit slightly different, addition to their knowledge.

The writing of this Attingham history in its fortieth year establishes, dubiously, how we all regard anniversaries. 1976 was the twenty-fifth anniversary of the School's founding. It was also the year that Helen passed over full directorial control to Helena Hayward. The control changed but the direction was to be still the same, inexorably, caring and efficient.

On Monday, 12 July 1976, a twenty-fifth anniversary party was given at Attingham and at the dinner a drawing was presented to Helen. In writing to thank Phelps for this Helen noted:

> I was tremendously touched by the letters and really felt they were sincere — more than most obituaries! Also I was glad that there were people there who would be led to understand that education lies *inside* the preservation problems and not outside.

Whilst wags have suggested to me one Appendix to this history might be 'Attingham and Sex', there is reason enough to record a happy meeting in 1976 leading to marriage! Hope Alswang from the Brooklyn Museum met Henry Joyce, a Leverhulme Trust scholarship holder and Curator of the Duke of Bedford's collections at Woburn. And of course there have been other 'Attingham' marriages. It is not to my purpose to follow up what a distinguished landscape architect said to me once at Attingham: 'Geoffrey, I get up very early in the morning; you would be amazed what I see.' I sleep the sleep of true innocents, and welcome that happy encounters of like souls lead occasionally to the altar. Apart from Henry and Hope Joyce (Alswang), I know of David and Linda Hollenberg (Samter), Jonathan and Tamara Thornton (Plakins), Jonathan and Sue Kinghorn (Whitman) and David and Sarah Meschutt (Bevan). I am sure there are others.

So many have been helped to attend Attingham by the award of scholarships. But in 1976 it was only a third of the number of those now awarded to American scholars. The Harry Grier Memorial Scholar for 1976 was Louise Ambler, Curator of Harvard's Portrait Collection at the Fogg Art Museum, and the Sir George Trevelyan Scholar, David Dangremond, was then a graduate Fellow at Winterthur.

Through the offices of Arete Schwarz (Warren) at the Royal Oak Foundation, support had been given both to Dennis McFadden at Columbia's School of Architecture and a Restoration architect, Martin Rosenblum. The National Trust in Washington helped their Education co-ordinator, Pat Williams, to attend, and the American Society of Interior Designers supported Professor Jim Harrington from the University of Georgia. The American Friends helped Judith Hawk. She was selected by the Society of Architectural Historians from the Architectural Technology Programme at the Northern Virginia College. The remainder paid their $525 or $575, depending on age, and the *alumni*, on the Third Week in Leicestershire, their $300. The administration of the course was helped by two assistant tutors for four days, Cindy Fletcher (Lady Shaw-Stewart) and Edward Saunders, with, in the Third Week, Phillis Rogers and Ros Savill, former Leverhulme Trust Scholars (both Att. '75), as 'Editorial Assistants'.

There is no means of knowing whether the Class of '76 developed a nose for agricultural smells, or the ability to be adroitly 'down wind'. Apart from starting at the Harper Adams Agricultural College, the Third Week (20–27 July) was at Brooksby Agricultural College, near Melton Mowbray. Spirits were, however, high (and were perhaps also 'downed') for the following song to be composed for the final party. May Stone has supplied the text, sung to the tune of 'Bali Hai':

Attingham, Attingham, Attingham —
> Miss H. Lowenthal will come calling
> Every morning, every day;

Better hop upon the red coach
Or dear George will drive away.

Mrs. Hayward will be laughing
As she points to chair and chaise
Then she'll take you to the next room
As she sweeps you on your way.

Our own country house —
It's up on a hill,
Surrounded by sheep
That are there from Repton still.

Rosemary Lomax-Simpson
Graciously pays the bill,
Keeps us all safe from worry
Writing cheques from the till.

Our own country house
High o'er the river Tern,
Attingham our school,
Fortress strong, a place to learn.

As we weave through the country,
Sighting turrets and spires,
Massive piles of grey granite
That adorn the country miles.

Attingham, Attingham, Attingham —

On 20 September 1976 Phelps wrote to Helena:

The first thing I want to do is to tell you how greatly successful was your
first solo Director flight of 1976. Numerous notes come in here from
wildly enthusiastic students.

Further enthusiastic support came in the form of letters, signatures on
'group cards', and visits from itinerant *alumni* carrying the good wishes of
the Winter Reunions. In January 1976 Helen, Helena and Rosemary had
sent a tape-recording to be used at the party being arranged in New York by
Jeanne Butler Hodges and Nick Pappas. Both had been members of the
Classes of 1974 and 1975 respectively.

In late November 1976 Helena sent a copy of the year's accounts to
Phelps. Amusingly he said he would pass them on to Treasurer Clyde
Snyder, 'who consumed them like cucumber sandwiches'. Phelps said he
was delighted to see that a little reserve (a little over £8,000) was building up
— 'we both have need for a nest egg against that rainy day'. He further
noted that *Antiques Magazine* were to carry a publicity piece about the 1977
School. As for fees, I do not think anyone will mind, and the historian in me
dictates, to admiration for the modest sum taken by Helen, Helena and
Rosemary — a total of £750 for all three! It is that selflessness which has its
place in the Attingham story even if all recognized always the eventual aim
of better, if still modest, remuneration.

Helen had hoped to be present at the 11th Reunion on 18 March 1977 at the offices of the American Federation of Arts. But she was, alas, ill and fifty-four persons signed a card under the heading:

Dear Helen
We miss you very much tonight and are deeply sorry to hear you had to cancel your trip. All of us who sign below send greetings and best wishes for a swift recovery.

She would have wanted to announce what she had known for some time — that the Class of '77 would be able to return to Attingham. Frank Bell's Educational Trust had taken up its lease and Frank had written to Helen on 8 November 1976.

I indeed hope that all goes well for your Summer School. I can assure you that we will try very hard indeed to have things as you wish.

Thoughts of change were being studied on both sides of the Atlantic. The return to Attingham for 1977 was announced by Phelps at the 20 May Annual Meeting. He lamented that Lydia Bond Powel, so long a valued Chairman of the American Friends, was ill and in a nursing home. When she had retired in 1976 Phelps wrote:

Many of the more recent Friends will know Mrs Powel by name only — her name appeared on our stationery since the earliest days — but others will recall her as the redoubtable Keeper of the American Wing at the Metropolitan Museum during which time she introduced Atting- ham to its American audience, bestowed upon the School the benefit of her strong personality and the prestige of her position, and even, single-handedly enrolled its first classes.

Later, when the Friends and the School teetered on the brink of a purple-haired abyss, Mrs Powel staunchly advocated and supported the professional cause. And the fact that the Friends has developed as a professional organization for professionals is largely due to Mrs Powel's leadership.

Her leadership capacity notwithstanding, it is probable Mrs Powel, a large woman of imposing presence, will be best remembered for her wit and inexhaustible fund of quotations and stories, always humorous, apt, and inclined to be deliciously wicked.

I am moving beyond my chronological slot. Mrs Powel died in Connecticut early in January 1978. There is a single page of tribute about her by Helen and so redolent is it of *déjà vu* that I quote it in full.

She loved England and her many friends here, and she visited country houses with discriminating enthusiasm. When the idea of the Atting- ham Park Summer School was first foreshadowed in the early 1950s, Lydia backed the plan with constructive support. I well remember visiting her in her charming New York apartment to enquire what she thought of the concept of a Summer School to investigate English houses; the result was that she recruited the entire body who attended — somewhat apprehensively — the first school at Attingham in 1952. She and her cousin Hope Harkness (formerly Mrs Hare Powel; she had married, secondly, Alfred Harkness) were the first of a long series of powerful ladies who aided the enterprise in many different ways.

Lydia had worked at the Rhode Island School of Design before she undertook her highly important post at the Metropolitan Museum. She became an early curator of the American Wing and helped to make it a valuable department full of new ideas on education. Through the American Wing, many new American citizens in the melting pot of New York were introduced to American culture. Museum broadcasts were among her innovations and she had a lasting interest in methods of museum teaching.

Lydia was a person of abounding charm and vitality with friends of all ages who never forgot her sympathy and wit. Her taste in art and her capacity to create delightful surroundings were memorable.

The Class of 1977 assembled at Attingham Park on 6 July for the opening of the 26th Summer School; thirty-nine Americans, five from Great Britain, Miklos Mojzer from the Hungarian National Museum in Budapest, an international expert on painting, Zafie Alber from the National Museum in Cracow, and then seventeen *alumni* for the Third Week. The number of lecturers, tutors and administrators, led by Helena, had increased (for various dates) to eight. Phillis Rogers and Rosalind Savill helped to prepare the 'Notes on Houses' and the 'Bibliography'. The American contingent included Tony Atkin, the Philadelphia architect, Roger Berkowitz, now Director at Toledo Museum of Art, Paul Gardner, then Curator of Ceramics and Glass at the Smithsonian, Charles Hammond, Curator of Gore Place, Alice Levkoff from the Historic Charleston Foundation, Tom Parker, Director of the Boston Society, David Robb, Curator of Kimbell Art Museum at Fort Worth, Don Stover, then about to move from the Winterthur programme to the Fine Arts Museums of San Francisco and Philip Zimmerman, doing his PhD at Boston (later at Winterthur).

The British scholars included Jeannie Chapel (Hobhouse), then cataloguing the paintings at Holloway College (and who was to give invaluable help in later years, shepherding Third Week members), Christopher Allan, who moved from the Whitworth Art Gallery, Manchester after the course to the Hunterian Art Gallery in Glasgow, Charles Truman, a research assistant in the Department of Metalwork at the Victoria and Albert Museum (subsequently Christie's until 1991). The first two held Leverhulme scholarships and Truman was the 'Alec Clifton-Taylor Scholar'. The National Trust nominated Christopher Rowell (now the Historic Buildings Representative for the South; and a tower of strength to each year's 'Attingham' at houses such as Petworth). For the first time the Historic Houses Association also made a nomination — Annabel Webb (Westman) as the 'Jonathan Vickers Scholar'. Annabel was then working at Cawdor Castle on the north-east coast of Scotland, helping with organizing its opening to the public, and later, to co-ordinate its part in Heritage Educational Year. As noted elsewhere in these pages, she is now much involved with Attingham's organization and its important tutoring role.

West Dean College, Sussex, Helen Lowenthal was a Trustee for several
years. The School visited it on and off, and since 1984 has started each
course there.

The return to Attingham after what, in Civil War terms, might be
termed 'The Interregnum' was fraught with difficulties. The domestic staff
was inexperienced and the preparatory arrangements woefully inadequate. At first the food was deplorable but there was a great improvement
in the service and catering in the last two days of the stay. The course was
opened by Helen and the progression of chronological lectures and visits
followed with lecturers from five universities as well as from The National
Trust and the Victoria and Albert Museum. An outstanding visit in the first
week (as so often) was to Mawley, Tony and Angela Galliers-Pratt's house.
The afternoon at Croft Castle, with an unplanned visit to delicious
Rococo-Gothick Shobdon Church with Lord Croft was also a great success.

In the final week the party moved to West Dean College, the
'Attingham' in the south as it has become for all Schools since the Class of
1984. Visits to Broadlands, Parham, Petworth, an evening visit and party at
Uppark. Rosemary Lomax-Simpson's arrangements for this were, as usual,
faultless and thanks were due to Frederick Crowell, a member of the
course, for his generosity in financing the party.

In November 1977 Helen Lowenthal made a trip to America. She had
been prevented by illness from going in the spring. She recorded:

I have spent the last three and a half weeks in Chicago, Texas, Lexington (Virginia) and New York. I suppose I saw fifty or sixty ex-students in that time. All talked with appreciation and enthusiasm of their time at the Summer School. I asked for critical comment and there was practically none. There is great enthusiasm in the States for the work of the Friends . . . and it was pleasing to hear the younger students voicing appreciation of what the Friends had done for them . . .

And what was done for Helen was a reception at Phelps' house on 15 November — a 'fiesta' confined to 'Officers, Directors, Sponsors, Past and Present', a 'semi-official do'. But there was already conversation and memoranda on the great change about to come. In June 1977 Phelps had written to Helen to say:

We will renew with the American Federation of Arts until June 30, 1978. But after that date we shall lose the office at 41 East 65th Street, and also the services of Anne Sharkey.

At the 4 May 1978 meeting of the Directors of the American Friends it was offered, seconded and passed by unanimous vote (and then read by Morrie Heckscher):

WHEREAS Anne Sharkey has, for the ten year period, 1968–1978, served as Executive Secretary of the American Friends of the Attingham Summer School; and

WHEREAS steadfastly through that period she has brought to that office a profound devotion to the Friends' purposes and the effective pursuit thereof; and

Anne Sharkey, Executive Secretary of
The American Friends, 1968–78.

WHEREAS to that pursuit she has also brought secretarial skills of the highest efficiency equalled only by ungrudging sacrifice of time and energy; and

WHEREAS by personal qualities of tact and charm as well as the consistent high level of her performance, Anne Sharkey has earned the friendship and admiration of Attingham Friends across the nation and of the Attingham Committee overseas; let it therefore be —

RESOLVED: that this Board records its deep appreciation of Anne Sharkey's inestimable contribution to the Friends; and records further both its gratitude to her and the unbounded affection which she has inspired throughout the Attingham community; and orders that this Resolution be read at the Annual Meeting of the Friends, May 25th, 1978, and a record thereof be spread upon the Minutes of that Meeting; and that it be published in the Friends' next general mailing in the United States, and that copies be forwarded to the President, Chairman, Director, and Administrator of the Attingham Summer School Trust in England.

Phelps made various approaches to other bodies — the British Art Center at Yale, the Society of Architectural Trusts and the National Trust in Washington. The last had some disadvantages as it received Federal money with, as Helen put it, 'accompanying bureaucratic disadvantages'. Of course there was little the English directorate could do to aid these deliberations, except to display discretion. As Helen said, wisely: 'To be remembered: we need students from all over the States, of Academic Quality. We need the approval of people in powerful positions. We need to maintain the existing amicable relations now existing'.

In November Phelps Warren made his usual annual appeal to all 'the American Friends of the Attingham Summer School'. He noted that in the twelve months since the previous appeal 254 former students had donated to the Friends. This record — an approximate 47% — 'is astonishingly high, will you help to maintain this record . . . we are interested in dollars, of course. But we are proud of the number of our supporters and we don't want any former student to hesitate to send a small "dues" because he can't send a large one . . . it is the aggregate of the smaller ones which makes for bones and sinews'.

Late in 1977 in New York, funds in significantly large amounts restricted for scholarships, were received from Hortense Feldblum (Att. '66), Frederick Crowell (Att. '77), Melvin Seiden (Att. '75) and (in memory of Caroline Wright [Att. '63]) from Mrs Frederick Frelinghuysen. It was therefore possible to vote four full scholarships for the 1978 School, one designated 'The Sir George Trevelyan, Bt., Scholar'. With funds under-written from the Gerald Watland (Att. '58) bequest, a fifth scholarship was available, and the seventh award of the Harry Grier (Att. '57) scholarship was funded by the Association of Art Museum Directors. For the third consecutive year two scholarships were awarded by the Royal

Oak Foundation, bringing the total number to eight. Additionally, it was expected to have scholars funded by the National Trust and the American Institute of Interior Designers.

In England the end of 1977 saw the reporting of an excess of income over expenditure of almost £1,000 due to Frederick Crowell's generous subsidy of the final party. The dollar parity was, however, not in English favour and was predicted to lead to financial difficulties in 1978. Whilst fees for that year were raised by twelve to fifteen per cent it was agreed to warn the American Friends that a small increase beyond that might be needed. It was agreed to invest a hard-won £7,000, with the advice of Singer and Friedlander, in an investment policy.

The 1977 brochure had been the last to include Lydia Powel's name. The Executive Vice-President under Phelps in 1978 was Stewart Johnson, and David Pettigrew and Margaret Stearns were Vice-Presidents. Alfred Mayor was Secretary, Clyde Snyder was Treasurer, George Nelson of Finch and Schaefler acted as Counsel, and Anne Sharkey was in her last months as Executive Secretary. There were changes in the list of Consultants. Jimmy Biddle remained concerned with National Trust matters, but Edith Standen became involved with General Enrolment, and Otto Wittman with the Scholarship Awards.

Despite the comparative discomfort and the problems of Attingham Park as a residence, it was felt the course should again be there in July 1978. It was difficult to see the State Rooms such as the Picture Gallery when the public was not present. However, as it transpired, the National Trust Historic Buildings Representative, Merlin Waterson (like all his colleagues over the years) improved this. The standard of service and food turned out to be excellent. Christopher Rowell put out some of the Berwick silver in the dining-room. But at Sheffield the food was disastrous, and Halifax Hall of Residence badly kept. Bitter complaints had to be mitigated by the splendours of Chatsworth and Hardwick. And then, a high plane again.

The Third Week was based at Pembroke College, Oxford and John Cornforth provided a list of houses which might be visited. And visited they were. In fact it was, according to the Director's 1978 Report, 'a really wonderful week'. It opened with a visit and reception at Balliol College, an exhibition of 'Design Sources' especially arranged in a private room at the Bodleian Library (with the chance to handle the exhibits). Visits to Queen's and All Souls the last arranged by Dr Kenneth Garlick), an evening reception in the Upper Library at Christ Church, Gibbs's magnificent interior of the Radcliffe Camera (an ascent to its roof), and a special evening opening of the Ashmolean Museum.

Frederick Crowell (Att. '77), invited to become a Patron through his generosity, again financed the final party at Kirtlington. In Christopher Buxton's great house everyone sat down to dinner at tables set out in several rooms. 'The food was excellent, the occasion comfortable and not at all noisy'! Then 'Preservation in London: a two day study' at the end of the

School, led by Helen Lowenthal with the help of the Greater London
Council's Historic Buildings Division. Separately costed (at £16) there were
talks on preservation law, special problems, recent successes and failures
and half-day visits under the tutelage of the architects and historians John
Earl, Frank Kelsall and Robert Chitham.

All of these riches were set out for the enjoyment of thirty-eight
American students, of whom twelve held scholarships (two, through
Helena's initial intervention, had come from Mr and Mrs Peter Minet's
Idlewild Trust). Six scholarships were given for British students. For the
first two weeks the student body numbered forty-five in all, with
twenty-one *alumni* joining for the Third Week. Over forty per cent of the
American young people were under thirty, and whilst this was in many
ways, encouraging, several were lacking in architectural knowledge. It is
fascinating to look down the Director's membership list with its pencilled
aids to identification — Undashing; Classics; curly hair; moustache;
moustache and beard (and) red hair'. The list gave the precise terminology
— 'interior designer, volunteer assistant, graduate, architect, preservationist, Associate Professor, Curator'. It included Edward Diestelkamp,
then a post-graduate student and now with the National Trust in London;
Joan Gorman of the Brandywine River Museum; Pat Hurley from the
Rhode Island School of Design Museum of Art and one of the authors of the
subsequent 1984 Attingham *Alumni Directory*; Sarah Latham (Kearns; now
the American Friends' Secretary); Cathy Lippert at the Indianapolis
Museum of Art; Frank Masson, a restoration work architect, Matthew
Mosca, then with the office of Historic Properties of the National Trust in
Washington; Karin Peterson (surely smiling, then, as now?) from Historic
Annapolis Inc., Francis 'Bill' Puig, until recently at the Minneapolis
Museum; Darrel Sewell, Curator of American Art at the Philadelphia
Museum, and Christopher Wilk, the Museum of Modern Art, then Brooklyn
Museum (now Curator of the Furniture and Woodwork Collection at the
Victoria and Albert Museum) and joint editor, with Pat Hurley, of the 1984
Alumni Directory.

The first (and only?) Japanese student to the School was Tsune Sesoko,
a journalist and exhibition organizer. The seven British scholars included
the architect Andrew Arrol (soon to be helpful to many Schools on walks
around Shrewsbury); David Beevers from Tredegar, the great seventeenth-
century Welsh house of the Morgan family; Lisa Clinton (Lady White), then
in the Furniture and Woodwork Department of the Victoria and Albert
Museum (recently the author of *A Pictorial Dictionary of British 18th Century
Furniture Designs*); Julian Gibbs, working for the National Trust at Blickling
(now at Attingham); Lindsay Morrison, working in Scottish country
houses; the architect John Redmill, responsible in recent years for fine work
at Sir William Chambers's Charlemont 'Casino', near Dublin, and Giles
Waterfield, then at the Royal Pavilion, Brighton and subsequently a
Chairman of the Attingham Scholarship Committee, a Council Member

and the distinguished Director of the Dulwich Picture Gallery, housed in Sir John Soane's spatially exciting building.

The Third Week *alumni* included the textile designer Alan Campbell (Att. '73), the collector Lillian Hirschmann (Att. '54), Paul Gardner, Ceramics and Glass Curator at the Smithsonian Museum (Att. '77), Lisa Terrace (Koch), a preservationist (Att. '74), Alice Levkoff, Historic Charleston Foundation (Att. '77), Pauline C. Metcalf, then in the Historic Preservation programme at Columbia (Att. '66), Nick Pappas, an architect, then in Washington (Att. '75), Merribell Parsons, Chairman, Curatorial Division, the Minneapolis Institute of Fine Arts (Att. '69), David Pettigrew, Associate Director of a private New York gallery (Att. '70), Anne Sharkey, Executive Secretary, the American Friends of Attingham (Att. '71), Patti Foos Whitelaw, Historic Charleston Foundation (Att. '65), party-giver Fred Crowell (Att. '77) — Fred was an architectural historian by training — Jim Buckler, the Smithsonian's Staff Horticulturist (Att. '75), the garden historian Julia Davis (Att. '73), Ruth Jackson from the Montreal Museum (Att. '72), Ann Kennan, Director of the English Braintree School System (Att. '71), Arline Leven, Assistant to the Director of Washington University's Gallery of Art (Att. '77), Raymond Levra of Cochise College (Att. '71), Margaret Machell, Keeper of the Grange, Art Gallery of Ontario (Att. '76), Tom Parker, Director of the Boston Society (Att. '77), and finally Contessa Loredana da Schio from the Centro Palladiano at Vicenza (Att. '60). I have given the list in full to show the range of background

J. Stewart Johnson, President of
The American Friends, 1979–82,
photographed without his
knowledge at Sissinghurst
Castle, July 1990.

expertise such a group could add to the School's deliberations. Only numbers gradually toppled the system, as dazed owners took in the sight of a Class of sixty-five eager inquisitors.

After the 1978 Summer School was over, activity in an administrative sense was present both sides of the Atlantic. Phelps visited Washington in early August to sign a contract with the National Trust by which Mrs Pauli McClanahan became the Executive Secretary of the American Friends, based at 740 Jackson Place NW in Washington, DC. It was agreed that the National Trust name should not appear on brochures or stationery. As Phelps noted in his 1979 retirement note, it had been a move which was made under the benign influence of loyal Attingham *alumnus* James Biddle (Att. '58). Stewart Johnson and others pressed that students should be presented with a 'Certificate of Attendance', and this idea was added to the preparations for the 1979 Class, with the Third Week to be within walking distance of the centre of York.

In May 1979 two significant events happened in New York. At the Annual Meeting in New York on 15 May Phelps Warren retired, fifteen years to the day after he had been elected president of the American Friends. He was succeeded by J. Stewart Johnson. In issuing an appeal to the membership to subscribe to a 'Phelps Warren Fund' Ferris Megarity, then Vice-President, Development noted:

> True to form, Phelps has said he wants no plaque, silver tray or gold cuff links as thanks for his service to the American Friends of Attingham. He is more concerned that we find a way to assure a firm future for the organization, and to overcome the pressures of the steadily rising costs of all operating expenses due to inflation. With this in mind, the directors have asked me to head a committee to raise an endowment fund for the Friends in Phelps's name . . .

From Phelps's 'Historical Notes by the Retiring President' in the same document there are perhaps two points. After discussing the profound influence of Lydia Powel 'on the Attingham-for-and-by-professionals doctrine', he commented on the action each year of the Scholar and General Enrolment Committees.

> The influence of these committees goes far beyond the selection of the members of a given year's class. The committees are not only the arbiters of enrolment but the guardians of the Friends' and the Summer School's professional standards.
>
> The Friends' organization came of age with the development of enrolment procedures. However much these may be improved in time to come, as they have been changed and we hope improved in the past, our procedures have established the Friends as an organization set apart. Attingham membership is a privilege; Attingham people are *selected* people, deliberately screened and chosen. It is a satisfaction to me that the guidelines for enrolment for carrying out the Powel doctrine in the United States were laid down during my term of office.

Helen sent the following rhyme to Phelps:

To dear Phelps we send our greetings
O'er the wide Atlantic wave,
We remember all our meetings —
Attingham that notion brave.
All those years of your devotion
All those 'students' young and old,
Made that early scatty notion,
Into something firm and bold.
Complications came up yearly,
Dearest Phelps you never quailed!
Skirted round the rocks so clearly
Calm good humour never failed.
Now we know that you are moving
From the centre to the wings
We shall still continue loving
All your help and what it brings.
And as onward move your minions
Bearing Attingham along,
So we hope for new opinions
But a loud continuous song,
Praising still our common culture,
Working to maintain it still,
Though inflation is a vulture,
We uphold a former will.
Lift our glasses to your health, sir,
Thanking you with ringing praise,
Wish you all content and wealth, sir
Attingham is yours always.

Coda. Byron: But who forgives the senior's ceaseless verse
Whose hairs grow hoary as his rhymes grow worse?

In May 1979 the Trust's Committee met also, in London to 'report the changes in the administration of the Friends of Attingham in New York and to discuss the future policy of the school concerning British candidates and the related question of fund raising'. In a paper proposing various ways of fund-raising Helen suggested the appointment of someone who could write to Trusts and possible benefactors. She suggested Mrs Sylvia Stevenson for this appointment. I shall return to Sylvia's vital Attingham role.

Hot as a sinking orange sun the bright 1979 brochure set out the inexorable pattern pursued over almost thirty previous years; Attingham, Sheffield, and, for the Third Week, forays out from Hepworth Croft, York. As inexorable was the gradual rise in fees, $775 (under 30), $840 (over 30), with $405 for those attending the Third Week.

Chatsworth. A statue of Bacchus forming a caryatid on the Dining Room fireplace. Drawing by Kent Brinkley (Att. '89).

The scholars were as bright as ever. Barbara Brand was in from the Hammond-Harwood House in Annapolis and Debby Barker from the University of Kansas. Michael Brown journeyed from the Museum of Fine Arts at Houston and John Cherol from the Newport County Preservation Society. Ed Cooke, then at Concord Antiquarian Museum (now, Boston Museum of Fine Arts), took as keen an interest in furniture as anyone, as did the English scholar Frances Fox-Robinson (Collard), now at the Victoria and Albert Museum. The librarian Bill Dane was fascinated with the Chatsworth Library, as was Mrs Murray Douglas of Brunschwig et Fils with many textile collections. Allison M. Eckardt (Ledes), now Editor of *Antiques Magazine*, was (I venture to assume) knowledgeable and irrespressibly cheerful, and Nancy Hirst (I venture to suggest) was ever-busy with her excellent camera 'eye'. The preservationist (and Counsel to the American Friends) Huyler Held attended, as did the Executive Secretary Pauli McClanahan, the European decorative arts scholar from the Boston Museum, Jeffrey Munger, Deborah Shinn, a MA candidate, Jane Strauss from Colonial Williamsburg, Audrey Michie, then at the Museum of Early Southern Decorative Arts and Professor Suzanne Turner from Louisiana State University.

In compiling lists of names to mention here I try to give some balance. The 1984 Attingham *Alumni Directory* and subsequent lists are fuller. All who attended have an honoured place in this story, and lists of their names are given in the Appendix hereto. Attingham remained as a 'lifeline' to East Europeans, with Jiri Kotalik from the National Gallery in Prague joining, animatedly, the English scholars Christopher Beharrell (National Trust), Martin Chapman (Victoria and Albert Museum, now Los Angeles County Museum), Frances Collard (as previously mentioned), Greer Crawley (Buckinghamshire College of Higher Education), Anne Eatwell (Victoria and Albert Museum), Sarah Medlam (the Bowes Museum, Co. Durham), Michael Pearman (Librarian at Chatsworth) and Carola Stuart from the National Trust.

Let the last word about the Attingham Class of 1979 be its own words, in its final party song:

> There once gathered a class at Atcham
> All but one of whom arrived by a tram.
> Between gardenly walks
> And ruinous talks,
> We all 'et' tea, scones, and jam.

> Not once did our enthusiasm fade
> And shortly friendships were laid.
> While King Huyler sat
> In the Paradise flat,
> We had to frequent the pub called Mermaid.

> From Shrewsbury it was on to Sheffield
> Where under togas much was revealed.
> Helena of Troy,

A Senator — no boy;
A few sheets and the group was congealed.

> With Rosemary we woke with the the bell
> And were herded to the coach pell mell.
> Duke, Lord, Marchioness
> Had us duly impressed,
> But the pinnacle was one certain Sitwell.

And so onwards it was to York
Where one seldom picked up a fork.
Trips far to the North,
Manifestoes from Cornforth
Provided much fuel for discussion and torque.

> This week our class is augmented
> But younger members remain demented.
> Football until one
> And pun after pun
> One hopes this limerick will be amended.

On 4 December 1979 Tony Galliers-Pratt attended a dinner in Phelps's honour in Park Avenue, New York. Stewart Johnson was in the chair, and the President Emeritus was presented, by Tony, with an 'Attingham Certificate'. Pleasure obviously given to Phelps, but there was business too. Tony later attended a meeting of the Council of Directors at Ferris Megarity's, and spoke on the problems of financing Attingham in the future. The American Friends were worried about the rising costs for students, but believed there were difficulties in approaching large Corporations for money, because of the School's small (albeit, important) position. They returned to England for Christmas with much to ponder.

AT ATTINGHAM COUNCIL MEETINGS in London in January and April 1980 discussion centred again on financing Attingham in the future. The American side, as noted, was worried about the rising costs for students, but believed that it would not be helpful to approach large corporations for money, because Attingham altogether was too small. The American Council had suggested that one solution might be to shorten the main course to two weeks and, as noted, to have a Third Week devoted to fund-raising; a course for wealthy newcomers which would be more luxurious than a main course and costs could include a donation to the Attingham Trust. The two advantages to this idea would be that the unwieldy numbers of the third week, as then arranged, would be reduced and that financial problems would be eased and the future of the course assured. Subsequent discussion led to the conclusion that it would be wiser to retain the basic course as at least one of eighteen days and to have a separate fund-raising week. By April this idea had been established. Helen Lowenthal agreed to launch the 'new' week and Mrs Sylvia Stevenson was asked to organize it, which she did with great style and efficiency.

The first idea of a title was the 'Attingham Sponsors Special Tour'. It was suggested that it would have up to forty members, who would consist of those already on the main course who would like to stay for a further week, the *alumni* and those from England, America and Europe who were interested. Each member would make a donation to the main course, and plans were laid to launch this in 1981. Meanwhile the 1980 Summer School was well in hand, with its Third Week in Cheshire at the College of Education at Alsager.

From Attingham, on 6 July, the group set out for a fascinating day seminar at Tony and Angela Galliers-Pratt's Mawley Hall. These 'seminar days', really the innovation of Helena Hayward, have been a good feature of Attingham in recent years, still pertaining at Petworth and Chatsworth. The restoration of house and garden were discussed by Tony and Angela, Helena spoke on the outstanding inlaid woodwork and furniture, and Ros Savill and Charles Truman discussed the porcelain and silver. Then, seated in the attractive Orangery buildings, John Cornforth led a discussion on attitudes to preservation.

It had been a suggestion of the American Board that its new President, Stewart Johnson (Att. '65), should attend the full 1980 Class. To partly earn his place, welcome as his genial presence was to all, was the insistence he lecture on 'Palladio in Italy, England and elsewhere'. But amongst all the happy chatter, the congenial and rewarding visits, the lectures, the instruction, a heavy hand was laid by the tragic death in a climbing accident on 14 July, the last 'free' evening in Sheffield, of Stuart Platts from Manchester City Art Gallery's neo-Classical Heaton Hall, in north-west England. The entire 1980 School subsequently took up a collection so that they would be able to offer a special scholarship in his name for an English student in 1981. Further, John Cushion, the affable and knowledgeable ceramics tutor to the course over the years, was unable to attend due to his wife's illness. Mrs Cushion had died before Stewart Johnson's report letter from his 'Desk' in November, and he also had to announce the death in a motor accident of Eloise 'Missy' Childs. Again her classmates of 1975 took up a collection to award an ongoing scholarship in her name — 'ongoing' for some years, because a number of Missy's professional friends pledged to donate annually a consultation fee to the fund. As Nick Pappas wrote to Helen, 'Attingham was a turning point in her life'. It was also the first year a scholarship was offered through the bequest of Edward Maverick (Att. '52), and there was news of a bequest from Catherine Bohlen (Att. '61) which was destined for scholarship awards. A suggested wording for such bequests had been prepared by the new Counsel (from September 1979), Huyler Held (Att. '79).

What of the members of the 1980 Class? I have mentioned the great sadness they all felt at Stuart Platt's death. 'They' included sixteen American architects or environment consultants, eight from museums in an educational or curatorial capacity, three professors or associate professors, and so on — as Helena noted in her 1980 Report, 'a well-balanced group in terms of age and range of experience', although she noted, percipiently: 'I would be happy to see a few more museum curators since we have so much opportunity on the course of studying the decorative arts'. There were only seven British students, as against nine in 1979, all supported by scholarships. Three of these scholarships were given again, generously, by Jonathan Vickers, by Rudi Verspyck and by Rosemary Lomax-Simpson in order that two scholars from provincial museums and one architect could attend the Summer School.

In compiling this account I have been conscious that I have selected names to comment on in each Class, but not every name. They are given alphabetically in the 1984 *Alumni Directory*, the 1991 computer print-out (for American and Canadian members) and in a more restricted way in the Appendix later in these pages. My aim had been to show the range — all are worthy of mention, all cannot easily be so commemorated. Ann Brubaker was Director of Education at the Nelson-Atkins Museum of Art in Kansas City and she had a few curatorial colleagues — Christina Corsiglia from the Boston Museum's fine 'European' Department (Christina subsequently had the task of collecting the American contributions to the Platt Memorial Fund, as Annabel Westman did in England), Elaine Evans Dee from the Cooper-Hewitt Museum (elected, in 1991, President of the American

Friends), Crosby Forbes, founder and Curator of the American China Trade Museum (now at Salem), Stewart Johnson, as noted, then Curator of Design at the Museum of Modern Art in New York, and Joanne Platou from the Historic New Orleans Collection. Among the graduate students were Kim Rorschach at Yale, Tom Savage at Cooperstown, Marc Simpson at Yale, Debra Mancoff, Northwestern University, and John Wilson at New York University. The several architects included Mark Hewitt (since, the historian of 'The American Country House'), Frank Sanchis of the New York Landmarks Preservation Commission and Mark Wenger at Colonial Williamsburg. The educationalists (but aren't we all that?) numbered Hank Dunlop from California.

The varied American group was joined by John Lewis (now Chairman of The Attingham Trust), Jane Legget from Leicester (a faithful worker in subsequent Attingham Society events), the architect Nicholas Thompson, Stuart Platts (as mentioned), Anne Manningham-Buller from the Victoria and Albert Museum, Hugh Mellor as National Trust Scholar, and Christine Tindale, then Assistant to Chatsworth's Librarian. In fact, what would each Attingham year have been without the help and knowledge given by the Duke and Duchess of Devonshire and the successive Keepers of Collections, Francis Thompson, Tom Wragg and Peter Day? It is a privilege that cannot be over-estimated, and in this complex pattern Christine, and the Librarian, Michael Pearman, have played their part.

Almost as faithfully as the annual Chatsworth help was the long contact built up with the National Gallery in Prague. 1980 saw Eva Zikova

Chatsworth, Long Canal and Emperor Fountain before the south front.
Drawing by Kent Brinkley (Att. '89).

attending, as many of her colleagues had done before and have done since. Vonny de Mist from the Rijksmuseum's Department of Coins and Medals completed the selection of scholars from Europe. Lucy Knox (Abel-Smith) and Annabel Westman attended the course as administrators and tutors, and both, in their various roles, have, for many subsequent years, always put Attingham at the forefront of their busy lives.

In her 1980 report Helena Hayward dealt in detail with 'The Future'. To help her deliberations on European scholars she organized the setting-up of a Scholarship Committee, chaired by Ros Savill, with a supporting membership of Jeannie Chapel, John Lewis, Charles Truman, Giles Waterfield and Annabel Westman. Secondly she turned again to the idea of the Sponsors' Week in celebration of the thirtieth anniversary of the foundation of the Summer School. This was to commence on 3 July 1981 at Attingham Park, thus offering the unique opportunity for *alumni* to return to the house in conditions similar to those on their own year. Before leaving for Stamford they would meet the incoming members of the thirtieth Summer School for a celebration lunch.

Financial arrangements were still tight — hence Helena's concern for each Class account. In 1979 a surplus of £2,644 had been earned on the year, to add to net assets of £15,528. In 1980 the surplus was but £307. Of the 1980 expenditure of £25,966, some £17,527 had been spent on accommodation and meals, £1,405 on tutors and lecturers, and £2,579 on travel. Scholarship income in Great Britain only amounted to £3,416. With the American Friends of Attingham a three-year analysis of operating income and expenditure, 1979 to 1981, was issued in September 1981.

> May 1979   Income $9,858   Expenditure $7,760
> May 1980   Income $19,203   Expenditure $9,250
> May 1981   Income $16,174   Expenditure $10,300

The three-year cumulative surplus was $17,928, but of this amount $11,000 represented the result of the appeal in honour of Phelps Warren. With most of its other assets locked away for providing scholarships, there was a considerable dependence on the annual appeal to *alumni*. In fact, in his Presidential Letter in 1977 Phelps Warren summarized what remains true to this day:

> Contributions to the Friends make up the bones and sinews of our organization. Because the Friends have only this sedate yearly Appeal and don't have financial drives or 'go after' foundation support, people might think we are privately funded. Not so. We exist on the bounty of Attingham's former students . . .

And yet perhaps but a quarter of the *alumni* were responding in the early 1980s. The by-laws state that each Attinghamite must make a contribution at least every five years. It was a subject near to any Treasurer's heart and I shall refer to it again.

During the autumn of 1980 much thought was given in New York to the thirtieth anniversary in England. The overall donation above cost for those attending was to be set at $300 per person, but five places out of the thirty were to be reserved for younger professionals. They would be asked to donate only $100 each. Assuming all thirty places were filled, a donation of $8,000 could be made. This could be used as a capital fund, the interest from which would support the future administration of the course. It was also realized that the School in England was being run without realistic compensation to those most involved and that the special anniversary week should accurately reflect actual costs in the basic fee. However, by September 1981 it was noted in the Director's report that 'although this principle of a capital fund is agreed as far as New York is concerned, no formal arrangements to this effect have been put on paper, still less implemented'.

The blue brochure for the thirtieth Summer School, 6 to 24 July 1981, has been issued as usual in the preceding autumn. It stated that after the usual venues for the first two weeks, Attingham Park and Sheffield University, 17 to 24 July would be spent in Norfolk, based at Keswick College, a few miles out of Norwich. As some measure of the increasing costs of general enrolment it can be noted for the years 1952, 1961, 1971 and 1981:

	Under thirty years	Over thirty years
1952	Not applicable : one fee of $150	
1961	Not applicable : one fee of $275	
1971	Under 32 : $395	Over 32 : $450
1981	Under 30 : $1,330	Over 30 : $1,370

The officers in New York in 1981 were headed by Stewart Johnson as President and Morrison (Morrie to everyone) Heckscher as Vice-President. The Vice-President for Development was Ferris Megarity, and David Pettigrew held this status for 'Events'. Sibyl McCormac Groff was Secretary, David Nathans Treasurer and Huyler Held, Counsel. Pauli McClanahan (who has been most generous to the Attingham Trust in subsequent years) remained as Executive Secretary in Washington. The Directors now included Miss Isabel Benham, the President of Printon Kane Research Inc. Her financial experience was to be very valuable in the succeeding year or two. Phelps Warren maintained his interest as Chairman Emeritus, and as one of the eleven Patrons heading the English committee's structure.

Whilst patrons may be, in some circumstances, merely a listing of their names on letterheads, Attingham's patrons, headed by the Duke of Grafton and the Duchess of Devonshire, have always been active, and most supportive. They help with arranging introductions to other house-owners, and, as I have noted elsewhere in these pages, our two annual visits to Chatsworth are made most congenial by the Duchess's help and

Annabel Westman (Att. '77), Assistant to the Director from 1980; Secretary to The Attingham Trust and Tutor on Textiles.
Photograph: Tony Frederick (Att. '89)

hospitality. Equally, other patrons, in various years, such as F. St John Gore, Sir John Summerson, Sir Trenchard Cox, Sir Brinsley Ford and John Cornforth have given lectures or tutoring assistance at many houses. Furthermore, from his wide knowledge, John Cornforth has frequently suggested houses to visit (or, conversely, a few not to), in counties less well known to the organizers. He has also written some house notes (for example, Scotney Castle) for us, and has taken part in discussions on estate duty and other issues which complicate house-owners' lives.

Concurrently with the 1981 brochure a leaflet issued in New York noted 'A Very Special Program for the Thirtieth Anniversary of the Attingham Summer School, 3–10 July 1981'. The basic cost was now set at $750 but the additional donation had been revised to $100 and $200 for non-alumni. 'These donations will be tax deductible and will be used by the Friends to offset the rising costs of the School'. The paperwork for these extra thirty applications was undertaken by one of the Directors, and former Executive Secretary, Anne Sharkey. In England Helena Hayward appointed Annabel Westman (Att. '77) as 'Assistant to the Director'. She still devotes a considerable part of her busy life to Attingham. As well as remaining Assistant to the Director, she also acts as Secretary to the Attingham Trust (a post conferred in December 1982).

No Attingham Chairman, or Director, since the early 1980s, can imagine the Trust, or its Summer School, without Annabel's careful and resourceful work, done always with patience, good humour and flair. However, over recent years too, Annabel has also established a reputation as an Historic Textiles Consultant. She has been involved in some restoration tasks at, for example, Arundel, Osterley, Kenwood, Blickling and Petworth, is Tutor on Textiles to the Summer School, and to the Study Centre for the History of the Fine and Decorative Arts, established in 1964 by Erica O'Donnell.

I cannot give a list of all those who attended the thirtieth anniversary week, but in my divisive way I will list a few. Alan Campbell (Att. '73) was joined by Bill Doneghy (Att. '66), Hortense Feldblum (Att. '66), Lillian Hirschmann (Att. '54), Florence Montgomery (First Class, '52), Karin Peterson (Att. '78), Wanda Radcliffe (Att. '66), Mr and Mrs David Stockwell (First Class '52), Lucy Sydnor (Att. '69), Charlton Theus (Att. '67) and Phelps Warren (Att. '59), for the Attingham days only. As for the programme, it started with drinks in the Hall at Attingham and an enthusiastic welcome from Sir George Trevelyan. On Day Two — 4 July — there were visits to Powis Castle, Linley Hall and a special showing of films on Ludlow and Stamford with Alec Clifton Taylor as commentator, both on film and in person. The group visited Ludlow on 5 July and after lunch on the 6th and a discussion (with John Hayward) on the Berwick Silver, left for the *George Hotel* at Stamford. Helen led the week with the help of Sylvia Stevenson (whom she was steering towards running such valuable special events) and John Cushion. The Burghley archivist (and family doctor!), Dr Eric Till, led the group around Burghley, and on successive days visits were made to Boughton, Lamport, Grimsthorpe Castle (Vanbrugh's last 'great fine house'), with a final dinner party in the hospitable house of Mr Edmund and the Hon. Mrs Marian Brudenell, at Deene Park. The group dispersed on Friday morning, 10 July, after a visit to Althorp.

I mentioned earlier that on 6 July, at Attingham Park, the 'Special Week' merged with the incoming 30th Summer School members. They had been attracted by the usual high standard of programme. Their Class was formally opened by Florence Montgomery. Of the American members, thirteen worked in museums or for historical societies, while nine were architects or architectural historians, including one Professor of Architecture. There was one Associate Professor of Landscape Architecture and three members were teaching at school or in adult education, one of whom was an Associate Professor of Art History. There was one Professor of English, one antique dealer, six students and five others variously occupied, 'making a well-balanced and remarkably well-integrated American group'. There were six British members supported by scholarships. Two of these worked for The National Trust, by whom they were funded. Three scholarships were offered to candidates working in provincial museums (at Manchester, Salisbury and Glasgow). Funds to support these candidates came again from Jonathan Vickers, Rudolph Verspyck and John Lewis. Donations were also gratefully received in memory of Stuart Platts, whose tragic death on the 1980 Class I have noted previously.

Helena Hayward, in her careful report, regretted that the usual practice of the Victoria and Albert Museum to fund two junior members of their staff was discontinued by the Director, Sir Roy Strong. It is not really to the purpose of this history to fully examine the matter. Sufficient to say that Helen Lowenthal had criticized in *The Times* (2 December 1980) the closure of the National Slide Library at the Victoria and Albert Museum. Altogether some seventy-five organizations made representations about this and the Library was finally saved. However, Sir Roy declared Helen *persona non grata* in perpetuity' at the Museum. The matter flickered on through letter and counter-letter. Helena Hayward wrote finally to *The Times* after a Council Meeting on 5 April 1981, and crisply indicated the long support given to Attingham by Sir Roy's predecessors as Director — Sir Leigh Ashton, Sir Trenchard Cox (still an Attingham Patron) and Sir John Pope-Hennessy, and her regret that personal feelings prevented the Director supporting junior members of his museum from receiving scholarships. The matter was resolved finally in 1989 when the Museum, under its present Director (Mrs E. Esteve-Coll), supported one of its staff again attending each year. Amusingly, the file in Helen's papers recording these transactions was inscribed 'Roy Row'.

But who were some of the members of the 1981 Class? Bill Butler, then at Winterthur, was the Edward Maverick Fund Scholar, and as his fellow student members he had Tom Jayne (then University of Oregon), Tom Michie (Yale), Stephen Pallrand (Oberlin College) and Patrick Youngblood (Courtauld Institute). The more senior members included Betty Starr Cummin (then University of Pennsylvania), Gaylord Dillingham from San Francisco, Mary Louise Fazzano at the Rhode Island School of Design, Wendy Kaplan (Boston Museum), Richard Milhender (the Boston collector and Trustee of the China Trade Museum, a long-time supporter of Attingham and a member of the Advisory Committee to its Study Week), Gloria Ravitch, then at the De Young Museum, San Francisco, and Liz Tucker from Charleston. They joined Belinda Cousens from the National Trust Regional Office at Attingham Park — Belinda is the Assistant Historic Buildings Representative working for Julian Gibbs (Att. '78) — Tiffany Hunt, then at the Salisbury Museum (now The National Trust), John Lewis (attending part-time as a member of the Attingham Council and the Scholarship Committee), James Lomax, then at Manchester Art Gallery (as the Stuart Platts Scholar), Juliet Kinchin (Pollok House, Glasgow) and Sue

Collingridge, The National Trust's Assistant Historic Buildings Represen-
tative in Cornwall. Dr Stephen Barkoczy came from the Museum of Fine
Art in Budapest (funded partly by Sotheby's), Dr Jarek Stoklasa from the
National Gallery in Prague, and for the Third Week only, Contessa
Loredana Da Schio (Att. '60) joined the group.

The 'lecturers, tutors and administrators accompanying the course'
included Helena Hayward as Director, her Assistant, Annabel Westman,
Rosemary Lomax-Simpson, John Cushion, Helen Lowenthal, Dr Rosalys
Coope, and Lucy Knox. Faithfully, this team (as with earlier teams in the
preceding years) did everything they could to smooth progress and
tempers, instruct minds and manners, and befriend the friendly and
friendless. As for the programme, by now in this account it is clear that
Attingham, the Peak District houses (Chatsworth, Hardwick, Kedleston)
could only be enhanced by visits in Norfolk to Holkham and Houghton.
Whilst the catering at Keswick Hall was poor, the fine medieval churches
and wonderful Palladian houses overcame thoughts of dreary food. The
final party at Heydon Hall was in any case splendid and hilarious; the
cementing of impressions and friendships into one pervasive memory.

In organizational terms 1981 saw changes in New York and London —
Pauli McClanahan finished her services as Executive Secretary in Washington and Helen Hamilton (Att. '75), living in Princeton, took over such
duties. In England Helen Lowenthal was acting as President and 'Acting
Chairman' as Tony Galliers-Pratt had resigned as Chairman in November
due to his increasing business commitments. It was arranged that on behalf
of the Council the valued support of Tony and Angela Galliers-Pratt should
be commemorated by making a presentation of a tree to be planted at
Mawley Hall.

With the future in mind it was decided to invite someone with good
business experience to join the Council. Alexander 'Sandy' Stirling was
eminently eligible, being Chairman of a London broking house, and as a
Liveryman of the Worshipful Company of Goldsmiths he was additionally,
much interested in period and contemporary silver design. He was
therefore elected in November 1981, together with the Historic Buildings
Secretary to The National Trust, Martin Drury. As one of his first duties Mr
Stirling was asked to chair a Financial Committee (Helena Hayward,
Rosemary Lomax-Simpson, John Lewis and Annabel Westman) to look at
ways of raising money, part of which would be given to paying more
realistic salaries for the staff. John Hayward was elected as a Patron in view
of his long-standing support to the Summer School. His place on the
Council was given to Ros Savill, the first Chairman of the Scholarship
sub-committee.

The 1982 document which Sandy Stirling and his colleagues produced
in May 1982 (partly revised in September 1982) was a cogent document. It
firstly summarized the present situation, noting that the Trust was
covering its costs, but that the accumulated surplus from operations, plus

Alexander 'Sandy' Stirling,
Chairman of the Attingham Trust,
1982–88.

some donations by May 1982, was £26,000 for thirty years' work. The American Friends had $80,576 capital for their scholarship fund and an operating surplus to May 1981 of $17,925. The School had an established reputation, the support of The National Trust, enthusiastic and efficient direction and the support of some 1,050 *alumni* scattered in America, with about eighty from England and various European and 'Iron Curtain' countries.

In most arguments or organizations there are weaknesses. Mr Stirling's team listed these as the comparatively small assets after thirty years, inadequate funds to provide the desired number of British scholarships, the fluctuation of annual income due to the $/£ exchange rate, the dependence on co-operation of the Concord College tenants of Attingham Park's administrative areas and plans for succession among officers needing to be made. Further, there was a limit on the number of students, an annual School because of other commitments of part-time staff, and the charitable status of the Trust imposing certain constraints. The 'Proposals' to achieve the principal objective of advancing knowledge of the country house in Britain and their collections were simple to state. In principle it was felt the Trust should plan to generate enough income each year to cover its full annual costs and also to create an operating surplus to help in building up a reserve. Annual costs would be based on officers being properly remunerated, with the income generated by the reserve being used either to supplement the annual income and reduce the amount needed from fees, or for the funding of scholarships, or as the Council decided. The costs of the 1983 School were estimated at about £43,600. The ambitious target for a capital fund to carry out the long-held objects of the Trust in future years was set at £100,000.

As a part of the wide-ranging review John Lewis, Legal Adviser to the Trust, had undertaken a revision of the Rules. Helena Hayward and Annabel Westman were also much involved in the long hours of detailed discussions. The changes in wording suggested were accepted unanimously by the Council at its Annual General Meeting, held at the Sloane Club on 13 December 1982. The Council's warm thanks were expressed to all three and to Mr Peter Anderson, of Jacques and Lewis, who had prepared the Resolution to the Charity Commissioners.

At the same Annual General Meeting Sandy Stirling was appointed Chairman of the Trust, Martin Drury, its Vice-Chairman and Annabel Westman its Secretary. A month or two prior to this he had visited New York on business and took the opportunity to meet the American Board. With Stewart Johnson relinquishing the Presidency in May 1982 the Vice-President, Morrie Heckscher, Keeper of the American Wing at the Metropolitan Museum of Art, had succeeded him. A meeting was arranged by Morrie at his New York home on 4 October 1982.

After reviewing his previously circulated statement, the new Chairman directed discussion towards the 'Special Week' which had been devised as a profit-making scheme to increase the Summer School's

Martin D. Drury, Vice-Chairman,
The Attingham Trust, 1982 to date.

Rosalind Savill (Att. '75),
appointed first Chairman of the
Scholarship Committee, 1980.

reserves. It will be recalled that this grew from the 30th Anniversary Week in 1981 and its important role is described below. It was not possible under US tax law to regard the additional donations to the fee as tax-deductible and then transfer it to an overseas recipient, even if a charity. A donation would be made, however, in the sum of $5,000 for 1982 and ways sought to regularize this. A more sensible way might be for the Summer School Trust to build a profit margin into the fee for the Special Week. However, there was a concern that some advantage from this should come to the American Friends to increase their scholarship funds. It was worrying that the cost of the 1983 Summer School would need to be as high as $1,590 for students over thirty and $1,550 for those under. Whilst demand for places seemed strong enough to bear a realistic cost being applied, in the final account the amount proved to be unacceptable: it was still only $1,600 (and $1,550) in 1985.

It is time to focus on the Special Weeks which were so important in the early 1980s in contributing to reserves. How did they start? For some time it had been felt that, whilst *alumni* had been allowed to join the Third Week of the Summer School, there was room for a more comfortable and relaxed programme in addition — the so-called 'Special Week'. Sylvia Stevenson, who organized them with great skill and style, has kindly provided me with the following note to which, in parentheses, I have added some statistics. Sylvia writes:

The 'Special Week' was the brainchild [in 1982] of Helen Lowenthal; the original idea was not only to give pleasure to *alumni* and their friends but to raise funds — at that time badly needed — for the English administration of the Attingham Trust. Knowing of my great interest in Attingham, Helen invited me to join her in initiating this enterprise. I was, at that time, working whole-time for Christie's Education, but Helen knew that I was retiring at the end of the academic year, 1981, so it was arranged that I joined her at Stamford to assist her during the first Special Week [3–10 July 1981] and that in the following years I would take over the running of it from her, and she would help me; this I did for three more years [1982–84]. We had the greatest fun together from start to finish, and with the members and their friends who joined us and with John Cushion who did so much in every way — not just his specialised knowledge in ceramics — but carrying luggage, helping any members who had special needs and so on. I think most members would agree that the highlight of those four years of the Special Week were the two visits we made to Scotland, one based in Edinburgh [1–8 July 1982] and the other based half in Glasgow and half in Aberdeen-shire [June 1984]. In Edinburgh we had two wonderful private parties: one with my friends John and Elizabeth Clerk at Penicuik and the other at my son's house in Edinburgh where we celebrated the 4th July in real style — the stars and stripes of America painted all over one wall of the house — our hostess, dressed in red, and white and blue providing — in addition to a lovely dinner and superb wine — a wonderful cake with the American flag on it; we all sang American songs and had a very special evening. Earlier that 4th July we had visited — in a private capacity — my friends the late Lord Haddington and the Lady Haddington at Tyninghame; Gordie Haddington showed us all round personally and as we left made a special speech to the members about the 4th July — he was then over 90, and Sarah took us personally round the garden she had created and entertained us to a lavish lunch and tea in their beautiful home. Then back to Edinburgh, changed, and this really fun party at 29 Warriston Crescent. The other great event of that visit was a number of the very best seats were allocated to us by John Clerk, Lord Lieutenant of Midlothian, for the installation of the Order of the Thistle ceremony at St. Giles Cathedral. Similar sorts of events took place in Aberdeenshire and in Glasgow, where all the members contributed most generously to a great celebration of Helen Lowenthal's eightieth birthday [21 June] on the actual day; and we visited a number of houses, not available at that time to the public at all. It was, for me, and I know for Helen, and I hope for the members who came, four very happy weeks indeed, and despite the reference to parties above, we did do a certain amount of serious studying. I personally made many life-long friends, and I shall always be very grateful to Helen Lowenthal for having invited me to join her in this venture.

The 1982 Special Week then took place in Edinburgh. At its conclusion this was the utterance:

> Raise your glass — first — to Sylvia
> Who made us feel at home
> And who has taught her American cousins
> To say *Scoon* instead of Scone.
>
> And here's to bonnie Helen
> Stouthearted lass is she
> And with her we shall always
> Join hands across the sea.
>
> And certainly our many hosts
> Whose friendship we shall treasure
> For we have come so very far
> And have received full measure.
>
> Drink too, to John and Maggie [Cushion]
> Who shortly will be mates —
> And we will meet again this fall
> In our — and their — United States.
>
> And drink to one and all — good friends.
> We'll meet again sometime.
> And when we do, let's hoist a few
> For auld lang syne.

Due to Sylvia's care and the bullying of her friends for favours, free and *gratis*, profit of around £5,800 was made on a total income of £15,780. The profit, which to this extent was not intended, was largely due to the beneficial exchange rate, as well as Sylvia having her own home in Edinburgh (therefore avoiding hotel costs for herself) with John Cushion and his soon-to-be second wife, Maggie, as her guests, by using local

Morrison H. 'Morrie'
Heckscher (Att. '66),
President of The
American Friends,
1982–6.

part-time lecturers and by careful 'housekeeping'. This would allow a
reserve of, say, £2,500 for future 'Alumni Weeks' when the exchange rate or
other factors might be less favourable. It would be possible to give back £50
a head to each individual but it was felt most of them wanted to donate it to
the Trust. The weeks were in the best interests of Attingham and Sylvia
concluded her explanations to Helen with the words that 'hopefully the
main Trust can be assured of an annual income of £5,000 plus'. I will
describe the Special Weeks of 1983 and 1984 in their correct chronological
sequence.

In New York, late in 1981 it had been discovered that the American
Friends had not filed its tax returns for 1979 and 1980. This matter was
serious and came to a head finally. As President, Morrie Heckscher was
subpoenaed to appear. With the help of Huyler Held as Counsel and
financial advice from Isabel Benham it was stated in mitigation:

> Attingham is and has been since its creation a relatively small publicly
> supported charity governed by volunteer officers and directors
> interested in its charitable efforts. For approximately fifteen years until
> 1979 the President and Executive Secretary remained the same and
> during that time all tax returns were prepared by accountants and
> properly and timely filed. Unfortunately in 1979 the long-time President
> and Executive Secretary as well as the other officers of the organization
> retired. A new slate of officers was elected and more importantly, new
> arrangements were made to handle the day to day administration. In

1979 a contract was entered into between Attingham and the National Trust for Historic Preservation under which the Trust undertook for a flat annual fee to handle what the newly elected officers of Attingham assumed were all administrative and book-keeping functions. In 1981 Attingham decided to terminate the arrangement with the National Trust. An Executive Secretary (Helen Hamilton) was retained then to work on Attingham affairs.

It was then the mistake was discovered. Matters were not helped by casual external professional advice in completion of the relevant accounts.

But such troubles could not distort that it was Attingham's thirtieth year. The Council in London gave a small reception on 20 May at the Royal Society of Arts. It was, as Helen wrote in her letters of invitation: 'a chance for old friends to meet recent supporters of the School'.

With inexorable promptitude the 1982 Summer School could not be delayed by such matters, including those vital to the hard-pressed team in New York. They were required as usual to issue from Princeton the beige-coloured brochure to announce the 31st Summer School (5–23 July 1982) to be held at Attingham Park, Sheffield and Exeter University. It was the first occasion the School was to visit the true West Country with a promise of seeing Saltram House, where the Parker family employed Robert Adam, Powderham Castle, with its rich rococo plasterwork, and Castle Drogo, masterpiece of Sir Edwin Lutyens, c. 1900. The two costs of enrolment were at $1,300 and (for those over thirty) $1,370. A limited number of younger *alumni* would be accepted for the Devon period at a cost for the week of $550.

What came out of the New York selection committees was as fascinating a group as ever: highly competent specialists such as Sue Swan, Winterthur's Curator of Textiles, Alan Darr of the Detroit Institute of Art, and Charles Fleischmann, with one of the finest private collections of English miniatures. Laurie and Peter Fusco were in from the Getty and Los Angeles County Museums, and spirits were kept high by Hillman Holland from Atlanta and Louise Turner, the Regent of Gunston Hall. Caroline Sartor looked appreciatively at every scrap of landscape (she is a distinguished landscape architect), and Whaley Batson at everything she hoped daughter Barbara would also one day see (she made it to the Class of '89).

The European members included Susan Denyer and Jeffrey Haworth as National Trust scholars, Kedrun Laurie from the Geffrye Museum, Deborah Clark from Manchester City Art Gallery, Katherine Spencer from the Victoria and Albert Museum, Andrea George from Cusworth Hall and Tony Tibbles of Speke Hall, Liverpool, the great half-timbered house on the edge of the Mersey. Luboš Slavíček was the scholar from the National Gallery in Prague.

For the first time I was able to help, away from my University life, for all the final week, at Exeter. The Class was also joined there by Jeannie Chapel, who, as I have noted, made a valuable contribution over several

Lucy Knox (Mrs David Abel-Smith), President of The Attingham Society, and a frequent tutor and 'party-giver' to Attingham, 'on its progresses'.

years when *alumni* were present on the Third Week. Helen also came down to Exeter and John Cushion, Annabel and Rosemary were the usual effective support team. But whilst all seemed well there had been a considerable problem. Helena had been taken ill in June and was still recovering from an operation. At short notice Rosalind Savill took over the position of 'Acting Director' to steer the 1982 Class, the programme for which Helena had, of course, prepared with her usual care. Helena's work was further divided between Lucy Knox (as Director of Studies) and Annabel Westman (as Director of House Visits and Assistant Administrator); both would also tutor. In addition John Hardy gave a similar lecture on furniture to that which Helena would have given and John Hayward put in an additional lecture on furniture. Rosemary Lomax-Simpson, with her usual care, supervised all the minutiae of accommodation and travel.

Perhaps there is always something special about any final week. Helena was able to rejoin us towards its end. I recall talking on plasterwork and then taking the Class an hour later to see all the exuberant froth of it at Powderham. We walked in the evening on a conducted tour of Exeter, we gazed down at 'Lorna Doone' country from the ramparts of Castle Drogo, and enjoyed the great garden created by Lord and Lady Amory at Knightshayes Court. There was even time for a hardy few to sea-bathe at the end of the visit to Mothecombe and, if adroit, not to miss the picnic tea either. Even the names of the houses on subsequent days were evocative — Cadhay, Rockbeare, Forde, Bickleigh Castle (for the final Dinner) and then a return to London via Elizabethan Montacute on 23 July.

A little earlier in 1982, in June, Sibyl McCormac Groff had been in London armed with questions, principally from Isabel Benham, about financial information of use to both groups in New York and London. There was need to clarify the fact that money did not come from the Courtauld Institute or the Robertson 'jam' family — they had helped a 'Bath Summer School' with which Helen, confusingly, was also involved in the early 1950s — the nature of investments, the long-term plans for investing in the School part of the accumulated surplus, and the current thinking by Helen and her associates of retirement and prospects for succession. They were questions, as Isabel wrote, 'in order that we may better understand what we are about'. She was interested in the rate of exchange used for 1980 and 1981 in computing the American tuition.

It was left to Sandy Stirling as Chairman to answer such questions. After defining the nature of an English educational trust, with all profits, in the status of the Attingham Trust to be applied towards organizing educational courses, including the granting of scholarships, he turned to other relevant matters. He clarified the fact that no Robertson money had ever come to Attingham, but that any such sums in the past had gone to support scholarships. There had been no definite policy hitherto to build up a capital reserve. The Monument Trust had given £5,000 for scholarships but there was a need to address, firmly, building up reserves. The Trust needed to stand financially on its own and meet deficits from its own resources. It had no claim on money accumulated by the American Friends. A surplus had been made in 1981 when the exchange rate was favourable — conversely in 1980 the pound was high. As for succession, Helen had handed on executive responsibility when she became President. Helena was indicating her wish to move more to a consultative capacity after 1984.

In respect of annual accounts, those for 1982 showed a substantial surplus — arising almost entirely from the successful 'Special Week' — but in respect of the Summer School the surplus achieved in 1982 (and probably for 1983) was quite modest. As for the volatile rate of exchange — decisions were made by the Chairman (following careful discussion with Mr John Lewis) in September of one year in respect of funds which would not be converted from dollars to pounds until June the following year. If there was a suggestion to remit in pounds from America to take advantage, then equally the risk of disadvantageous movement in the rate would need to be transferred too. This risk has always been borne by the Trust in London, although it is correct to say that it was managed to the Trust's considerable advantage in the late 1980s. Out of chronology, it may be pertinent to note that costs for 1990 were calculated at the rate of $1.80 to the pound when the rate was nearer two dollars, with the loss calculated. So a difficult decision, but one any good financial observer such as Isabel Benham was certain to raise. The Chairman concluded his long letter with words (which are still as relevant) — 'it is our wish that we should work with the closest possible understanding between the Trust and the American Friends'. The review which had been inaugurated, together with the relevant financial information, were pertinent to the October 1982 meeting in New York, previously referred to.

I have explained that for two or three years Sylvia Stevenson's 'Special Weeks', apart from being excellent value, were a means of enhancing the Trust's income. This was not hidden from the participants in any way: they knew an extra 'loading' on costs was to help the Trust continue to be effective with its Summer School. The 1983 Special Week, 29 June to 6 July, was based at Cambridge (King's College) and Lincoln (*White Hart Hotel*). Again it had the advantage of visiting houses not normally open with a great deal of lavish hospitality which Sylvia had arranged with good friends. When Sandy Stirling gave his Chairman's Report at 30 September 1983, he noted that:

> The week is operated as a fund raising effort and it has, for 1983, produced a very satisfactory surplus of £9,552. In addition donations of £3,304 were received, most of which were in respect of the Special Week of 1982.

The Summer School naturally made a more modest surplus, some £2,660. The 1983 School opened on Monday 4 July. However, on the previous day the Scholarship Committee had arranged a Decorative Arts Study afternoon at the Victoria and Albert Museum. This was for those arriving before the opening of the course and was led by John Hardy and Charles Truman. On 15 July after the heady exciting days in the centre of England the group left for Durham via Richmond. On this scenic tour of England there were wondrous visits to Cragside, to Callaly, where the owner, Major A. S. C. Browne, shot around with great speed in his electric 'wheelcar'. He marshalled everyone with the efficiency of a first-rate shepherd. Then on a dark brooding day I introduced Seaton Delaval, Vanbrugh's great house with its soaring ruinous interior, mighty stable range and 'theatric' elevations. There was also time — always time — to view the Romanesque spaces of Durham Cathedral. Then on yet again, north to Edinburgh, with visits to Adam's castellated Mellerstain, romantic Abbotsford, mighty Drumlanrig Castle. There was, however, a temptation to be over-ambitious, and the wealth of Scottish houses, the generosity of their owners, made for a crowded if splendid occasion. Longer and more studious visits were promised by the organizers, to themselves, for 1984.

Thirty-six places had been allocated to American members. There were seven British scholars, all of whom received full scholarships but with each contributing £50 to the Summer School. The Scholarship Committee had discussed such a contribution in 1982 but reached no decision on implementation. When introduced for 1983 — the money is put towards scholarship funds — one member of the Scholarship Committee, Charles Truman, objected. However, the majority committee view had to prevail and in due course Mr Truman resigned. Such a sum of money (now £75) is still a condition of the award of an English scholarship, and helps to provide about half the annual fees for one place. But who were the lucky recipients?

I confess to some liking for the Class of '83. Perhaps to no more than I normally feel, but it had some good friends on it, and Helena called it 'a superb Class'. I have received many kindnesses in America. But Pam Armour, Ulysses Dietz, Diane Dunkley, Willie Graham, Jethro Hurt, Valencia Libby, David Reese, Kevin Stayton, Jonathan Thornton, Jeanne Vibert and Ghenete Zelleke who extended them were all Class of '83! In English terms there were more friends, Dorian Church, David Freeman, John Fuggles, Richard Gray, and with Tony Atkin, Charles Chevalier and Richard Milhender on the Third Week. Less euphoria in the scribe will make for more objectivity.

Perhaps the luckiest point about the Class of '83 was that they gradually realized they were to be the last to be residential at Attingham Park. Frank Bell's Concord College was attracting less paying students and it was to be easier for him to pay out his lease from The National Trust, fold his tent and drift away. This fact he announced, laconically, at dinner on the first night, sending Helena and Rosemary into immediate forays to other suitable places near to Attingham for the 1984 venue. After considering another school at Abbot's Bromley owned by Mr Bell, and thinking hard, it seemed that the Harper Adams Agricultural College, near Newport, specialists in down-wind piggy smells, would win the day at the expense of the olfactory sense. But I hasten a little too much, which is what people at Harper Adams were to do.

In October 1983 Morrie Heckscher, as President of the American Friends, sent out his Fall Letter. He noted that with the completion of the thirty-third consecutive year of the Summer School course some 1,500 people had attended Attingham, including about 1,250 Americans. His Board felt that an *Alumni Directory* should be published to include English and European members additionally to those in America and Canada. The *Directory* was to be prepared by an *ad hoc* committee consisting of Christopher Wilk (Att. '78) as Chairman, Bill Butler (Att. '81), Tom Jayne (Att. '81) and Pat Hurley (Att. '78). A questionnaire was circulated and was due to be returned by 30 November 1983 to Helen Hamilton in Princeton. The *Directory* was published in 1984 'in recognition of Phelps Warren (1906–1985), President of the Friends 1964–1979'. So to be bibliographically exact: it has '1984' on its title-page and the *verso* but came through to sale after Phelps' death in February 1985, allowing the tribute to be placed on its first page. It has been as invaluable to us all as he would have wished.

I have been able in this history to say little about American regional activities which keep the membership involved. But let's consider 1983. On 18 February the Mid-Winter Reunion took place at the New York residence of Mrs Rush H. Kress; in February also there was a reception for Williamsburg Forum and Virginia area *alumni* hosted by Nick Pappas and

Lucy Sydnor; on 16 April the annual spring meeting to three collections in Philadelphia; on 13 June a reception given by Phelps Warren, President Emeritus, in honour of members of the Class of '83; and on 16 June a reception hosted by Tony Atkin for Philadelphia area members at the Washington Square residence of Marion Carson. The fall outing to the North Shore of Long Island took place on 8 October.

Some changes in the list of officers in New York had taken place at the Annual Meeting of 26 May 1983. Isabel Benham was elected Vice-President, Finance and Clare Le Corbeiller (Att. '56), a most distinguished member of the Department of European Sculpture and Decorative Arts at the Metropolitan Museum, a Vice-President. Clare's long service to Attingham has an honoured place in this story, as does that of Edith Standen (Att. '56) and Barbara Wriston (Att. '53). Any of them would have made an outstanding President of the Friends but they have been content to serve in every other helpful post: currently Clare is Chairman of the (American) Scholarship Committee. Sibyl Groff remained Treasurer, with May N. Stone (Att. '76) as Secretary. The resignation of Ferris Megarity (Att. '68) as Vice-President for Development was accepted with regret. Among the new Directors was Bill McNaught (Att. '70) who was to eventually become the Friends' President.

Each autumn in England the Attingham Chairman and his colleagues on the Finance Sub-Committee (and particularly John Lewis) have agonized over setting the fees for the following year. This has to be done in mid-September in order that brochures can reach America a month later. What the dollar exchange rate is at in September as opposed to the following June, when dollars are received from New York on behalf of that Summer's class, is always a matter of concern. There was an obvious temptation to enter into a forward buying contract in order that advantage could be taken of advantageous currency movements. Equally there was a risk of loss. In 1983 the Main Course made a profit of about £9,600 of which sum £3,542 was accounted for by the voluntary waiving of fees to which they were entitled by the officers (Director, Treasurer and Secretary), and £4,162 arose from the favourable exchange rate between the dollar and the pound. The sum of £2,000 (actually £1,943) was operating profit. Investment income provided £5,162, the Special Week added £9,552, and miscellaneous income gave an overall total of £27,665. This sum helped in setting fees for the following year by only increasing them at 1.3 per cent and 1.9 per cent for Americans under and over thirty years respectively. Non-US students were increased by 2.2 per cent and Third Week *alumni* by 14.5 per cent. It was hoped the Special Week for 1984 would settle at about a 6.6 per cent increase.

The Attingham files in England are adequate testimony to the meticulous annual calculations which were made. Each service had a cost and in earlier days much of this had been uncontrolled, 'lost' in various ways or was slumbering to emerge as an unwelcome deficit. But for the selfless ignoring of responsible remuneration by the English officers over many years things could have been worse.

In February 1984 when the September calculations had been made at £1/US$1.65 the pound was substantially weaker and it was agreed by the Council to take out a forward contract to purchase sterling with $60,000 of the money expected in early June 1984. This represented about two-thirds of the total expected. Following that decision the pound continued to weaken (hovering at $1.41 to the £). A forward rate of 1.4205 would produce an exchange profit of £5,875. In the twenty-four hours taken over consultations the rate had moved to $1.447. The next day it was $1.4505. In forty-eight hours profit expectation was £5,001 instead of £5,875.

I am aware that there was American criticism of these arrangements but I do not endorse them personally. The risk could be undertaken provided reserves were adequate and the objective was to strengthen Attingham's reserves to award scholarships and secure the School, for want of better words, 'in perpetuity'. At the beginning of the 1983 financial year Attingham's total funds were £42,568. It was estimated that at the year's end they would be £51,168. But with a good wind, helped by currency movement and better than expected income, it had moved to £70,233 actual. Scholarship outgoings from investment income had been helped by the Monument Trust renewing its generous contribution, enabling scholarships to be again given, mostly to provincial museum staff.

It may be helpful, and certainly truthful, to show the build-up in Attingham's reserves in London for the five years 1984 to 1988. Naturally I cannot give every financial gloss or reason. Currency movement advantages (but these were never excessive; in 1983 a gain of £3,737 only), putting more to increase investments, improved performance there, keeping costs as prudent as possible all helped.

Accumulated surplus

31 August 1984	£92,425
1985	£111,964
1986	£119,311

(In 1986 there was a deficit on the cost of the Summer School of £3,325.)

1987	£144,609
1988	£165,819

The troughs in the value of the fixed assets can be noted with investments at cost of £142,384 on 31 March 1988 having a market value of £190,009 at that date. However, with a drastic stock market slump they had dropped to £142,383 (cost) at 30 September 1988. Nevertheless steady annual investment income, ploughed back, helped increase the reserves. There is ample evidence that the costs of the School in recent years have been held lower than is really wise, to help our English and American colleagues. However, with currency fluctuation no longer a sensible option, Attingham tries to seek enough external scholarship funding to allow its investment income to be ploughed back to increase the capital sum to a position where we can weather any adverse 'storm'. The operating fund, for example, made a deficit of £7,936 in 1990 and there may be a deficit in future years.

At the Annual General Meeting in December 1983 there was sadness that it was not possible to meet at Attingham in 1984; equally, sadness at the deaths of four distinguished patrons, Dr John Hayward, Dr Clifford Musgrave, Professor Sir Nikolaus Pevsner and Mrs Neal S. Wood. They had all given valued help and advice over many years. F. St John Gore and John Cornforth consented to become 'Members of the Association' on their retirement from the Council. The Members (now in reduced number) are that small group who would be responsible, if the Trust was ever wound up, for the distribution of its assets. Elections to the Council were Professor John Wilton-Ely and myself.

During 1983 the Trust had been able to provide the first scholarship from its own funds. With more substantial capital there would be room to increase the number. Nevertheless the budget for 1984 was forecasting a rise of 24 per cent over the previous year. This was mainly due to the rising cost of board and lodging and to the payment of more realistic fees for administration and tuition.

For the first time since 1952 Attingham Park was not available for residence and so the first week of the 1984 School (9–27 July) was, as noted, to be at Harper Adams Agricultural College. Its relative proximity to Attingham allowed the second day to be spent viewing the house, estate and the attractive 'estate house' of Cronkhill (to John Nash's design, and in part, attractively circular in plan). A local architect, Andrew Arrol (Att. '78), also led a visit to Shrewsbury to draw attention to its wealth of early timbered houses set around by later Georgian and other development. There was also a welcome visit to Erddig, superbly restored by the National Trust. Anyone who has not read Merlin Waterson's *The Servants' Hall* (reissued in paperback in 1990) is missing out on a slice of social history with Erddig as the exemplar. The first week ended with the usual fine visit to Mawley Hall with a long one and a half hour lunch break to savour both delicious food and the attractive garden. After Chatsworth, Hardwick, Kedleston — the perennial delights of the Derbyshire Peak — the last week was perhaps prophetic. The 1977 School had spent its final week at West Dean College, the great Sussex home of the James family turned into a residential crafts college, and now 1984 was there too. Clive Aslet of *Country Life*, and author of the delightful book, *The Last Country Houses* (1982), spoke on 'West Dean and the Edwardian Country House'. It proved possible to visit Woolbeding, home of the Hon. Simon Sainsbury, who, through the agency of his Monument Trust, has been outstandingly generous in making money for scholarships available to the Trust. Also, to journey from Portsmouth across to the Isle of Wight to see Osborne House and Appuldurcombe, the great early eighteenth-century ruin, formerly a Worsley family house, both being now in the care of English Heritage. There was also opportunity for good seminars at Petworth, Arundel Castle

Uppark, West Sussex. The late seventeenth-century house, beloved by all
alumni, was damaged by fire in 1989 but is now being rebuilt.
Drawing by Will Gwilliam (Att. '88)

(superbly led by the Duke's librarian, Dr John Martin Robinson), Firle Place
(which we were shown, devotedly, by Hazel and Deborah Gage) and to see
the rich silhouettes and interiors of the Brighton Pavilion, with dinner
afterwards in the Adelaide Suite, and a private view of the great collection
of silver-gilt plate. Time also for an evening visit to dreamy Uppark, and a
morning visit to see the Sèvres porcelain at Goodwood, described expertly
by Ros Savill. Attingham's tuition, always good, had been honed to
perfection under Helena Hayward's direction and, I hope, continues to be
so.

Long coach journeys could not have given the staff (Helena, Rosemary, Annabel, John Cushion, Lucy Knox and me) more companionable
'souls' to talk to. Debby Binder from St Louis, Jean Burks (talking often on
brass candlesticks!), Pat Gibbs, fascinated by Attingham, and her time after
on the Beaufort estate, researching Lord Botetourt, Ken Hafertepe, then a
doctoral candidate, Gail Homer from the National Parks service, brown-
eyed Shep Houston, the talented Philadelphia architect, Carter Larsen
from San Francisco, Frank Matero from Columbia University, Kathy
Meehan (almost lost at every great horticultural expanse, such as
Chatsworth), Stewart Rosenblum, fascinated by estate duty problems, Bill
Sargent, enthusing on Oriental Lowestoft, Mark Wenger from
Williamsburg and Henry Zimet from French and Company. And why
should I not include Chinx Noyes from Winterthur, Bill Neudorfer
(because he could chat daily to Sibley Jennings (Att. '69), whose company I
have also enjoyed) and Patsy Sands who showed me, subsequently, all the
great Long Island mansions, in her then role as President of SPLIA?

As for European members, who could forget the 'Fish Bathroom/
Bedroom' party for all at West Dean, hosted by Fausto Calderai, (the first

'John Hayward Scholar') — I have a dim memory of a staircase Bacchanalian photograph with us all in togas: Dr John Maddison, The National Trust scholar, Dr Richard Edgcumbe, then at Peterborough and subsequently the Victoria and Albert Museum, and Chairman of the (London) Scholarship Committee (1990–91) and John Sheeran and Julian Treuherz. With Giles Waterfield, John and Julian have also given expert tuition on paintings over several years. Giles in particular, as Director of the Dulwich Picture Gallery, has not only guided the Scholarship Committee as Chairman but given excellent lectures on picture collecting and patronage. He is also an accomplished summer wearer of a stylish Panama hat, perhaps only rivalled by those sported by Lady Scarsdale and the Hon. Simon Sainsbury! As for East European scholars, I have been remiss in not recalling those in 1983, as well as Gyorgy Frankl, an architectural historian from the Hungarian Academy in Budapest in 1984. In 1983 we enjoyed the company of Jaroslava Kopecna (Prague) and Jozsef Sisa (Department of Ancient Buildings, Budapest). And as I look at the list of names and events again there was chat about furniture with Sarah Nichols and Philip Duckworth (both now officers of the Attingham Society), listening to a talk on the Shugborough temples by Michael Bellamy, admiring Hilary Bracegirdle's modern jewellery and watching the urbane progress of Major Nick Lawson, MVO, owner of Longnor Hall, but on the three-week stint.

In October 1984 the Chairman wrote to all members of the Council about the important role of the Summer School's Director. Helena needed some assistance of a kind which might ultimately lead, at some future date albeit, to identification of a successor. No clear solution had then emerged and he invited comments with a view to someone taking over more of the load in 1986. There were also changes afoot in New York. A Five-Year Planning Committee had been set up, composed of Isabel Benham, Phelps Warren, Tony Atkin, Mrs Murray Douglas, Lucy Sydnor and Hilary Brown, with the President (Morrie Heckscher) *ex officio*. It was imperative, they felt, to increase operating funds. Since it was not possible to increase the number of American students attending the Summer School, the Committee recommended increasing the fees, beginning in 1986, as follows: (a) raising the application fee from $10 to $15, and (b) raising the processing fee from $15 to $100.

'Autumn 1984' was the date put on the Friends' new *Newsletter*. The idea for one had been proposed by Helen Hamilton, the Executive Secretary from 1981 until 1 July 1984. Helen had stepped down to pursue a growing real estate business and her place had been taken by Mrs Sybil Bruel. Sybil, a graduate of Wellesley, was an admitted Anglophile in that she had lived in England whilst working for the British press. Then in New York she had done editorial work for Visnews Ltd, later running her own travel service, 'At Home in England'. The Attingham 'office' had therefore moved, conveniently, from Helen Hamilton's home at Princeton to Sybil's in Manhattan.

Sybil Bruel, Executive Secretary
of The American Friends 1984
to date. Photographed at
Scotney Castle, Kent, by
Geoffrey Beard, July 1990.

Now Sybil brings her acute mind not only to bear on private editorial
work but on Attingham's many-faceted activities in America. Additionally,
she, and her family, are always most hospitable to members of the Trust
visiting New York. The Friends' and the Trust's work would undoubtedly
suffer grievously if Sybil decided instead to write novels, although I'm sure
they would be most readable ones.

In further personal terms the *Newsletter* reported sadly on the death of
David Pettigrew (Att. '70) and Ferris Megarity (Att. '68). Both had been
recent Vice-Presidents, and Ferris left a generous bequest of $25,000, 'the
income therefrom to be used for a scholarship to be named [after his
parents] "The Nina and George Primm Harris Scholarship"'. This was
welcome support to total assets of which, as Miss Benham noted, only
about '$80,000 are in unrestricted funds, which should instead be in the
300,000 to $400,000 range'. But the *Alumni Directory* was ready to distribute
and there were several social events planned. Helena Hayward was to be
the guest at the February 1985 Mid-Winter Reunion at French and
Company. There was a need to see that *alumni* in outlying regions from

New York should feel catered for — the *Directory* would allow, with its valuable listing of members both alphabetically, by year of attendance, and by state in which they resided for the setting-up of regional *alumni* groups.

For the fourth successive year a Special Week was provided for June 1984 for Attingham *alumni* and their friends. Whilst a little less strenuous and spartan, the week, spent in comfortable hotels in Glasgow and Aberdeen, again benefited from Sylvia Stevenson's large circle of Scottish friends. What was seen was completely fascinating, ranging from the Whistlers and Art Nouveau of Glasgow to the ducal splendours of Inveraray Castle. There were picnics (without Scotch eggs) in Scottish ruins, welcomes from noble owners, delicious food. Everyone who participated had the satisfaction of knowing that his or her tax-deductible extra payment would be used to benefit students on the Summer School. The Special Week contributed about £2,000 to the Trust's reserves, and with a good job done Sylvia Stevenson retired. The Chairman's 1984 report noted that the Special Weeks had been Sylvia's great contribution, pursued with care and energy. She was invited to be a Member of the Association.

The year of 1985 opened sadly for the American Friends with the death on 2 February of its President Emeritus, Phelps Warren. A Requiem Mass was held in New York at the church of St Mary the Virgin at West 46th Street, on 6 February at 11.00 a.m. In lieu of flowers, contributions could be sent to Sybil Bruel for the credit of 'The American Friends of Attingham' which Phelps had served for almost a quarter of a century. He was survived by a sister, three nieces and a nephew. The 1985 Annual Meeting of the American Friends on 8 May opened with Morrie Heckscher reading a tribute to Phelps, written by Helen Lowenthal. A further one was written by Christopher Monkhouse (Att. '66) for circulation to the *alumni*.

The meeting heard further that Helena Hayward would be stepping down as Director after the School of 1985 but would remain as Consultant Director. Two people had been appointed to replace her: Professor John Wilton-Ely of Hull University as 'Director of Studies', and Dr Geoffrey Beard, formerly of Lancaster University, as Principal Tutor. Sylvia Stevenson's role in organizing Special Weeks was taken over from that for June 1985 by Mrs Mary Stirling, wife of Attingham's Chairman. There was also much discussion about a pilot scheme to set up a Williamsburg-Richmond *alumni* group. It also proved possible from the tax-deductible donations of those on the Special Week to send a $2,000 contribution to the Summer School Trust 'in recognition of last year's superb course', as the President called it.

One of the advantages of starting the School at West Dean College, apart from its excellent organization, food and accommodation, was the chance to have Sir Brinsley Ford as an opening speaker. This distinguished art-historian had consented to talk firstly to the 1984 School (as he did until 1988) on 'Italy as the Climax of the Grand Tour' on which he is the acknowledged authority. With flawless English his address was delivered in a delightful way with shafts of ironic humour hidden in well-chosen phrases. *Alumni* will perhaps never hear its like again — age, upbringing, scholarship in a rare blend of elegant commentary.

For the Third Week of the 1985 School the members left on 15 July for the wild silhouette and neo-Baroque interior of Harlaxton Manor, built in the mid-nineteenth century for the ineptly named Gregory Gregory. Harlaxton is the English campus of the University of Evansville and, as one member put it, 'was truly uncomfortable. The rooms were small and crowded, the food was miserable and the plumbing didn't work'. Then

Helena Hayward, Geoffrey Beard (as 'Groucho Marxentius') and
Annabel Westman in (rare) toga dress at Harlaxton, July 1985.

there was inequality — a baronial room on the south front for some, a garret for others, with some routes to WCs mysteriously lying on the route through other bedrooms, with presumably puzzled onlookers. But a mile or two from Grantham, it allowed consideration of the riches of Belton and Grimsthorpe, and it did itself look magical at the end of its San Simeon-style mile-long drive. We could all revel in the painted excesses of Burghley House, hear Gervase Jackson-Stops talk about 'The Influence of Daniel Marot on Architecture and Furniture', see Boughton and Drayton, and still have heat enough for a heated session on 'Modern Conservation' chaired by Jonathan Thornton (Att. '83) of Cooperstown. Then the most perfect final dinner at Deene Park: log fires, cream, silver, white napery and the joyous laughter at the wonder of it all. Finally off to London, with a call on

Professor John Wilton-Ely
'Director of Studies', The
Attingham Summer School,
1986.

Diane Nutting at Chicheley Hall, long a friend of Attingham and sometime Council member, and, as many young swains thought, beautiful too.

Then what is this at the foot of the programme? 'Mr. John Hardy, with the cooperation of the Victoria and Albert Museum and the National Trust, has arranged an evening private view of Osterley Park: transport, visit, light supper, £10.' What the group was unprepared for was a masterly performance by John, dressed in eighteenth-century costume from wig to buckled shoes, chiming repeater watch in hand, welcoming all as 'Mr Child', Adam's banker patron, faultless on every mythological nuance of the great house, lighted for its guests as it had been from the 1760s. Of such stuff are Attingham memories made. Who were some of those who enjoyed it, as the Class of '85?

Michael Adams alphabetically leads as he did with his straw hat and great weighty volume of *English Homes* throughout — for the final party he gathered peacock feathers for his headdress, like someone from a Beauvais tapestry. There was Steve Andrews from 'Pres. of Virginia Antiqs'; the irrepressible Hilarie Faberman from Yale, heavy into the career of Augustus Egg; the late lamented Terry Garfield, one of the nicest people one could ever know; the energetic maverick of the pack, Grace Gary; Maureen Cassidy Geiger, later of the Met. Museum, nice Lorraine Gilligan, mystified still, I'm sure, by Buffalo Bill at Coe Fields; Liza Gusler, neat, always neat; Margize Howell with her final party headdress of garlic corms; David Maxfield, then editing the *Smithsonian News*, Lee Miller from San Francisco, and since the leader of the *alumni* on the west coast, Paul Parvis,

'What is underneath?' — a cartoon by Harriet Jordan (Att. '85).

Jeff Pond (who gave me his Paul Smith tie because I liked it), the splendid Strauss girls, Linda from the Getty and Monica at the Cooper-Hewitt, knowledgeable Gib. Vincent from Cooperstown, tape-recording fiend Lydia Thomen, representative of the best Winterthur has always sent. And so many: Beau Perkins, Penny Sander, Breffny Walsh, and Michele Marincola, as good as any Boston MFA has ever sent us. Non-mentioned few, forgive me, because you were all swept in with thirteen Europeans: Geza Entz from Budapest with his wonderful cameras, Dr Gabriela Simkova from Prague, our present Council member, Adrian Sassoon, Pam Wood from Nottingham, Christopher Hartley from Scotland's National Trust, Peter Brown, good friend from Fairfax House at York, Susan Bourne, ever good on oak furniture, Mary Goodwin, the specialist on paper conservation (who had stolen away to London to get lovely and suitable presents for the staff, given at Deene Park), cheerful Harriet Jordan, now Secretary to the Attingham Society, and leading 1991's Attingham through the Chatsworth gardens, Jane Farrington, in the long succession of Manchester City Art Gallery staff, Andrew Greg from Newcastle and textile specialist Barbara Heiberger. The token Australian architect (we had had Clive Lucas and Ann Toy from there in 1983) was Ian Stapleton (whom I recall setting off the alarm system at Bolsover). We also had the pleasure of Sybil Bruel being with us, with Charles Chevalier, Betty Starr Cummin,

Gaylord Dillingham, Paul Green and Richard Milhender — a fine Third Week addition to a fine Summer School.

When the notice of Phelps Warren's death and Christopher Monkhouse's appreciation were sent out to *alumni*, additional contributions were requested to add to the proceeds of the 1979 Testimonial Dinner. On Friday 25 October 1985, the first Phelps Warren Lecture was given by Edith Standen on 'Tapestries in the English Country House'. The evening, dedicated in the main to the memory of Phelps Warren, had started with a brief business meeting. Morrie remained as President, with Clare Le Corbeiller and Barbara Wriston as Vice-Presidents, Sarah Latham Kearns (Att. '78) as Secretary, Sibyl Groff as Treasurer and Huyler Held as Counsel. It was noted that the response to the 1984 Appeal had raised $12,100 for general purposes and $1,872 for scholarships.

In England there was interest in the forthcoming 'Treasure Houses of Britain' exhibition in Washington (with Gervase Jackson-Stops as its Curator) as a focal point for publicity and a possible joint visit to Washington with the American Friends. David Maxfield had written an article on the forthcoming 'Treasure Houses' exhibition, and having been on the Class of '85 he had mentioned Attingham. It had been distributed by the Smithsonian News Service to 1,500 American newspapers and periodicals. Annabel Westman arranged for 2,700 Summer School programmes for 1986 to be mailed and there was an air of excitement about the impending great display in Washington.

I mentioned that after Sylvia Stevenson's amazingly successful organization of the Special Weeks, 1982 to 1984, that the week for 1985 was undertaken, with characteristic energy, by Helen Lowenthal, with administration in the capable care of Mary Stirling. Based at Chokerford near Hexham, for exploring Northumbria in the first few days, the group would then move to Bowness-on-Windermere for the beauty and interest of the surrounding Lake District. Another feature of early 1985 had been the formation of 'The Attingham Society', to band together *alumni* in Europe. With Lucy Knox as Chairman, David Freeman as Honorary Treasurer and John Fuggles as Honorary Secretary, an interesting programme had already been set for

Mary Stirling, Administrator and Tutor, The Attingham Special and Study Weeks, 1985–9.

almost eighty members. Helena Hayward gave the first Attingham Society Lecture at the inaugural meeting held on 30 April at the great William Kent house, 22 Arlingon Street, London. She spoke on the subject of 'Patronage and the English Country House'. Ian Bristow and Nicholas Thompson showed the group round the house, now the headquarters of the Eagle Star Insurance Company. By June 1985, the first number of an *Occasional Newsletter* was circulated and tickets were being sold for the Osterley party at the conclusion of the Summer School. The minimum subscription was but £5.

At the conclusion of the 1985 Summer School Helena made her final report as Director. Percipiently she concluded:

> We must keep up our own standards both academically and in the accommodation we offer and make sure that as many suitable applicants as possible come forward from as wide a field as we can reach.

She noted that whilst in 1984 there had been over 100 applications for the 34 places, in 1985 there had been 78. Thirteen American members had received full scholarships and a further two half-scholarships. The course had a bias towards decorative arts and interior planning and design, and this, reflecting her interests and mine, has continued.

At the Annual General Meeting of the Trust in London on 14 November 1985, Sandy Stirling, as Chairman, presented Helena with Sir John Pope-Hennessy's book on *Cellini* and Morrie Heckscher's on *American Furniture in the Metropolitan Museum*. He thanked her deeply for her invaluable contribution to the Summer School as its Director for eleven years and for the time she had devoted to every aspect and detail of its running. Helena had indicated her willingness to assume a new role of Consultant Director and to direct a new 'Attingham Study Week', described below. The second *Newsletter* of the American Friends (Summer 1985) noted that Helena 'has led the Attingham Summer School with tremendous style and distinction for many years'.

In the autumn of 1985 John Wilton-Ely and Geoffrey Beard set in hand, with the invaluable support of Annabel Westman and Rosemary Lomax-Simpson, planning for the 1986 Summer School. Also, with the experienced help of Tim Westman, opportunity was taken to redesign all the Trust's printed material — notepaper, compliment slips and so on, and to come up with a new format for brochures and a poster. Much use was made as a design source of Humphry Repton's 'Red Book' for Attingham. Additionally, all the design work was provided free through the good offices of Tim Westman. It was an important catalytic action on which, with amendments and refinements, the present literature has been based. Meanwhile, in New York, the *Alumni Directory* had cost a one-time capital expenditure of nearly $5,000 for one thousand copies. The sale of 500 copies at $10 each was hoped for, but with the President noting that only 214 alumni had contributed to the Friends in 1985 hopes were not high.

Coincident with the succession to Helena of John Wilton-Ely and myself, the Special Week and the Third Week were rethought. The Special

Week, instituted in 1981, and its substantial tuition had been expressly intended to raise funds for the Summer School Trust. With that objective achieved, the Special Week was discontinued after that for 1985. The traditional 'Third Week' in which a limited number of lucky alumni were able to attend the final part of the main course, was also discontinued. Its life could not easily have been prolonged with the considerable opposition of house-owners to large groups and to the consequent difficulties in transporting everyone.

In place of the two additional events a new programme was to be inaugurated for 1986. Called the 'Attingham Study Week', it was to be under Helena Hayward's direction, with Mary Stirling as Tutor and Administrator. An Advisory Committee including three American alumni (Tony Atkin, Paul Green and Richard Milhender) was formed. Helena stated that she envisaged:

> the Study Week as a sort of mini-Attingham — a week with good tutoring and discussions and a lecture or two, with interesting private visits and a fully stretched academic programme. Living conditions will avoid the discomforts of university hostels while not being luxurious or expensive. We hope to price it to accord with the cost of the old last week of the main course (i.e. the Third Week). It should then be in reach of all *alumni* and we would like their spouses or friends to be allowed to come and also others who either cannot spare time for the full three week course or are not accepted for it. I want to give the *alumni* a new deal as I feel that since we limited their acceptance on the Third Week to very few, they have been discouraged.

I have noted that in the autumn of 1984 an American committee under the chairmanship of Isabel Benham was appointed to make long-range plans providing for the continuing viability and financial strength of the American Friends of Attingham. To achieve these goals, it was felt that there needed to be more involvement by those located in various parts of the States. The committee proposed that regional *alumni* associations, or chapters, be created. These would have a three-fold objective: (a) promotional, (b) organizing events, and (c) fund-raising.

A driving-force to set up the first of the Regional *Alumni* Associations was Lucy Sydnor (Att. '69), living at a splendid house, 'Dancing Point', on the James River near Williamsburg. Lucy invited all relevant *alumni*— some 54 of them — to her home on 8 September 1985, a wonderful, hot day. The Mid-Atlantic Chapter of the American Friends of Attingham' came into being, by ballot, after too good a lunch. Annual dues were set at $5 per person through 1986. Two members of the Class of '85, Liza Gusler and Steve Andrews, with Carl Lounsbury (Att. '81), then made comments on the Dumphries Courthouse archaeological excavations and Mark Wenger (Att. '84), also on the staff of Colonial Williamsburg, presented an overview of a diary written by a travelling companion of William Byrd on an English country house tour in the eighteenth century.

The committee members helping Lucy Sydnor set up the chapter were Nick Pappas, Carl Lounsbury, George Green Shackleford, Christine Meadows, Dennis Halloran and Maria Tabb. But O, dear ones, do you still meet? Is your area too wide? This history cannot become rhetorical, but to my knowledge the tight 'community' of twenty or so *alumni* in the San Francisco area and a budding Connecticut one are the only active *alumni* associations at 1991. Prove me wrong, by all means. Certainly attempts to start a Washington-Baltimore one have been felt to be counter-productive to efforts in New York. I have attended the occasional meeting in Boston, and there have been events arranged in the Williamsburg area. What is in existence is, inevitably, the only stuff of which history can be made.

Let me conclude this section with the 'Ballad of Attingham' compiled by Barbara O'Brien (Att. '80) in attendance on the last Special Week of 1985:

THE BALLAD OF ATTINGHAM
Dedicated to Helen Lowenthal and Mary Stirling

Is it Calvin or Salvin?
Is it Wyatt or Paine?
James Adam or Robert?
Please, tell us again!

Is it Holker or Dalemain?
Where ARE we, at Levens?
Is Hutton-in-the-Lake or Forest?
We're at sixes and sevens.

Is this molding baroque?
Did the carpenter plane it?
Whatever it is,
Please, Helen, explain it.

Is this tapestry Beauvais,
Or Mortlake, or what?
Please, Helen, please tell us
What it is or is not.

Oh, what lovely embroidery,
What beautiful knots,
This must have been done
By Mary, Queen of Scots.

Helen, what are you saying?
You say it's not true?
What about Geoffrey,
Does he reject it, too?

Oh, Geoffrey, look at this
Just perfect, no nicks.
A sixteenth century agent's table . . .
What, you say 1806?

What's in this little cupboard,
Minton, Chelsea or Bow?
John, *you* pick it up
And let us all know!

What was that about Flodden,
Which uncle was killed?
Who *were* all those ancestors
Around whom we milled?

'Now, group, say goodbye
To Lady Inglewood.'
Oops, it's the wrong name
(But Lady Howard understood).

What time are we leaving?
And when do we eat?
And Mary, explain
What to put on our feet.

What a dear little village
May we get out to shop?
Mary, why are you shrieking
'No, Driver, DON'T STOP!'

Through mist and o'er lakes
The cavalcade rolls,
Muffled in raincoats
With dampening soles.

A few have pneumonia,
Though claim they're just cold.
But Attingham sheep
Are made of stern mold.

We've survived, we're much wiser,
We've got lots of new knowledge.
We're proud of our stamina.
It's tougher than college.

So three cheers for the collies
From all of the sheep.
It's been a great trip,
With memories we'll keep.

VII · STRENGTH ON STRENGTH
1985 to 1991

THE ATTINGHAM SOCIETY had got off to a good start in 1985, with its inaugural meeting on 30 April with, as noted, a lecture by Helena Hayward. Then on 30 October John Wilton-Ely continued the patronage theme with a lecture on 'William Beckford and Fonthill: The Romantic as Patron and Collector'. This took place at the Apothecaries' Hall in London, an impressive late seventeenth-century interior incorporating particularly fine carving. But, with 1986 in view, plans were afoot for the Society to join with the Amercian Friends, and the Furniture History Society, with a visit to New York, from 13 to 19 February 1986. This was to coincide with the important exhibition, 'The Treasure Houses of Britain', at the National Gallery of Art in Washington. The American Friends 'Mid-Winter Reunion' was scheduled to take place at the British Embassy there. Sir Oliver Wright, the British Ambassador, and his wife received some 220 Attinghamites and others in the splendid ballroom of Lutyens' embassy complex. Guests of honour included Sandy Stirling (the Attingham Trust Chairman), Mrs Stirling, Helena Hayward, Lucy Knox (President of the Attingham Soceity) and Rosemary Lomax-Simpson. It was a reunion greatly over-subscribed, and one which owed a great deal to successful co-ordination by Sybil Bruel and by the help of Gary Scott, who also arranged for the American Board to have lunch and a Board meeting at the Arts Club.

In announcing plans for 1986 in the fourth *Newsletter* of the American Friends I noted that John Wilton-Ely and I, on separate visits to America, had met *alumni* in New York, Washington, Colonial Williamsburg, Kansas City, Chicago, St Louis, Los Angeles and San Francisco. I also commented on the fact that Helena Hayward was to lead the new Study Week in June with Mary Stirling as Administrator. It was in the spring already over-subscribed, with a waiting list. The Summer School itself was to have the pleasure of some attendance as a tutor by Helena Hayward, with a lecture on Sir Walter Scott by Helen Lowenthal.

At the Annual General Meeting on 14 November 1985, Rosemary indicated her wish to retire from the office of Treasurer and Administrator after the completion of the 1986 Summer School. Generations of Attingham *alumni* have much cause to be grateful for her care and attention to the working details of each year's course. The Executive Committee felt themselves fortunate to have had her services. In a delightful supplementary way Rosemary's great skill as a professional flower-arranger added much to each final party. I recall a great baroque display of flowers at Uppark, which was worthy of being a Dutch still-life by Jan van Huysum.

Catherine Norman, Treasurer and Administrator,
The Attingham Summer School, 1986–91.
Photograph: Christine Boydell (Att. '90)

They nominated Mrs Catherine Norman, who had had much experience in organizing conferences and visits for the Furniture History Society, to succeed Rosemary and to act as her Assistant during the first half of 1986 and on the Summer School. She would then be responsible for administrative arrangements from 1 September 1986. Catherine is a photographer and is knowledgeable on heraldry. Further, as with Rosemary before her, each year's class owes much of its material comfort to her careful attention.

In preparing our 'first' Summer School, the 35th, of 10 to 29 July 1986, John Wilton-Ely and I had some apprehension. Whilst the 1983 School had spent part of its final week in Edinburgh the School had been 'booked-in', some time previously, to be again in Scotland, on its west coast, at Ayr. Both of us adored Scottish houses but we knew less abot them than their English counterparts. We were therefore grateful to Lucy Knox for her great help in arranging visits to memorable houses, with equally memorable hospitality. Has the tea at Caprington Castle been bettered, as the members strove valiantly to clear constantly replenished tables?

Because I am interested in printing and layout we made a marginal amendment to the actual programme — giving it a Renaissance border — but a fundamental one to the explanatory brochures for the Summer School and the Study Week. The process had been started by the 'graphics rethink'

William 'Bill'
McNaught (Att. '70),
President, The
American Friends,
1986–90.

under Tim Westman's careful gaze. For the 1986 brochures we chose a detail of Knyff and Kip's 1715 engraving of Wimpole Hall for the Summer School, and one of Vivares' engraving of Stourhead in 1777 for the Study Week. 'We' in this case was Annabel Westman and I: together we continue to plan and see through the press all the Attingham publicity material and that for use by the members as folders, badges and so on. As for the first programme venue, we had 'played ourselves in' at West Dean College and there was the delight that one of its Senior Trustees, Helen Lowenthal, was both Founder and President of Attingham.

It was seemingly coincidence that as we assumed our new roles Morrie Heckscher announced his retirement as President of the American Friends. I had known Morrie since 1966 and it had been a particular pleasure to me to have his hand at the helm in New York. The Nominating Committee of the Friends, under the chairmanship of Kevin Stayton (Att. '83), listed for President, Bill McNaught (Att.'70), head of the New York office of Archives of American Art. At his appointment on 3 June 1986, at the Metropolitan Museum of Art (where Morrie was, and is still, Keeper of the American Wing) Bill presented Morrie with a drawing of Chatsworth as a token of appreciation from the American Friends. In England, Sandy Stirling noted in his Chairman's Report for 1986:

> Morrie Heckscher has earned our warmest thanks for giving so generously of his time and for his leadership of the American Friends in their great support for the work of the Trust.

THE ATTINGHAM SUMMER SCHOOL

THE ATTINGHAM SUMMER SCHOOL
1986

The newly-designed Attingham leaflet, and front of the Summer School
Programme, 1986.

On Thursday 10 July 1986, Helen Lowenthal addressed the Summer
School at West Dean on the subject of 'Attingham and 40 Years' Experience
of the British Country House'. There was chance too, in the crowded first
few days, to hear Sir Brinsley Ford speak on 'The Society of Dilettanti and
the Grand Tour' (Sir Brinsley was the Society's Secretary), Gervase
Jackson-Stops on a retrospective view of organizing 'The Treasure Houses
of Britain' exhibition, and to survey architecture from the vernacular
examples at the Weald and Downland Museum, the great Tuscan-
columned ruin of The Grange, dreamy Uppark and the Baroque splendours at Petworth. And what a tutorial team for the last house — Martin

Drury, the indefatigable Historic Buildings Secretary to the National Trust, one of the finest exponents of its rich group of houses, and our Vice-Chairman since December 1982; John Hardy, then in the Furniture and Woodwork Department at the Victoria and Albert Museum dealing, with me, with furniture; Terence Mullaly, Art Critic of the *Daily Telegraph*, and John Sheeran of the Dulwich Picture Gallery describing paintings; Dr Richard Edgcumbe from the Victoria and Albert Museum's Metalwork Department talking about the silver; John Fuggles, Libraries Adviser to the National Trust, showing members rare books, and the large sculpture collection talked about, *in situ*, by John Wilton-Ely. Finally there was an exhilarating ride on tractor-drawn hay-waggons around 'Capability' Brown's landscaped park, with the great south front rising and dipping from sight, and an atmospheric dash across the front of us by a herd of deer, mewing and excited at the unlikely invasion of the distant reaches of their sylvan territory. That night Lord Egremont, who lives with his family in the private wing at Petworth, spoke on his predecessor, the 3rd Earl of Egremont, as a patron of J. M. W. Turner and as a collector. The circle turned full on a fine day.

There are perhaps always 'first time' events that cheer individual members of each Class. The first time they had seen a miniature by Hilliard, the first time they had been on the roof at Hardwick or posed in 'The Temple of Ancient Virtue' at Stowe. So it was in 1986. The School arranged for a short programme of chamber music, as the first to take place in the newly restored Music Room of the Royal Pavilion at Brighton. And then away to Halifax Hall at Shefield University, the settling-in and the first of several annual deliveries by John Fuggles of a brilliant and amusing lecture on 'Bess of Hardwick and the Cavendishes'.

On the long journey north to Scotland the School called at Levens Hall in Cumbria, where there is a famous topiary garden. I had apparently promised a member of the School that I would find out a little more for her how it was all done. Growing tension in her (which may well have happened anyway) caused an 'explosion' and she almost leapt on the owner, Annette Bagot, shouting that 'Geoffrey had told her he would find out about the topiary'. 'You cut it, dear, you cut it', was Mrs Bagot's advice, as the members fell on their tired mercurial colleague. She was one of the very few I recall who didn't quite make the eighteen to twenty days and left early.

On Tuesday 22 July we set out for Drumlanrig Castle, home of the Duke of Buccleuch. On the way in the coach we were all treated to one of the finest and most lucid descriptions of what was to await us, given by Lady Shaw-Stewart. The new President of the American Friends, Bill McNaught, was also with us and there seemed a rosy glow about it all; good friends, good tuition. Lucy Knox had arranged for us to visit several little-known houses, Rowallan Castle, Caprington Castle, the ruined Auchinleck where we met the present James Boswell, the ruined Adam

Levens Hall, Cumbria, a northern pele-tower house, drawing
by Ralph Harvard (Att. '86).

house of Dalquharran and fine visits to Blairquhan, the home of James
Hunter Blair, and, under the expert care of David Learmont and Chis-
topher Hartley, to the Scottish National Trust properties of Culzean Castle,
on its cliff top, and Brodick Castle on its harbour. Hard-working as ever, the
'faculty' was writing its thank-you letters on the long ferry crossing from
Ardrossan.

Those on the 1986 Summer School will remember for many a year the
amusing episode surrounding Basil Skinner's lecture on 'Portraiture in the
Scottish Country House'. As he was ready to begin in the lecture
hall-cum-theatre of Craigie Hall, Ayr, where the group was in residence, I
went backstage to dim the house-lights. I pushed what seemed to be
appropriate buttons and returned to find nothing had happened, so I went
backstage again. In that split-second timing, immortalized by Harold
Lloyd, John Wilton-Ely had dived to the secondary switches at the side of
the hall. Lights went up and down as each 'operator' pushed harder and
more frustratingly. As we leaped like Russian ballet dancers on to the stage
and off, the audience was rolling with helpless laughter, as much at Basil
Skinner, who, old friend that he was, entered into the spirit of it all and
moved his head from side to side at advancing Geoffrey and disappearing

John, neither knowing what the other was doing. It was also, finally, a good lecture!

Those who enjoyed Scotland in particular numbered Mary Lee Allen, Assistant Director at Gunston Hall, David Barquist from Yale University Art Gallery, Lou Brady, a fine gilder, Charles and Mary Grace Carpenter, 'father and mother' to the School and much-loved scholars, Ed Chappell, Director of Architectural Research at Colonial Williamsburg, Debby Federhen with her Associate Curator colleague, Don Fennimore, both from Winterthur, Ralph Harvard, whose drawing of Levens Hall is reproduced (p. 118) from his amazing sketchbook, Ron Hurst, Curator of Furniture at Colonial Williamsburg, Daniella Kisluk-Grosheide from the Metropolitan Museum, Melissa Meighan from the Philadelphia Museum (and one of the winners of the 'Best Hat' competition at the final party at Pollok House, Glasgow), Derek Ostergard, Jon Poston and Sumpter Priddy, all keen on diving under furniture, were in excellent form.

When I visit Alexandria I have the pleasure of staying with Nancy Richards of the '86 Class. She has shown me most of Historic Annapolis in several visits. Molly Smith, a Vice-President of Dillingham & Co. in San Francisco, I don't see often enough, and I keep promising myself I will look more into Shaker artefacts with June Sprigg from Hancock Village or find out with Anne Van Ingen what the New York State Council on the Arts really does.

'The European members attending the Attingham Summer School, 1986' is not quite tidy enough, for there was Miriam Hamilton from Old Government House in New South Wales, Australia. Also the pattern of our East European friends coming to see us was maintained by Barbara Gratkowska-Ratynska, Curator of Furniture at the Royal Castle in Warsaw, and Dr Ferenc Batari from Budapest. Who did they join? Scholars like David Bostwick of the Sheffield City Museum, who still helps each year as part of our Hardwick tuition team, Caroline Carr (Whitworth), then at Bolling Hall, Bradford, Clare Latimer from Manchester, the irrepressibly cheerful Sarah Levitt at Bristol Art Gallery, John Miners, ever-ready to confirm 21-inch fabric width, the architect Giles Newby Vincent, Anthea Palmer from The National Trust, Thom Richardson of the Royal Armouries, who delighted with his quiet expositions at Hardwick and Culzean. I paraphrase:

> The Bengal helmet at the far end of the Hall is really upside down: the bayonets are cut off just as they go behind the shield [curator peers in astonishment].

And lastly, and far from least, Lavinia Wellicome, Curator of Woburn Abbey. She will not mind me raving about her portrayal, with Ralph Harvard, as Muses, pieces of sculpture, all covered in white, who danced attendance at each stage of the final party's gifts to the staff — there was a special gift of two Spode flower-painted plates, c. 1820, as a retiring present to Rosemary Lomax-Simpson — and Lavinia's kindness at giving, at cost to herself, of scholarships in subsequent years that others could enjoy and learn as she did. I append the poem I wrote for the final party on 28 July. The title was based on Malcolm, as our coach driver, always needing to be asked, in unison, for 'Air', for the visit to Ayr, and for animal hair in the plaster. Let me confuse you further.

The Class of '86, or 'Malcolm: Air', 'Ayr, Hair?'
When the class of '86
Crossed the Rubicon and Styx
And came to Sussex by the sea
All thoughts of nervous, tense disporting,
On the lawns, c.v., reporting,
Were banished by the Earl Grey tea.
'Who was that with gaudy ties?'
Or professorial with smiles?
Are you 'Mr Benhamou'?
Ralph from Yale, or merely Harvard,
Thom, with an h,
Who studies 'h'armour,
'That Melissa is a charmer',
Will we ever — Polish whisper,
Master "Gratkowska-Ratynska"?

Samsons heaving Samsonites
Up the footprint Jamesean flights
Had us soon in whitest whites —
'Could I have a double gin?'
'Are you Alison, or Kim?'
'Do you come from Cold Spring Harbour,
Are self employed, adjunct Professor,
President of someone's Inc.?'
Am I really Maverick Scholar? —
'I've left my undies in your sink.'

Stirling 1 and Stirling 2
Even Sterling Silver too
Lowenthal and Wilton-Ely,
Not yet Helena, but Drury
Uppark bound, we're Dilettanti
Divided now, or was it fancy?
'Is it Monday? Am I Nancy?'
Tell me Catherine, 'At The Vyne
Will they have a gin and lime?'
'Should I dress up for the Grange?'
'Deb's backless dress is such a change.'
'Will the Duke drop me a curtsey?'
Attributions are by Mullaly
Ferenc Batari: how *very* strange.

Conservation, room arrangements,
Country Life in xerox form,
On the Fowler yellow lawn.

Porridge on the Sheffield menu,
Rosemary recommends the prunes.
Touching all with sticky fingers
'Is there time to have a shower?'
Seminars and private wings,
Buying ever stranger things
I know I'm slower in the loo,
No, Lou, not you, not you.
Is my ASA still showing?'
'Did I hit you with my Nikon?'
'Derek, was it really, *real* glue?'
'James C. Jordan, is that you?'

Piped across the Scottish border
This poem, sun-like, fades away
'Quick, quick, mush mush,
I'm Hunter Blair.'
'Break that tree down, stop just there.'
'Surely you've got things to say.'
Round by the organ — down that way
Johnnie Corbett, Lucy Knox
and Jamie B: some are 'chappies' —
Who was that with hair in plaster?
'Poll' Revere's the one in nappies.
Laths akimbo, ruins with no inner door,
One drunken night at Craigie Hall
'Did I inherit 'Auchinleck' or 'Woburn'?
'Lavinia tell me, tell me, more.'

The final days are now upon us
But I have my new found knowledge
'Lattice panes are all by Rennie
Many fall-pipes? — Hasn't any.'
'Sauchiehall' is: Land of Willow'.
But 'my Mackintosh' is: 'in the Hall'.
Train noise I'll miss and Scottish money
'God, I need a second pillow.'
Ed has put his tie all funny,
Porridge, guide books, votes by many,
'Daniel Marot? Daniella?'
Carpenters so very clever,
That they've joined themselves together.

Crenellated near *Alumni*,
Eating raspberry meringues
When I cross the Rubicon,
I tell my wife I do kiss many,
But no, my dear, '*no one* called Jenny'.
Her smile is sweet, decaffeinated.
She has heard my dreaming trances.
Her voice nuanced, drives me near giddy.
'Tell me, for God's sake, tell me,
Who, but who, is Sumpter Priddy?'

The new and first Study Week took place a few days before the Summer School, from 29 June to 3 July 1986. Based at Cumberland Lodge in Windsor Great Park, it could acquire the atmosphere of an English country house rather than a hotel. The food was excellent, the service welcoming and efficient, and the twenty-seven who joined in were eager to start 'work'. The programme had been planned to illustrate the theme of royal and courtly patronage starting with an excellent study day at Hampton Court under the tutelage of John Thorneycroft, an Architectural Adviser to English Heritage, followed subsequently by a privileged private visit to Windsor Castle conducted by the Surveyor of the Queen's Works of Art, Geoffrey de Bellaigue. Other visits included Hatfield House, an admirable introduction to Gorhambury by Lady Verulam, Woburn Abbey (with a picnic on that day at 'The Menagerie' kindly permitted by Gervase Jackson-Stops whose explanation of his restoration work there was both learned and delightful), Stratfield Saye, Polesden Lacey and Ham House, the latter introduced by John Hardy.

The evening lectures had been planned to illustrate the theme of the week. Helena Hayward talked about 'Eighteenth-Century Patrons and Collectors in the Classical Tradition', Selina Ballance dealt with 'The Historic Buildings of Eton College', and there was a lively panel discussion on 'The Care and Presentation of Historic Houses'. Chaired by Helen Lowenthal, there was lively debate by Phillis Rogers of the then Historic Buildings and Monuments Commission, Terry Empson, Director-General of the Historic Houses Association, Edward Fawcett of The National Trust, Hugh Roberts, then Head of the Furniture Department at Christie's, and the architectural historian and conservationist, Joe Friedman. A dinner on the final night was held at Chicheley Hall. Helena and Mary Stirling had done their estimates carefully and the Study Week yielded a profit of about £3,500 to the Trust. Whilst more 'outsiders' than *alumni* had been attracted, everyone enjoyed the week and viewed it as a success. However, in the concentrated period of one week the useful lesson had been pointed up that it was essential to select houses to visit and lecturers to lecture with extreme care.

During the autumn of 1986 as English universities continued to have to cut their arts and humanities activites under government pressure on finance, it became obvious that John Wilton-Ely's Department of Art History at Hull University was threatened. I had had a similar situation in 1982 at Lancaster University, and rather than preside over the slow decline of what it had taken me ten years to build up I took my full pension and ran! It was a complicated decision but one I have never regretted. There was therefore much anxious talk at every opportunity between John and myself, each to the other friend and colleague, then and now. On 10 January 1987 John wrote to advise the Chairman that he would have to relinquish his post as Director of Studies. He had been appointed Director of Educational Services at Sotheby's from 1 May 1987. Meantime, across the

Dr Geoffrey Beard, Director, The Attingham Summer School, 1987 to date.

anxious hiatus in the autumn of 1986 I had been planning the 1987 School with the very experienced help of Annabel Westman. On 1 January 1987 I was appointed Director of the Summer School and was mindful of the high standards set by my three predecessors, Helen Lowenthal, Helena Hayward (acting still in the valued capacity of Consultant and as Director of the Study Week) and, briefly, as Director of Studies, by John Wilton-Ely.

One of my first tasks was to read through many of the reports submitted over the previous ten years by members. It could well be proved that the suggested improvements cancelled each other out by the apparent need to cater for each interest — more free time, more on gardens, more on conservation, fewer houses, fewer lectures, do not deviate from country houses; retain visits to churches, more museum visits, simple instruction on far-from-simple cameras — 'an experience almost too intense', 'to be able to cross the ropes and look closely at certain works was very satisfying' — there was a whole vocabulary and the file almost talked. Trying to achieve the correct balance was a difficult task. But in minor ways it was possible to improve an already finely tuned experience. The reading list could go out (after the letters of acceptance) with the joining instructions, the list of *Country Life* references could be modified to omit the earlier, less informative house accounts, there could be reasons given for choosing a particular house and speakers could be introduced more fully. Statements about a house could in many cases be done in the coach on the way to it, allowing extra time in the house itself, and in an unguarded moment there might even be free time planned so as to give a whole afternoon!

A Class is made by its members, carefully selected each year in New York and London. Clare Le Corbeiller continues to head the Scholarship Committee in New York. In London at an Executive Committee meeting on 22 September 1986, Giles Waterfield was thanked warmly for his seven years' service since the formation of the Scholarship sub-committee, three of them, latterly, as its Chairman. This valuable period of service had also been given by Lucy Knox who retired at this time from the Scholarship sub-committee. The Committee agreed to approach John Fuggles, Libraries Adviser to The National Trust, to see if he would assume the chairmanship. His acceptance of the post was confirmed at the Annual General Meeting on 20 November 1986. In subsequent years many intending participants to the Summer School wrote of John's encouraging and sympathetic letters to them about their scholarship offer or the lack of one. These were done in a fine hand, and, befitting his bibliographic knowledge, always with apt and telling quotation. John's infectious good humour too, during his active years in office, was much enjoyed by the members of many Attingham Classes in the late 1980s. We wish him well from recent bad health.

As part of the changes in the Trust's administration much thought had been given to Attingham's future role and its policies. It was agreed in July 1986 that the trust should continue to accumulate its capital fund with the target at £200,000. The income would be used to finance more scholarships, more tutoring on each Summer School and more realistic fees for the staff. Helen Lowenthal also thought consideration should be given to a course in the winter in addition to the Summer School and the Study Week. All the ideas were set in train by papers circulated by the President and the Chairman, who referred back to the important paper he had overseen in May 1982. That had as objectives:

(i)   To maintain the Summer School as the best course in its field.
(ii)   To build up a capital fund of £100,000, the income from which would be used to fund the scholarships.
(iii)   To ensure the confidence and cooperation of the American Friends of Attingham Inc.

By May 1986 all these objectives had been achieved and it was time to reassess future plans. The success of the Trust in the past (and present) had depended upon five things:

(i)   the inspiration and dedication of Helen Lowenthal, the founder, and Helena Hayward and a small band of devoted supporters;
(ii)   a sufficient demand from those interested in the course in America, Britain, Europe and Australia;
(iii)   the willingness of the *alumni* in America to maintain the activity of the American Friends of Attingham;

(iv)   the willingness of owners to allow visits to their houses and treasures;
(v)   the supply and willingness of lecturers and tutors of sufficient quality.

At May 1986 there was capital of £130,000 producing an income of over £8,000 per year. Factors the Chairman asked his colleagues to consider, were:

(i)   care by the Council to choose people for key roles;
(ii)   demand exceeding supply of places on the main course but a fall in the number of applications. Was this due to a rising level of fees: if not, what else?
(iii)   a need to be more successful in the policy of attracting Europeans to the School;
(iv)   whether the Trust should undertake in future a more leading role by running additional courses, collaborating with other organizations (implying an enhanced administrative burden), merging with The National Trust to become its educational arm;
(v)   providing a national centre for advice on display of houses and training guides, as well as advising on guide books;
(vi)   creating a conservationist political lobby.

There was talk about an office, a secretary, public relations, better liaison with other groups, the vitality of the Attingham Society; the fevered throw-out of ideas. The Chairman's colleagues reacted with considered papers outlining further ideas and reactions.

A considerable amount of attention was naturally given to Helen Lowenthal's paper 'The Attingham Summer School — the Way Ahead?' She wanted a continuing concern to be expressed about the role and situation of country house owners — an informed lobby of information and even political pressure. Secondly, Helen asked, with the percipience of long years, 'Has the time come when we could contemplate an enlarged School admitting West Europeans?' Was the School to be limited, after thirty or more years, to the numbers convenient for Attingham Park 'when, alas, we are no longer there?' She suggested an increase in numbers of a third. Due, largely to the efforts of Tony Galliers-Pratt and Sandy Stirling, as successive Chairmen, Helen thought that a 'respectable capital fund' had, at last, been established. She felt that one day there would be need for a central office, however modest, and for the services of paid office staff. She referred further to her pleasure at the successful launching of The Attingham Society and to the friendly relations with the American Friends.

John Lewis, as Legal Adviser to the Trust, addressed the problem of the capital fund. Whilst this had reached an admirable level it was not yet sufficient. He was also against any commitment to an office and staff, 'but we must have the financial resources to be able to do so if necessary'. John Wilton-Ely and I, after discussion, gave full answers or suggestions. John, with an informed knowledge of other courses, thought a fall in the Summer

School applications was attributable to many other competing entities such as Sotheby's, Christie's, Southampton University's Summer School, courses at Strawberry Hill, Boughton and elsewhere. He suggested launching a concerted recruitment campaign in Western and Eastern Europe, organizing annual *symposia* to keep Attingham in the lead as a forum for the projection of the country house, annual contact with Attingham USA by funded visits, the maintaining of Attingham as an independent organization, the writing of special articles about the Trust and, importantly, the need for accreditation by the linking with an academic institution able to award credits for use by participating Americans in their own institutions.

As Consultant Director Helena Hayward was strongly in favour of considering the country house as a whole — the estate, historical influences, architectural planning, furnishing and equipping and the creation of collections. She wondered whether the fall in the number of applications was due to the length of the course. Would a fifteen-day Summer School be better, with an eight-day Study Week and an additional eight-day couse in the Winter? She wished to see more Europeans on the course and to develop our relationships with The National Trust, the Historic Houses Association, the British Council and the Victoria and Albert Museum. She concluded:

(i)   We need to continue to raise money.
(ii) More secretarial help was needed.
(iii) The Attingham Society and the Scholarship sub-committee should be on more firmly organized lines. She recommended the appointment of a secretarial assistant.

The main idea I tried to explore myself was one drawn from Helen's paper when she asked whether an enlarged school could be contemplated. It would be possible for two Summer Schools: one to consider architecture, conservation, the planned interior and the landscape setting of the country house, and another to deal with the fine and applied art collections. However, I equally pointed out the pitfalls in this — more tutors, more funds to support scholars, more secretarial and administrative help. I wanted the long association with The National Trust, from the founding in 1952 to continue, but to maintain the Trust's independence. There was need for a small Publicity Committee, and to pass over the need for repayment of the initial loan of £300 from the Trust to the Attingham Society.

In the series of papers submitted, the Director's assistant, Annabel Westman, also Secretary to the Attingham Trust, thought the School should only move to new directions if they came logically and naturally. She approved of trying to find out why applications had fallen in number and there was need to offer perhaps a European scholarship to encourage wider participation. Care should be taken that if 'Attingham' expanded its uniqueness and strength was not lost. However, there was always room for in-depth study and having optional visits to suit different needs. She had a keen interest in improving publicity and in having someone from the American Board attend the Summer School. Finally Annabel wanted guidelines given to the Scholarship sub-committee, of which she had been an inaugural member, in 1980, in order that careful selection of scholars could be made and the members retire on a proper rota system. She concluded with words with which no one has ever disagreed:

Attingham must always be kept alive and maintain a pioneering role.

In New York there was understandable concern that as the fees approached the $2,000 level — for 1987 they were at $1,800, plus a $100 processing fee — that this might prove too great an expense, when the chosen members added the air fare. It was agreed that accommodations were not extravagant and that one of the few ways of reducing cost might be to reduce the length of the School. I was able to sit in on this meeting as an observer in that I was to give the second Phelps Warren Lecture on 29 October 1986, at the Abigail Adams Smith Museum, by courtesy of its

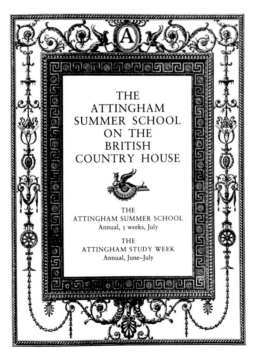

The front of the green and white 'Adam-style' Attingham folder, introduced in 1987 and copied through in 'house-style' to the annual programme, poster and Certificate of Attendance.

Director, David Reese (Att. '83). I had elected to talk on 'The Economics of Taste: A Study of Noble Patronage'. Phelps Warren had been a supporter of the House and the lecture site was therefore particularly appropriate.

One of the ways of improving the shortage of secretarial help might be the employment of efficient machinery. In March 1987 the American Board gave first consideration to purchasing a personal computer for use by Sybil Bruel. The response to the Annual Appeal had been satisfactory, with forty-eight contributions over $100 and several in excess of $1,000. The Vice-President for Finance and Development, Alan Campbell, stressed their concern with the need for a capital fund drive and the difficulty of attracting foundation grants for endowment puposes. To know where the *alumni* were was also vital and discussion had taken place with Christopher Wilk over the several options for updating the 1984 *Alumni Directory*. The most attractive suggestion seemed to be use of a computer to use for membership mailings and to update addresses to serve as the master for a *Directory* to be printed out and multiplied by offset copies.

For both the Study Week and Summer School in 1987 the programmes used by members were given a printed front page of an avowedly 'Robert Adam' nature, and this was matched in house-style to new green and white name badges in plastic holders and to a new green and white folder to contain 'Notes on Houses Visited' and other literature. 'House-style' had come to an organization dealing with house style. The Study Week (25 June to 3 July) was to be at two centres, Blandford Forum (The Crown Hotel) and Bradford-on-Avon (Leigh Park Hotel). Helena Hayward and Mary Stirling devised a programme that, apart from being over-subscribed, concentrated on landscape history and garden architecture (with visits to Stourhead, Belcombe Court and Badminton House), apart from the wider concerns of studying houses such as Kingston Lacy, Longford Castle and Melbury.

The professional affiliations of the Study Week members showed that half of them were museum board members, curators or assistants, and that in twos and threes the others were as varied as archivists, university teachers, National Parks Service staff, antique dealers and interior designers. It was a pleasure to have as members Graham Hood, the distinguished Chief Curator at Colonial Williamsburg, Dr Dagmar Hejdowa, formerly Director of the Decorative Arts department at the Museum of Fine Arts in Prague, and Miss Edith Standen, the Curator *Emerita* of Textiles at the Metropolitan Museum. Outstanding members of the younger generation were Kim Rorshach, who was working on her Yale doctorate on the artistic patronage of Frederick, Prince of Wales, and Tom Savage, Chief Curator of the Historic Charleston Foundation. My selection of a few names should not, of course, lessen appreciation of the high standard of the members.

At the conclusion of the Study Week Helena thought that the interest shown by *alumni* was encouraging, particularly from younger persons. There was, however, not enough interest shown by British or European

The front pages of the Summer School and Study Week programmes,
introduced in 1987, but changed in colour (annually) and in image
(from time to time).

candidates — for whom the course might seem expensive. However, an
increased and welcome grant to the Trust from Simon Sainsbury's
Monument Trust meant that a scholarship could be funded for a British/
European applicant. Whilst the Study Week made a profit of a little over
£3,000, Helena wanted in future to relate fees to costs rather than to a need
to look for profits towards further fund raising.

The 1987 Summer School met somewhat later than usual, not starting
at West Dean until 18 July, and terminating in Bath on 5 August. Apart from
the usual programme of house visits, seminars and lectures, there was an

attempt to stengthen the conservation theme, not only in discussions with Dr Ian Bristow, John Morley, Peter Smith and the Hon. Anna Plowden, but in encouraging owners to talk on special problems or methods of running their estates. In this respect the Duchess of Devonshire's talk was outstanding. In an administrative sense lecturers had been sent clear contractual letters setting out precise details of location, fees, expenses, equipment. This was much appreciated and has been continued and improved. It also proved possible, by Catherine Norman's efforts, to distribute most National Trust guide-books in advance of visits.

Nothing really went wrong on the 1987 Summer School except that members ate too much at West Dean (both salads and hot meals rather than either/or) and their efficient Bursar thought 1988 charges to us should correspondingly rise. We thought better directions to each 'queue'. What, otherwise, did we do, apart from eating well? Apart from our usual study day at Petworth we applied the same formula to Goodwood House. Ros Savill, Adrian Sassoon, Annabel Westman and I dealt, respectively, with Sèvres porcelain, French furniture, textiles and English furniture. Ros and Adrian also stayed on excellent form to excite the group by their enthusiasm and knowledge at Firle Place.

A special feature of our second week was to have the Chippendale authority, Christopher Gilbert, talk to us at Nostell Priory about the important furniture there. We also had the pleasure of visiting Lord Scarbrough at Sandbeck and enjoying his laconic commentary in the entrance hall — 'nothing much here — a dog [Stubbs], a landscape [Cuyp], my grandmother [Sargent]'; of seeing the precious Lumley Inventory of 1590 with its drawings of furniture and sculpture, and appreciating the problems an owner faces with acid rain attacking the elegant magnesium limestone façades. With careful preparations by Annabel Westman and myself, our annual Hardwick visit has been honed to near perfection. It has always been a high point in the Summer School's progress and we are indebted to our friends at The National Trust Regional Office at Clumber Park and to the Hardwick administrator, Ian St Clair Hughes (and his wife, Helen) for all they do annually to make Hardwick a special experience.

Then in the Third Week away to Bath, where I choose to live. Living in with the School in Somerset Place caused amusement to my neighbours as I would motor in for some clean shirts late at night and leave again. 'Do you know the Beards are living apart?' might be the scenario, and this is perhaps the place to thank what my wife calls the 'Attingham Cinderella Club': Margaret herself, Tim Westman and Jack Bruel, who, respectively, give support to me, Annabel Westman and Sybil Bruel in all we get involved in for Attingham. Bath is a city that lends itself to walking, and Dr Tim Mowl, who knows every back street and façade, led us on a fascinating tour from Lansdown Crescent to Queen Square, tumbling down the gradients surrounded by honey-coloured stone crescents. On Friday

31 July, John Morley conducted a controversial session. His basic thesis was that it was often better to leave an interior alone than to 'conserve it'. As he decided to do his lecture on the basis of 'interrupt me if you don't agree', it got very lively and I think never finished. What it did, whether one agreed or not, was to create a lively 'buzz' throughout the School, which the delights of the party at Quenington, given by David and Lucy Abel-Smith (Knox) did everything to enhance. The group photograph was taken before the north front of Badminton, which the Duchess of Beaufort opened for us, and she led us on an excellent, highly individualistic tour, with dogs being called in through the windows to bound before us up the stairs to view the Linnell japanned furniture.

Finally, because there is always a sad realization that Attingham, for another year, is over we paced the walks of Stourhead on a perfect sunny morning and then to the American Museum at Claverton Manor where the Director, the late Ian McCallum, showed us his splendid apartment with its wonderful views up the wooded valleys and we talked and, yes, ate everything the final party produced. In preparing for my plasterwork lecture earlier in the course I had leaped into the shower and grabbed a setting-gel bottle in there rather than shampoo (I only use the latter!): my hair came out very rigid (hair in (a) plaster!). The group had noticed this, and from the depths of her cleavage (this is 1991!) Mary Schoeser produced a lock of hair in a 'gel container', kept warm and supple. What can be done with such dear friends, but who were they?

Let me stay near the end of the course for a moment. No group was better trained in their final party songs because of the presence of Sally Gant of the Museum of Early Southern Decorative Arts, who is an accomplished musician, with her own choir. And who could fault the enthusiastic singing of Robert Domergue from San Francisco and the compelling negro melodies with thumping foot in unison from Jack Lindsay from the Philadelphia Museum? So good were the 'choir' that they needed to repeat part of their performance at the optional party at Syon House, the day after the School had finished. The back of the bus was controlled by my favourite Yale'ie, Robyn Asleson, who had the support of Molly Moreno, Sue Whitman, Simon Tickell and Nina Stritzer — or is it all some dream? No, the list of members notes they were there, with Bill Bartle, a freelance writer, elegant Beverly Brandt, with whom Sir George Trevelyan shot off to see Arts and Crafts furniture — George had joined us at Dyrham, and like the Old Testament prophet he resembles had the audience spellbound. Not so much what he says but the way that he says it. Was Ross Francis dressed too in Brunschwig et Fils fabrics — she is their Vice-President for Development and New York has the long-time commitment of its Mrs Murray Douglas (Att. '79) to its scholarship cause. Peter Hammell represented Winterthur, as the Head of its Division of Education. Barbara Hammond, the Assistant Director at Lyndhurst, was one of the two Royal Oak scholars. The other, Mary Ellen Hern, talked well at

Chatsworth about the table glass, and Bill Hickman and Larry Jones talked restoration problems, befitting their skills.

When I go to Boston I still see Diana Larsen from the Museum of Fine Arts, and Betty Leviner decided the course was so heady she returned to Colonial Williamsburg and got married. Melissa Marsh has shown me Historic Annapolis and I have since met Leslie Morris at the Rosenbach Library in Philadelphia. Vals Osborne since the course has left Sotheby's Education and Betsy Panhorst has left Kenmore. Sue Pittman was first with her vote of thanks and Barbara Shellenberger carried back many stories to the Winterthur guides. This was the year Sue Whitman met Jonathan Kinghorn from Glasgow: she is now Sue Kinghorn. Finally, because I always miss a few out to keep editorial control, there was one of our few special Zs, or Zees — the 1984 *Alumni Directory* shows only five in forty years, to which Europe adds five — Alice Zrebiec, the distinguished Associate Curator of Textiles from the Metropolitan Museum.

The 1987 Class was as fortunate with its European members as always. The National Trust scholar was John Chesshyre, then its HBR in the East Midlands, keeping up with his correspondence on the coach, guiding us the back way to Hardwick Hall, ever jolly and courteous. Elain Harwood (English Heritage) got so excited at leading us in the Chatsworth gardens that we lost her. Treve Rosoman (also English Heritage) was splendid over finding ships' chairs (they fold!) at Arbury, and in master-minding the intricacies of the projectors. Delightful Mary Schoeser I have mentioned, then Archivist to Warner and Sons. There was Ruth Shrigley, as good as any Manchester had ever sent, and brave after a major operation, Sue Newell was as nice as the Wallace Collection had led us to believe. Marjorie Trusted from the Victoria and Albert Museum was, as the seventeenth century would have it, 'heavy with child' (the birth was in September), but I recall being instructed by her in Spanish sculpture and how to say 'Valladolid' — the intermesh of human life and great knowledge of her subject. Graeme Rimer from the Tower Armouries was as knowledgeable as all his colleagues there when the Duke of Norfolk told him to tell us about the Arundel arms and armour. Was any Museums Association oral ever as demanding? Tim Wilson, a National Trust Land Agent in the Severn Region, was fascinated by 'land', obviously, and by estate management. Our 'foreign' colleagues were Dr Pavel Preiss, the leading Baroque expert at the National Gallery in Prague, Selysett Somorjay from the Ancient Monuments Department in Budapest, and a Danish Student at the University of Copenhagen, Anne-Sophie Fischer-Hansen.

During the Summer School the chairman and I had issued a jointly prepared questionnaire. Of the forty-seven given out, thirty-eight were filled in. We asked:

(1)   How did you hear about the Summer School?
(2)   At what approximate date did you send in your application?

(3)   Were the dates of handing-in an application (January 31) and of
      being informed of the result of it (second week in March) —
      (a)   convenient?
      (b)   would you have preferred dates earlier? If yes, by how many
            weeks, 1, 2, 3 or 4?
      (c)   or would you have preferred dates later? If yes, by how many
            weeks, 1, 2, 3 or 4?
(4)   Since the present fees do not fully cover costs the fees will have to
      be increased in 1989. In your opinion would a fee of, say, $2,400 —
      (a)   seriously reduce the number of applications, or
      (b)   signifcantly change the typical characteristics of applicants?
(5)   An Attingham Winter Week in London is envisaged. The cost
      might be in the region of $1,400. In principle, would such a
      programme attract support?
(6)   Any further comments.

I analysed the results as follows:
   Q1   How did you hear about the school?
   A   (a) From *alumni*: 28
        (b) Notice boards: 8
        (c) Adverts in *Antiques Magazine*: 2
One comment: 'In 13 years work in US Museums I had never seen the
flyer.'
   Q2   At what date did you submit your application?
   A   November: 2
        Mid–late December: 6
        Mid–late January: 17
        Mid-February: 10
        After deadline: 3
   Q3   Were these dates convenient?
   A   (a) Yes: 28
        (b) Later dates?
            3 (2 weeks)
            1 (3 weeks)
            1 (4 weeks)   (Several 'no firm view')
   Q4   Present fees — would they (a) seriously reduce applications
   A   No: 29
        Yes: 4
        Maybe: 3
        Don't know: 2
Frequent comment: 'Scholarship Funds would have to increase.'
        (b)   Alter nature of applicants —
              No: 21
              Yes: 9
              Probably: 4
   Q4   'Yes' comments about higher fees and attendance —
        *   Many scared by fear of rejection already.
        *   Older group the result of higher fees
        *   Cut costs of food/entertainment rather than raise tuition fees
        *   Maybe, depending on salaries, level and number of scholar-
        ships available. Course needs to always attract young scholars.

*   Those who wish to attend will always determine some way to raise fees — the higher they are the more exclusive and older the group will be.
*   Scholarships remain the vital requirement.
*   High fees would increase the number of interior decorators.
*   I hope it won't change. I don't want this programme full of people who are taking it for a tax deduction.
*   Give more publicity to scholarships that are available.
*   Scholarship support must remain substantial: if it declines the profile will change and this would be detrimental.

Q5   Would an Attingham Winter Week attract support?
A   Yes: 32
     No: 5
*   It would be different and have its own appeal.
*   I think it is a lot of money.
*   Depends on audience you are seeking.
*   Absolutely, but wrong time of year for work release.
*   It would be great to get to London in the off season.
*   Sounds like it would appeal to established museum people.
*   Who is your anticipated audience? There would need to be lots of 'behind the scenes' to lift it out of normal.

Q6   Further Comments
*   Make more use in Britain of *Museums Bulletin* for publicity.
*   The programme has an excellent reputation and will attract applicants whatever.
*   A foreign Study Week (France, Italy) would be a great idea.
*   What people spend whilst on the course is amazing, so don't worry about fee increases.

As the questions and answers analysis is set out it is sensible to show a few things we took note of. *Alumni* continue to be the best publicists, but we do also send out a poster in America and England. Fees have risen, but scholarship support is constantly maintained and sought. We did a Winter Week on Historic Textiles, noted below, and the 1991 Study Week was over-subscribed for eight days in Paris — an Attingham 'first' in a foreign setting.

All this activity merits a few words about finance. I have noted earlier that by the start of 1988 the Accumulated Fund in London stood at £144,609, with investment income of £17,938 and a surplus of £3,272 on the Operating Fund pushing it forward to £165,819 at 31 August. When one bears in mind that the £3,272 represented the surplus after the Summer School and Study Week had been paid for and salaries and other expenses met, little contingency was built in. Investment income from a growing capital base is the only way to cushion against deficits or unexpectedly needing to finance scholarships when other Trusts reallocate expected support. In New York the Treasurer Sybil Groff reported, however, that the Friends' future investment income could not be as healthy, due to the lower investment interest rates she expected. Amidst all these considerations there was a happy occasion in London. At the conclusion of its 4 June meeting the Council gave a dinner at the Sloane Club in honour of Rosemary Lomax-Simpson who had served Attingham so faithfully over sixteen years as its Treasurer and Administrator.

There was still concern in New York, expressed at its September 1987 Board Meeting, at the projected rise of $200 in the Summer School fee for 1988. The Summer School, whilst having good reserves, had made a loss in 1986 and a modest profit only in 1987. There was irritation that the original projected increase in the Study Week fee represented a nearly fifty per cent increase. The profit made on the 1987 Study Week was approximately £4,000. Meanwhile, in late November Deborah Gage, of the family long seated at Firle Place, gave the Phelps Warren Memorial Lecture on Charleston Farmhouse in Sussex, the home of Vanessa and Clive Bell and Duncan Grant from 1916 to 1978.

In October 1987 a meeting with the American Board by the Trust Chairman, Sandy Stirling, and myself, was possible as we were both in New York. I can but say it was a tense meeting with worries expressed about rising fees and the benefits accruing through currency movements: 'playing with the Futures market' was one phrase I recall. There was concern to study the balance sheets for each programme, to perhaps set the tuition fees in pounds (this was felt to be cumbersome) and that escalating fees might change the make-up of the participants. It was a feeling which simmered on and the chairman devoted a three-page letter to explanations in September 1988. I shall refer to it after discussion of other events in 1988.

At February 1988, when the selection meetings were due in New York, there had been 187 requests for application information and 97 requests for information on the Study Week. The beige brochures had obviously done their work again but it was decided that different colours were to be used for the Summer School and Study Week brochures from 1989. The Study Week was, as in 1988, to be in two centres, Ludlow (27 June–1 July) and Moreton-in-Marsh (1–5 July). Ludlow, visited by so many generations of Attinghamites, is laid out on a medieval grid-system: broad streets, lined with timber-framed houses, many now with Georgian façades; they tumble down from the crest of a hill dominated by a great Norman castle. Accommodation was to be at *The Feathers* hotel, a splendid example of a seventeenth-century timber-framed house.

From Ludlow it was possible to visit Powis Castle, confronting dramatically the Welsh border with its ancient fortifications built on an escarpment, adapted in the seventeenth century to create spectacular terraces. The baroque interiors, the newly-opened museum displaying Indian exotica collected by Lord Clive of India were certain to excite. A quieter but still lively contrast would be the Georgian 'Gothick' decoration of Croft Castle and the overpowering mock defensive Norman revival architecture of Eastnor Castle (1812–20) with its furnishings by Pugin and

Crace. Here we were tutored by John Hardy, and there is no one to equal him for the enthusiastic and accurate flow of relevant information, given with great generosity of spirit.

For the second half of the programme the group would move to the *Manor House Hotel* in the long main street of Moreton-in-Marsh, a main street which was once part of the Roman 'Fosse Way'. This is seventeenth-century Civil War country, and there would be an opportunity to visit Chastleton, a romantic Jacobean house with many original furnishings, haunted all by Royalist memories while Broughton Castle, home of the Saye and Sele family for six centuries, was a Cromwellian stronghold. Rousham was defended for Charles I by General Dormer whose descendants employed William Kent to Gothicize his old house. Finally there were the Islamic arches, onion domes and minarets of Sezincote, designed by Samuel Pepys Cockerell for his brother, a retired Indian Civil Servant. Repton's Indian-inspired garden complete with lotus pools, sacred stone bulls and shrines created exactly the setting 'Attingham' loves for a remarkable house.

The cost of the 1988 eight-day course had been $1,225, but it was, in Helena's view, still not attracting *alumni*. Another discouraging tendency was for applicants to be 'interested visitors' rather than members whose work, whether amateur or professional, would benefit by attending the week. She felt that a change of emphasis in plans for 1990 might have to be made to provide for the needs of the large number of museum curators in America concerned, or interested at a lesser level, with the study of European decorative arts. The final accounts showed a surplus of £2,746. The income was as budgeted and the expenditure was within 5 per cent of budget. Increases in hotel accommodation often did not neatly coincide with estimates made.

While we were at work planning the final stages of both Study Week and Summer School there was delight at a special award made on 9 May to Helen Lowenthal. This was given by the National Art Collections Fund to commemorate her services to

A Gothick Sanctuary Chair at Croft Church, Herefordshire, *c.* 1755. Drawing by Jim Abbott (Att. '91)

furthering art education and helping the National Association of Decorative and Fine Art Societies and the Attingham Trust. There are so many who have profited over the years from Helen's unfailing pursuit of truth about the past and her wise advice about the problems likely in the future.

The 1988 Summer School was calculated to attract with its final week being in York. The School had been there previously in 1968 and 1979 — the School's cycle of returning anywhere is about ten years. I noted at the head of the programme:

> The Summer School will have its usual concentration on the decorative arts. However, on visits to five of England's great houses it will also be possible to arrange specialist groups and to consider many topics from architecture to the life of the household staff. Attention will also be given to landscaped parks, monastic ruins (perhaps the finest in England at Fountains Abbey) and to a walk (and free time) in the walled city of York. We shall even visit the Mausoleum at Castle Howard, but promise to leave it, for lunch . . .

When the group assembled at West Dean on 8 July 1988, our first speaker was to be Helen Lowenthal talking on 'The Early Days of Attingham', as she had done in 1987. In 1987 I had decided to tape-record her and in a great hurry arranged it all. I swathed the microphone, to Helen's disgust, around her neck, and as I had hoped, in thirty seconds she had forgotten it and talked away spontaneously for forty minutes. Later in the year I added to the tape of Helen a commentary by Sir George Trevelyan and one by Helena Hayward. The tape was then issued for sale in New York and England and I recall Gloria Ravitch (Att. '81) writing to me that she had played it over and over as she tried to park her car in San Francisco! It so recalls the early days when Helen was in full possession of her memories, and there are still copies to be had, I'm sure. Following Helen belatedly that night was Mavis Walker, reading from Mark Girouard's *A Country House Companion* (1987). When I went into the West Dean Library very late that night, to check over the projectors for the next day, I realized that it had perhaps been one of the happiest days of my life. Like Eve biting the apple, I wanted so much more of it all, mindful always that what any of us had done for Attingham returned to us a thousand-fold in the form of lasting friendships and superb company.

In 1988 we were privileged to have Angus Stirling, Director-General of The National Trust, address the Class at West Dean. His 'Thoughts' provoked many more and proved how valuable is the work the Trust does, and how Attingham benefits from close links with it, not least in its vice-chairman, Martin Drury, being the Trust's Historic Buildings Secretary. The Attingham staff had earlier spent some time thinking out the Uppark afternoon. We based Sir Brinsley Ford in the saloon to talk about the Grand Tour paintings, Martin Drury, Christopher Rowell and I were peripatetic, roaming the house to instruct people scattered on their 'free flow' progress; Gillian Darby was doing the same about the ceramics, and

Annabel Westman the tapestries and upholstery. We should have had
Sarah Levitt discussing the kitchens and role of the servants, but Nature
had decreed that her impending baby had to take priority.

The 1987 Summer School had not visited the Royal Pavilion at Brighton
due to its all being swathed in scaffolding. So in 1988 we redressed the
omission, giving members, in one of three groups, either a memorable
journey to its fantastic roof, to marvel at the care on the restoration and
conservation of the interior, or to gaze in wonder at the furniture collections
and the set-out Banqueting Room table with its extensive array of
silver-gilt. A final tea party in the Great Kitchen gathered all three
awe-struck groups together.

There is a casual tendency to regard an Attingham Second Week as
only having Haddon, Hardwick, Chatsworth and Kedleston! Some would
be content with only those mighty four. But additionally there was a good
visit to Vanbrugh's Grimsthorpe Castle and a fine party with Henry
Thorold at Marston Hall. Henry, both a clergyman and a distinguished
author, threw open his house and delightful garden and the splendid
ladies of our caterers, 'Fabulous Feasts', travelled from the south to entice
us with cold salmon and other delicacies. As if that was really necessary.

It is perhaps few groups that are allowed into the crypt of the Castle
Howard Mausoleum, Hawksmoor's great building a mile across the park
from the house. Even to walk 'in a crocodile' towards it was humbling: then

Richard Robson talking to the Class of 1988 from the steps of Vanbrugh's
'Temple of the Four Winds' at Castle Howard. Catherine, Helena, Geoffrey
and Sybil are discernible, if you have good eye-sight!

to hear Richard Robson describe the ceremony for the burial of a family member and, finally, to go silently and reverently down to the burial place of the Earls of Carlisle was moving. The 1988 Class was on its best behaviour and I was proud of them. Time enough to drink coffee in Colen Campbell's Banqueting House of the late 1720s at Studley Royal, to hear a spirited talk on Fountains Abbey by Dr John Maddison (Att. '84) — surely the best exponent ever of medieval architecture — a lovely picnic with Nigel and Malise Forbes-Adam at Skipwith Hall, and an impeccably timed visit to Hovingham Hall. We had been asked by Lady Worsley to arrive at 4.00 p.m. We pressed the bell as the clock struck.

Every member of the Class of 1988 will recall the visit to Fairfax House where Dr John Shannon, Chairman of the York Civic Trust which owns it, was our host. His son-in-law, Peter Brown (Att. '85) had arranged not only that we saw the house and the Terry Collection of furniture under privileged conditions, but he and his staff provided, again, wonderful food. There was an excellent, if somewhat expensive, private visit to Harewood House where Christopher Gilbert was present to decribe the documented Chippendale furniture. He was also responsible for one of the finest Study Days Attingham has ever had — at Temple Newsam House, Leeds, of which he is Director. With his colleagues James Lomax (Att. '81), Sarah Nichols (Att. '84) and Anthony Wells-Cole, we were allowed to see furniture, ceramics and silver of unparalleled quality. To be within inches of the Paul de Lamerie tea equipage (1735), the Harewood Chippendale desk (1771) or the array of eighteenth-century Leeds creamware was memorable indeed. But for myself I recall, additionally, the quiet tranquillity of Lady Stoddart-Scott's garden at Creskeld Hall, where I both 'lost' and 'found' myself in the mirror perfection of its pools. All that awaited me after my deep reverie was the 'weary' business of eating more fabulous food and reacting to the great kindness shown to me and my colleagues: fine ties for me and lovely scarves for Annabel and Catherine.

So gifts were given, but from whom were gifts given? Carol Baker, a Senior Guide at Winterthur headed the list, closely followed by Tami Bitter (Scalamandre Silks) and the cheerful Stuart Chase from Raynham Hall at Oyster Bay. Not that Stuart had a monopoly on being cheerful or indeed being curious or perceptive. In writing of the Class of '88 in the American *Newsletter* (No. 9) Harvey Rosenberg noted his:

> feeling that for the first, and perhaps only time I was surrounded by many with the same interests, curiosity, passions and obsessions as mine.

Sharing, then, were Jennifer Esler, Executive Director of Cliveden, Alan Fausel, then at San Francisco and now at the Taft in Cincinnati, Debby Fillos at the Florence Griswold Museum, Stephen Frith at Columbia, doing his doctorate, Robyn Asleson's Yale friend and as irrepressible, too — Catherine Futter, the light of the coach back seat, Stephen Grout who knew

all about textile design, as befitted his professional post at the Philadelphia
College of Textiles and Science, and Bob Guffin from Winterthur.

So many fine drawings came from the pen of Will Gwilliam from
Colonial Williamsburg that several are reproduced in this book. Lynne
Hastings from Hampton, neat, knowledgeable and cheerful, Jane Hirsch-
kowitz who gave a splendid vote of thanks in the Farquharsons' garden at
Hare Park, Bulmer, almost in sight of Castle Howard. May I go on?
Elizabeth Igleheart, keen on Robert Adam (the eighteenth-century one),
Nancy Iliff from Lexington, Jas Jasik restoring furniture at SPNEA, in
Boston, Robert Joyce doing architecture at Yale, kind Peter Kaellgren from
the Royal Ontario Museum, always carrying what others didn't want to do
for themselves and delighted by being able to examine the silver toys in the
Dolls' House at Uppark (Ontario has a fine collection, too), Josh Lane,
helping at the Garvan Collection at Yale, and the urbane Mills Lane,
publisher of elegant and infomative books on the architecture of the deep
South. He is the distributor of this present study, on Attingham's behalf.
Jo Lawson looked at architecture as an architect should, and Chris Loeblein
from Charleston looked at everything. Jennifer McKendry from Toronto, a
PhD student, gave Canadian support to Peter Kaellgren. David McKinney
was studying architectural history at the University of Virginia, and while
David Meshutt was studying at Cooperstown he found time on Attingham
both to work hard and study Sarah Bevan from the Tower Armouries. They
are, as noted previously, now married and living in America. Ed Nickels,
he of 'Shakertown at Pleasant Hill', came alphabetically before Debby Rau,
an architect, and Cheryl Robertson, then at Winterthur, now at Sotheby's
Education in New York. Harvey Rosenberg of FIT, I have mentioned, and
he often renews acquaintance on his English visits. Talented Stephen
Saitas, with his own design company in New York, Joellen Secondo of that
splendid team at the Boston MFA, and Judith Straeten, kind when we
muddled her archives at Brunschwig's. Who else would I wish to sell me
books in New York than Jane Stubbs — her husband John had done the
School in 1976 — and finally Vicki Vinson from the Dallas Museum, who, in
giving the vote of thanks in Sir Thomas Worsley's eighteenth-century
Riding Hall at Hovingham had coincidentally been able to say that she had
been born on a horse ranch in Texas.

The European scholars now numbered fourteen, making a class of
forty-eight overall. Andrew Barber was the National Trust scholar from the
East Midlands Region which cares for Hardwick, Kedleston and Calke. I
have mentioned Sarah Bevan, the Keeper of Edged Weapons at the Tower
Armouries, 'impaling' David Meschutt or vice versa, but one of our most
knowledgeable scholars too, Tom Campbell, already expert on tapestries,
Simon Cottle from Glasgow, abounding in common sense, Howard Coutts
from the Royal Museum of Scotland, Ruth Guilding, 'Pre-Raphaelite' in
black, but so very delightful, Emmeline Leary caring for Sir John Soane's
Pitshanger Manor, Philip Sykas, a textile conservationist, bright (and

cheerful) Ros Westwood, and Lucy Wood, working hard on the Leverhulme Collections at Port Sunlight. Our East European friends were Danuta Luniewicz-Koper from the Royal Castle in Warsaw and Janos Zakarias from the Ancient Monuments Department in Budapest. Together they gave a wonderful vote of thanks to Lady Stoddart-Scott at Creskeld. Finally, from Italy, there was the Princess Corsini — 'Giorgiana' to her many friends, Vice-President of the Historic Houses Association of Tuscany, and delightful red-wine lover Dr Burkard von Roda from the Historisches Museum in Basel, holding the Villiers David Foundation Scholarship. I have left to the conspicuous end the pleasure I and my colleagues took in having Sybil Bruel, the splendid Executive Secretary of the American Friends, with us as the School's guest in the final week. She could explain, listen, intervene and enjoy all at the same time, and we valued the real contact, then as now. The American Friends are lucky to have her care and devotion to the cause.

In the early autumn of 1988 the chairman took another long look at Attingham's structure in the light of the spirited meeting in New York the previous October. Concern had been expressed then about the level of fees and he felt it helpful to set out 'a few points of mutual interest' in a letter of 23 September to Bill McNaught, the Friends' President. As a charitable educational trust Attingham could grant scholarships but only by using money received from donations or from the product of accumulated surpluses from the past. I can but *précis* a long letter. When the Chairman had been asked to help the Trust in 1982 the accumulated capital after thirty years of activity was only about £20,000. The Council agreed to try to build that up ten-fold with the income from the fund as its capital grew being used to provide scholarships, and to some extent stabilize fees. It was agreed that to maintain the academic quality of the course, fees paid to lecturers should be in line with market rates. Each course had to earn its own costs and not be subsidized from capital. This had not always proved possible and so the capital had to come from surpluses from the four successful Special Weeks, the Study Weeks, and in years when the dollar was strong, and by small surpluses from the Summer School itself.

Attention was then given to the accumulation of money by currency movement. Fees has to be set and printed in the brochures in September but they were not received until the following May/June. So in consultation with bankers, and with John Lewis, the chairman took a view of the likely yield in sterling of the dollars to be received some eight months later. In some of the years, 1982 to 1988, the dollar had risen in value between September and May, giving an unforeseen sterling bonus. This enabled 'windfall surpluses' to accrue. In other years the dollar had fallen in value, sometimes dramatically, after fees had been set. To counteract this, and after careful advice as noted, a forward contract with a bank would be taken out. This was designed to counteract the future value in May being lower than estimates made. The contract in effect fixed the rate of exchange at whatever the bank offered at the date of the contract. The disadvantages were that no benefit occurred if the dollar subsequently rose in value and secondly, the Trust had contracted to produce a large sum to the bank in any circumstances, even if for some reason (which had, of course, never occurred) the School had to be cancelled or if there were to be no subscribers. It was a risk consciously taken. By these means it had been possible to protect funds and build them up. In October 1987 the Chairman had set the fees with caution and had to impose a significant increase. The view was vindicated a week later with the Black Monday crash, largely brought about by the United States deficit in balance in payments. The usual contract had been taken out in London, however, an action which, with investment income of £11,200, bank interest (£3,288) and donations towards scholarships (£3,450) had given a good result to the year.

Finally, for 1989, it was announced that such a policy allowed the fees for the year to remain at the same level as 1988 and there could be an increase in the handling fees retained in New York, from $100 to $150 per head, nearly 7 per cent of the fee. The chairman stated: 'nobody is profiteering: the professionals receive only a meagre compensation for their time and the rest of us do it for love — as you do. The contribution of the Amercian Friends is essential to the continued success of the venture in which we both cooperate'.

At the end of 1988 the Balance Sheet of the American Friends showed that the operating income was $22,417 with expenditure of $17,473, leaving a slender balance of $4,944. Investment income totalled $10,081, and with special and non-recurring income, after expenses of $3,911, the 'unrestricted surplus income' for the year was $18,936. Of this amount $6,326 had been used for scholarships. Unrestricted funds totalled $147,647. In the 'restricted funds' charged with providing income for certain scholarships there was a total of $74,489. Together the two funds totalled $222,136, which one might note was within $26,000 of the English funds of £165,819 held at the same date, if a conversion rate of $1.50 to the £ ($248,728) is used.

I am always interested in what the longer effects of Attingham have been, well beyond its immediate impact on individuals. When the American Friends made a visit in Columbia County in September 1988 they called at the 1713 Dutch home of Rod Blackburn (Att. '76), an anthropologist and scholar of Dutch and English heritage. As a counterpoint Rod had constructed a Palladian pavilion in his garden, which was influenced by what he saw on Attingham. There is also little doubt that the period rooms in some American museums have been modified after a return from 'Attingham'. Further, in Wales, David Freeman (Att. '83) owns Attingham as a positive influence in setting out the great Baroque house of the Morgan family at Tredegar. More examples will occur to many *alumni*.

At the Annual General Meeting at the Sloane Club in London on 8 December 1988, the Chairman, Sandy Stirling, did not seek a third term of three years in office as Chairman. He had joined the Council in 1981,

John Lewis (Att. '81), Legal Adviser to The Attingham Trust, and its Chairman, 1988 to date.

became Trust Chairman in December 1982 and felt, with his main aim of increasing, substantially, the Trust's Capital Fund that it was time, after seven years, for 'new blood'. He wished to turn to new matters, in which Mrs Stirling would join, as she had relinquished her post as Study Week Organizer. Accordingly the Chairman, supported by his Vice-Chairman, Martin Drury, had approached, successfully, the Trust's Legal Adviser, John Lewis (Att. '81). He then proposed Mr Lewis to the office of Chairman, a resolution I seconded, and the meeting confirmed this. At the meeting Martin Drury and Annabel Westman also offered themselves for re-election to their respective offices of Vice-Chairman and Secretary and this was confirmed, in each case.

A word or two about the new Chairman. After some twenty years of practise as a solicitor Mr Lewis retired from this in 1985. He continues to act as a consultant to Jaques and Lewis, one of the leading London firms of solicitors. He has collected European sculpture, mostly bronzes, since his school-days, at Shrewsbury School, and now has a substantial collection. Because of this interest John Lewis is much involved with the museum scene in England and America: he is a trustee of the G. F. Watts Museum at Guildford and a member of the Visiting Committee of the Department of European Decorative Arts at the Boston Museum of Fine Arts. John is also Chairman of the Heritage Committee of The British Tourist Authority, the general forum to which those interested in such matters pay keen attention. As Chairman of a private group of companies he was much involved in turning various properties in The Royal Crescent at Bath into one of England's leading hotels — likewise his group acquired Cliveden from The National Trust — and effected the same careful transformation. Any Attingham Trust Council member has had reason, at meetings over many years, to be grateful to Mr Lewis, not only for arranging them in the comfort of The Sloane Club, but for making the business palatable by the provision of wine and refreshments.

In due course Martin Drury approached each member of the Council and with their contributions he presented the former Chairman with a copy of Antoine Chenevière's impressive book *Russian Furniture: The Golden Age 1780–1840* (1988), and some wine. It was further recorded in the Trust's minutes of 8 December 1988, that the Chairman, Mr Lewis:

> thanked Mr. Stirling, on behalf of all the members, for the hard work he had put in to the Trust. During the time he had been Chairman, the finances and the structure of the organization had been transformed as could be seen from his clear and helpful report circulated at the meeting.

An important task for the Attingham staff during the Autumn of 1988 and the beginning of 1989 was to plan the first Winter Week. We decided to do this from 28 February to 8 March 1989, and to devote the week to the subject of Historic Furnishings. Using all our contacts it worked superbly but as each day dawned we realized that bad weather could have rendered

The first 'Attingham Winter Week' participants on the steps
of Osterley Park, March 1989.

it unworkable. Possible if restricted to central London, even in the snow, but we had planned journeys much further afield — to Knole, Penshurst, Castle Hedingham to see Richard Humphries' silk-weaving establishment, Woburn Abbey and, a little nearer, Osterley, the Queen's House at Greenwich (then emerging from its long restoration) and Ham House. On Saturday 4 March the group joined the Furniture History Society Symposium at the Victoria and Albert Museum on the specially chosen subject of 'The State Bed'. At this, Gervase Jackson-Stops, Peter Thornton, Wendy Hefford, Sheila Landi, Jenny Band and Annabel Wylie, outstanding experts, ranged over the various roles of the Beds — from somewhere to sleep, their place in Baroque ceremonial, to the many problems posed in conserving them.

And what a group of knowledgeable participants were gathered, with Florence Montgomery, Susan Swan (Winterthur), Linda Baumgarten (Colonial Williamsburg), Peter Day (Chatsworth), Charissa Bremer-David and Mary Ackerman (Getty Museum), Alice Zrebiec (Metropolitan Museum), Mary Schoeser (Warner's Archivist), Wendy Cooper (Baltimore Museum) and Audrey Michie (Tryon Palace). They joined Lady Goodison, soon to be involved in the Study Week and, from 1991, its joint Director, Dorian Church and Treve Rosoman of English Heritage, the upholsterers Angela Burgin and Carole Thomerson, Robert and Beth Domergue, the interior designers, Julia Leisenring and Cynthia Drayton, Richard Milhender, a Trustee of the China Trade Museum, Hank Dunlop from the California College of Arts and Crafts, George Glazer, a Director of W. Graham Arader III's Galleries, Ralph Harvard who specializes in 'Antiques Decoration', Karin Peterson from the Antiquarian and Landmarks Society in Hartford, and Larry Ray from Lambuth College's Department of Art and Fashion. As I've noted, a very successful week, owing a great deal to the ministrations of my two colleagues, Annabel Westman, herself a textiles expert, and Catherine Norman, experienced at arranging 'how, why and when' and without taking the gate piers away, stuck on the side of the coach.

The preparations for the Winter Week had to be fitted alongside the detailed work in planning the 1989 Summer School. But let me return for one closing phrase on the Winter Week which I penned in the American Friends' *Newsletter* (No. 9): 'There is something particular to the Attingham spirit to be in darkened Knole, with stag-antlered park rolling away, looking at a seventeenth-century chair of state in the swirling light of a dozen pocket lamps'.

I have often wondered if our planning would have been any better if we had had a computer? Annabel had her own word processor but the American Friends' accounts for 1989 included 'Computer and Printer'. There is something rather awe-inspiring about knowing that what you plan on its screen, people will do. If we leave at 8.50 a.m. for Chatsworth on 15 July then everyone will turn up with coats and cameras more or less to time. If we plan a picnic at Horton on 23 July at 1.00 p.m. we are unlikely to have anyone missing. So it had been for thirty-seven years, ranging from twenty-two members in 1952 to our annual forty-eight from the late 1980s. The responsibility this places on organizers is something we take seriously. Catherine Norman sets out on timing all routes in March–April and Annabel Westman and I write many letters to try to smooth the eventual visit, to see we have the relevant accompanying tutors and to persuade owners of houses to be generous with privileges. Then there is little more that can be done except nudge the group, like adventurous voyagers shooting the rapids, to plunge in and be carried along boisterously to the end. That we have in America and England another sixty souls each year, anxious to be included beyond those chosen is gratifying.

The 1989 Study Week now received the keen attention of Helena Hayward with Lady Goodison (Judith) as her new Administrator and Tutor. Judith had studied the fine and decorative arts for her degree, had taken the Study Centre Course additionally, and was a valued officer of The Furniture History Society. She edited its *Newsletter*, and was also co-author of a 1986 book about English furniture from 1500 to 1840. It had earlier been decided to base the week in Yorkshire, at *Whitwell Hall Hotel*, almost within sight of Castle Howard, for the first four nights (5–8 June) and at the *Royal County Hotel* in Ripon (9–13 June). It proved possible to fill the first hotel, taking all the rooms in the main house and the converted stables. Whitwell was an excellent centre from which to visit nine houses of the importance of Castle Howard, Sledmere House, Newby Hall and Hovingham Hall. On moving to Ripon it proved possible to see a further eleven, ranging in date

Lady Goodison (Judith), Administrator and Tutor 1989–91, and then Joint Director, with Helena Hayward, The Attingham Study Week, 1991 to date.

from the Middle Ages (Markenfield) to the nineteenth century (Bolton Hall). Studies were for the most part concentrated on the eighteenth century, with a special theme being the landscape garden and garden buildings. This was exemplified, splendidly, by the Temple of the Four Winds (1726) and the Mausoleum (completed 1736) at Castle Howard, both of which were especially opened, by the Rievaulx Terrace, high above the Abbey, and by the incomparable landscaped expanses of Studley Royal and Bramham Park.

The course had twenty-seven American members, of which thirteen were *alumni*, and two English scholarship holders, Judith Elsdon of the American Museum at Bath and Jeremy Howard, a paintings expert at Colnaghi's. Helen and Judith found that the standard of knowledge and experience was higher in general than in 1988 and there were, moveover, a number of young people. However, with six museum curators and museum volunteers, an experienced gilder, four antique dealers, three interior designers, museum board members and interested amateurs it was also a good mix of ability and there was an enthusiastic response to the course throughout. Much of this was due to what the Chairman, in his 'Review of 1989', called 'Helena's inimitable style which epitomises Attingham and which she brings to the week, as she did to the Summer School'.

Whatever else happens in an Attingham year, the main focus is always on the Summer School and the Study Week. In 1989 we spent the final week at Silsoe College, Bedford. The administrative team had been strengthened a little beyond Annabel, Catherine and me by using Mrs Mary Roberts to help Catherine, and Dr Tim Mowl to act as Tutor on Architecture. In addition to this we were able to use the services of forty-seven additional lecturers and tutors, perhaps more than on any other comparable course, and it gives Attingham a good lead. The School visited twenty-five houses, apart from thrilling to a wonderfully ethereal Evensong in King's College Chapel, Cambridge. Another privilege was the Duchess of Devonshire allowing the Chatsworth Silver Steward, Ian Fraser-Martin, to put out all the Devonshire silver in the Entrance Hall for Helena Hayward to talk to the School about it.

Four of the houses, apart from being important to study, served as venues for parties or picnics. At Lady Stoddart-Scott's at Creskeld (scene of a memorable visit in July 1988) we again enjoyed Yorkshire hospitality, graciously dispensed. Gervase Jackson-Stops allowed us, in his absence abroad, to visit the Menagerie at Horton with Bruce Bailey acting as our 'host'. At Chicheley, Diane Nutting provided a wonderful tea and even cricket, if we had time to watch, on a perfect sunny afternoon. Lavinia Wellicome guided us on our visit to Woburn and our final party was held there. It was also pleasant to welcome Council members, Marian Brudenell and Judith Goodison, to see the School 'in action', and to have two Presidents *Emeriti* of the American Friends (Stewart Johnson and Bill

McNaught) come to see us at Petworth, with Attingham's Chairman, John Lewis.

Especially memorable was our visit to see the garden buildings at Stowe, coinciding with what we had been told about (but not told enough) — the Austin-Healey car owners' rally. Everywhere there were excited throngs of onlookers, glistening machines, boisterous children, barking dogs and large coaches going the wrong way in the one-way system, with golfers trying to play golf but only us looking at architecture. It was delightful in contrast to have the riches of Luton Hoo all to ourselves, and to see the textile conservation work being done at Hatfield House, on a private morning visit, ending with a pleasant meeting with the Marchioness of Salisbury.

I twitch nervously at listing so many members of each School. Whilst they appear alphabetically in the Appendix it is only possible in these pages to indicate their cohesion as a Class. Moreover, Attingham is about people, and those attending after the issue of the 1984 *Alumni Directory* are only recorded in the annual class list and on Sybil Bruel's computer print-out. So, perversely, let me, for 1989's Class, go for a change to the far end of the alphabet and start with Ann Wood from the Museum of Fine Arts at Houston. She had, as curatorial colleagues from America, Barbara Batson (daughter of Whaley Batson, Att. '82) from the Valentine Museum at Richmond, Charissa Bremer-David, Gillian Wilson's assistant at the Getty Museum (Gillian herself, Att. '67), Bradley Brooks at the Willis-Moody House in Galveston, Kasey Grier, the award-winning furniture historian at the Strong Museum, Bonita La Marche from the Detroit Institute of Arts, Sarah Lytle at the Middleton Place Foundation as 'Colonial Wars Scholar', Kristan McKinsey at St Louis Art Museum, and Margaret Moore at the Clark Art Institute. There were architects and landscape architects — Charles Bergen studying it all at Yale, Mark Brinkley drawing as expertly as his Williamsburg colleague Will Gwilliam had done in 1988, Tony Frederick, who even supplied a key to the splendid group photograph he took, the architectural historian, John Larson, and Christine Matheu, who was also lecturing at the University of Pennsylvania. Conservationists, polemicists, experts in this and that, experts on conservation such as Mary Brooks at York City Art Gallery, Michael Podmaniczky at Winterthur, Susan Odell at the Boston MFA, Carl Stepan from Graz in Austria and Anna Rawa-Szubert from the textile Conservation Department in the Royal Castle, Warsaw. Let's make everyone expert, and certainly Rosemary Brandau was that, as Manager of the Historic Foods Programme at Colonial Williamsburg, diving away on a specially arranged visit to the Chatsworth kitchens and 'below stairs' area.

Educationalists of various kinds included Cathryn Campbell at Auburn University, Sabele Gray as a graduate student on the Cooper Hewitt-Parsons programme, Richard Iverson, a Professor of Ornamental Horticulture, Caroline King at Williams College, Geraldine Prince at

A 'coat of arms', given to Catherine Norman by the Class of 1989. Drawn, and with legend, by Martin Ellis.

The Achievement of Lady Catherine de Attingham
QUARTERLY
  1st: On a ground tea-cuppy, a tea-pot *pourant*
  2nd: *Gules*, on a bend *or*, between a coach *departant* and a cloud of dust, three alarm clocks *sonnant*
  3rd: *Or*, a *fesse* dancetty, azure *semee* de pork pies, with, in chief, three contented students.
  4th: *Vert*, on a chevron *argent* between three schedules tattered, six microphones *rampant*.
SUPPORTERS   A wine glass tipsy
                        A sheep surprised, *bleatant*.
CREST   The Attingham 'A' adorned with a *chapeau de paille* and crested
              with a sock *errant*, mantled *gules* concealing a nightie mislaid *or*
MOTTO   *Semper Punctilio*

The Petworth State Bed,
1759, drawing by Kent
Brinkley (Att. '89). A
copy of this drawing,
mounted, was given
by the Class to
Annabel Westman.

Edinburgh College of Art (who emerged as an efficient 'leader'), delightful
(aren't they all?) Debby Prosser, whom Carl Stepan threw in the pool at
Chicheley, much to her (and his ultimate) distress, for Debby had had bad
news of a family illness that day and was trying to be more than brave. Dr
Priscilla Roosevelt from the Catholic University in Washington was useful
in giving us the names of Russian scholars and we might well have two of
them in 1992. As Dr Scott Swank soldiered on, with everyone in 90° heat, he
already knew that his Deputy Director's post at Winterthur had been axed
in an economy drive. He is now the Chief Curator at Canterbury Shaker
Village in New Hampshire. His careful report allowed us to make some
useful administrative changes. We looked at things in a cheerful way,
especially when we were with Laura Evans from the Cooper-Hewitt
Museum — she was ever cheerful — and Linda Ellsworth from the National
Trust for Historic Preservation caused us to think carefully about management structure in houses open, and the 'nuts and bolts' of presentation.

Eloy Koldeweij from Leiden (when not explaining why a Dutch first degree entitles you to the prefix 'Drs' (note the 's')) was expert on leather, stamped, gilded, and there was never enough of it. Rarely do we have an archivist, but we had Christopher Marsden, in charge of the Chippendale archives at Nostell as part of the West Yorkshire Archive Service: he was also 'Master of Ceremonies' at the final party which included the presentation of many ornamental shrubs in pots to me for my garden. The choice was Richard Iverson's. I drove home with the car's front passenger window completely obscured by Latin-tagged greenery. It all thrives in Bath's rain and sun.

There are more, many more. Neat Nancy Packer from APVA (you know what it means), Emma Lou Powers, a Research Associate at Colonial Williamsburg, Martin Ellis at Aston Hall, Birmingham who drew up an amusing heraldic shield to give to Catherine Norman, and greatest secret of all, the fine drawing of the Petworth Bed by Kent Brinkley presented to Annabel Westman. Mary Brooks even gave it curtains and Tim Westman has secretly produced a *Country Life* view of it for Kent to work overnight on his drawing. The actual bed, carved by Whittle and Norman in 1759, we had seen at Petworth a fortnight earlier and Annabel had been responsible for its lavish textile hangings. So the Class had thought out what would please us, as we had constantly thought of what would please them. They had all enjoyed West Dean and Kent gave Catherine his fine drawing of that too, on behalf of the Class.

I had said that if I needed anyone to sell me French furniture it would be elegant Margaret Civetta of Rosenberg and Stiebel, that if I wanted to see nineteenth-century 'half-timbered' Bramall Hall I would ask Anneke Bambery, its then Keeper, and Alastair Forsyth would surely tell me about the great years of the Cunard liners from his research post at Southampton City Museum. John Hermanson would be a good furnishings consultant and Mary Anne Massie would keep my calendar, as she now does at *Antiques Magazine* in New York. Elizabeth Michelson as a freelance writer could be a very useful press agent, and Daru Rooke from Leeds City Gallery would teach me how to dress Edwardian. Marc Rabun from David Hanks would then approve all my ties, and Roger Whitworth, HBR, for The National Trust in Yorkshire, would smile, as he did, at my jokes. He was also a shrewd and invaluable member of the Class. Hana Seifertova was with us from the National Gallery in Prague. She found few Flemish paintings but at least she recognized all she did, with great knowledge. I told Lesley Jackson from Manchester City Gallery to tell her Director, Richard Gray (Att. '83) to get a new car. As Director he had. Finally, we had the pleasure of welcoming Louise Mitchell from the Power House Museum in Sydney, taking in the Class on her way home from being at the Cooper-Hewitt Museum in New York.

In the spring of 1989 considerable thought had been given by Helena Hayward to the future make-up of the Study Week. It had been obvious that the requirement for admission to the selection process for the Winter Week, being the submitting of a *curriculum vitae*, letter of application and letter of reference, had discouraged casual applications. To strengthen the appeal of the Study Week to Attingham *alumni* she felt it necessary to stiffen the entrance regulations and programme. The theme of the week could be focused carefully but still be wide enough in scope to interest the thirty good people needed. Under the general title there could be consideration, in four successive years, of:

      (a) Collectors and Collecting;
      (b) Furnishing and Domestic Wares, 1550–1700;
      (c) Design and Decoration 1700–1760;
      (d) 19th-Century Interiors and Furnishings.

Furthermore, for 1991, the idea of a week based in Paris could be explored, perhaps with help from the 'Association des Vieilles Maisons Françaises' and knowledge gained on Furniture History Society and Georgian Group visits to Paris in earlier years. To help the organization in a structured way Lady Goodison's position as Administrator and Tutor would be recognized by her appointment as a co-opted member of the Council and its Executive Committee, with the right to vote. This was approved at the 1 June 1989 meeting.

It might be thought that across all the years of its existence that 'The Attingham Summer School Trust' was a sufficient title. A moment's reflection will, however, suggest that no purpose or aim of the Trust was indicated. The first three lines of every letter to a house owner had to say, more or less, 'The Attingham Trust runs a Summer School devoted to the study of the Country House in Britain' to disabuse those who thought we patronized sick people or cared for dissolute curators. On further reflection . . . At the June 1989 Council Meeting it was decided, after a long short-list of suggested names had been circulated, to recommend to the Annual General Meeting in December that the Trust should be re-named 'The Attingham Trust for the Study of the Country House in Britain'. 'The Attingham Summer School' and 'The Attingham Study Week', as also the title of 'The American Friends of The Attingham Summer School Inc.' would remain unaffected. It may be tidier to record here that at the Annual General Meeting on 6 December 1989, this new title was approved. The retiring Scholarship Committee Chairman, John Fuggles, was thanked by the Trust's Chairman for his excellent work, since 1986. Latterly he had not been well so I acted as Chairman for the 1990 selection of the European scholars. At the conclusion I handed over to the Chairman-elect, Dr Richard Edgcumbe (Att. '84). He had agreed, against a busy life at the Victoria and Albert Museum's Department of Metalwork, to serve for no more than two years (1990–91). In that time, however, as I can testify, he was meticulous in Attingham's interests. His Committee also subsequently made a presentation to Mr Fuggles in the form of a silver spoon, specially commissioned from Hart's of Chipping Campden.

A

B

C

A. Jay Cantor (Att. '71) re-enacting the role of 'Lord Cuthbert Magnus Opus' (see p. 49). In January 1990 at the Helen Lowenthal Scholarship Fund dinner in New York.

B. Christopher Monkhouse (Att. '66), co-chairman of the evening's event in New York.

C. Charles Savage (Att. '72), Pauline Metcalf (Att. '66) and Sarah Latham Kearns (Att. '78) helping to re-enact parts of 'The Screw of The Tern'. Miss Metcalf also acted as co-chairman of the evening's event.

At this Annual General Meeting (as is customary each year) I outlined the itinerary for the 1990 Summer School. This was to take place at West Dean College, Nottingham University and Wye College, Ashford, Kent. But more to my immediate mind in December 1989 was an impending visit to New York. The American Friends, helped by a $7,500 donation from the Attingham Trust, had raised some $31,000 from *alumni* (as listed in their *Newsletter* No. 11) for an annual scholarship in honour of Helen Lowenthal. This sum was increased subsequently to about $35,000. She was feeling, then, at the age of eighty-five, a little nervous of the trip and I was to accompany her on the Trans-Atlantic flights and join the Trust Chairman, John Lewis, in New York. He had at a later point asked Helena Hayward to accompany us, and when in January Helen became unfit to travel he extended a further invitation to Annabel Westman and Catherine Norman. Uniquely, therefore, all five officers of The Attingham Trust were able to be at the memorable black-tie reception and dinner at the Cosmopolitan Club in New York on 26 January 1990. Let me quote what Pauline Metcalf (Att. '66) wrote about the evening:

> Toasts were given by Morrison Heckscher, former President of the Friends, Alan Campbell, President pro-tem, John Lewis and Helena Hayward. Geoffrey Beard, on behalf of Helen, accepted a hand-made medal, especially designed by Stephen Saitas, '88. With the after-dinner program, the entertainment began in earnest. Christopher Monkhouse, co-chairman of the evening, regaled the audience with tales of the early days, accompanied by slides of various classes, including the first year, and some wonderful candids of the founding fathers and mothers — Helen Lowenthal, Sir George Trevelyan, Lydia Bond Powel, and Phelps Warren. The evening's finale was the revival of a 'Lively Review' — 'The Screw of the Tern', written by members of the Class of 1971, most notably Jay Cantor, who performed and directed the players — Sarah Latham Kearns, Pauline Metcalf, and Charles Savage — in their respective incarnations as the Curious Culturephiles visiting Lord Cuthbert Magnum Opus at his stately Hodge-Podge Lodge.
>
> Numerous Attingham *alumni* made the evening possible through their generous contributions, including those of time and talent. Special thanks go to Alan Campbell for his donation of the invitations, Richard Nelson for providing the topiary table decorations and flowers, and Betty Landreth for writing the place cards.

Whilst the Attingham 'team' was in New York it was possible to meet the Finance Committee of the American Friends, to visit and talk business with many *alumni* and also to enjoy the New York scene, either from 'Pentop', the depths of the Plaza or Carlyle carpets, or the riches of the Frick and the 'Met'. At the Finance Committee meeting John Lewis stated (as Isabel Benham had done in December 1984) that he felt the American Friends should aim for a higher total fund of, say, $300,000 to $500,000 to enable higher payments for administration and to secure and increase the number of scholarships to say, twenty. Discussion then ensued on the ratio of scholarships to fee-paying places. Huyler Held advanced the view that the Friends should certainly endeavour to increase its unrestricted funds. The day might well come when it would be necessary to consider subsidizing students so that the total cost of tuition need not be borne by them. He went on to say a capital fund committee was ready to be set under the chairmanship of Mrs Lisa Koch.

This meeting was without the genial presence of Bill McNaught, who had been obliged to resign his Presidency of the American Friends in December 1989 on his appointment as Director of the American Museum in Britain. Alan Campbell (Att. '73) was acting as President, pro-tem. In the Spring 1990 *Newsletter* (No. 12) he announced that the Nominating Committee of Christopher Monkhouse, Hope Alswang, Allison Ledes and Stewart Johnson were recommending to the Annual Meeting of 22 May that Mrs Elaine Evans Dee (Att. '80), Curator *Emerita* of Prints and Drawings at the Cooper-Hewitt Museum, be elected as President. All the Directors cast their votes for the nominee and she was unanimously elected at the May meeting. News of this could be flashed to England more quickly through the generous gift of Betty Starr Cummin (Att. '81) of the cost of facsimile machines purchased for the New York and London 'offices'. With the subsequent acquisition of one for me, our chatter sessions are ever efficient and informed, or so we prefer to think.

Elaine Evans Dee (Att. '80), President of The American
Friends, 1990 to date.

For the 1990 Study Week Helena Hayward and Judith Goodison elected to base it (from 5–13 June) at Durham and Kelso. The theme was to be the nineteenth century in its various aspects — ranging from the influence of Sir Walter Scott's historicism and the romantic appeal of the Middle Ages to the renewed appreciation of the exemplar of the great Italian renaissance palaces. The group convened at the *Royal County Hotel*, Durham for the first four days. The thrill of staying in Durham is always evident, but the hard-working members journeyed out to Raby Castle, to the vast 'château' of the Bowes Museum, to Seaton Delaval on a suitably dark cloudy day, befitting Vanbrugh's dramatic house for the Delavals, and to Palladian Rokeby, although Scott frequently stayed there and drew on its romantic landscape for his poem, *Rokeby*. Evenings were occupied with lectures and with the inevitable chat. On the first evening Judith lectured on 'Nineteenth-century idealistic trends and their influence on furniture and interior decoration', whilst I led a group discussion a day or two later on 'The problems of restoration and upkeep of historic houses'.

Then away for the next five nights to Kelso, with memorable visits to the former Trevelyan home of Wallington, to Floors Castle, with its amazingly complete Playfair dining-room and good tapestries (expounded on with her usual authority and verve by Edith Standen (Att. '56), to Bowhill, Alnwick, Cragside, Mellerstain, Lennoxlove. And so much more to see and do — a party with Tim and Jane Clifford at Tyninghame and lunch with the Earl and Countess of Rosebery at Dalmeny. But not only

The Attingham Study Week, 1990, assembled at Cragside, Northumberland.

eating: to see and think, to learn and memorize, to capture in the mind or by the ever-clicking lens. At the end of the course the various threads were woven in place by Helena talking on the sources of the Gothic revival in the eighteenth century and contrasting them to the rich excesses of the following century.

A welcome trend, and one to be ever encouraged, was the presence on this Study Week of the first scholar sponsored by the American Friends (Dr Anne Woodhouse (Att. '78)) and two scholars sponsored by the Monument Trust and the Attingham Trust, Pippa Mason, an authority on picture frames, and Belinda Cousens (Att. '81) of The National Trust at Attingham Park. They were 'model students' and confirmed the view that carefully chosen candidates will always enrich the conversation and observation pursued by members of the increasingly rigorous Study Weeks. Its very name dictates that there will be serious concern but blended with rare friendship and sheer fun.

The 39th Summer School of 6 to 24 July 1990, was the fourth for which I had the overall responsibility, but ably backed by my splendid colleagues Helena Hayward, Annabel Westman and Catherine Norman. We were to journey down to Wye College in Kent for our final six days. The brochure issued in October 1989 had indicated that in our first week we would visit Uppark, 'a romantic house of 1690 with interior decoration and furnishings virtually unaltered since they were gathered on the Grand Tour in the early 1750s'. But a few weeks after the 1989 Summer School had sat before it, a tragic fire had all but destroyed the house, but by untiring effort most of the contents were saved that fate. The 1990 brochure was left unaltered but it was a very saddened Attingham which, after viewing a video on the fire, gazed at its scaffolded and storm-sheeted walls and at the trays of carefully labelled fragments of the most dream-like of houses. All *alumni* of recent years had found Uppark to be their favourite house, their fondest memory. It is missed like a faithful and loved friend: we are grateful that it will be, at least, well restored.

The great seventeenth-century Sackville house of Knole is always a prime consideration when visiting Kent, but the county is rich in other important houses and gardens — Penshurst, with its Great Hall dating from 1340, the romantic landscape garden surrounding moated Scotney Castle — where we were graciously received by Mrs Christopher Hussey — and Sissinghurst. Here Nigel Nicolson, on an idyllic hot summer's day, guided us to his mother Vita Sackville-West's study in the tower, explained the planting and let us picnic in his private garden. John Maddison taught us the architectural intricacies of Canterbury Cathedral (with Evensong to follow), and we giggled, just a little, at some of the 'public attractions' of Leeds Castle, whilst enjoying its incomparable setting in the centre of its lakes. But again on a rare hot day, blue azure sky, wheeling birds, strutting peacocks, the Palladian overwhelming richness of Colen Campbell's Mereworth Castle, one of the homes of His Excellency Mahdi-Al-Tajir, and maintained in impeccable splendour. The introduction had been arranged by Robyn Asleson (Att. '87). We were glad that Sybil Bruel and Lisa Koch, representing The American Friends, were with us for a week, and we had as guests for the day two of its Presidents *Emeriti*, Stewart Johnson and Bill McNaught. I know they were days I was hardly ever myself. I over-stared at everything, I over-photographed many things at Old Wilsley and Sissinghurst, but I was granted a pardon. They were a fine Class but who were they?

Tracey Albainy from the Cooper-Hewitt Museum stayed ever immaculate and calm, while Dr June Hargrove (University of Maryland) bubbled with enthusiasms and incisive comments. Betsy Lahikainen from SPNEA was under every upholstered chair, sometimes with her husband, Dean (Essex Institute) and sometimes with me, whilst Isabelle van Tichelin (Musées Royaux, Brussels) looked for weavers' marks on tapestries. 1990 was characterized by the presence of a number of senior curators who had found it difficult to be away in earlier years; Peter Spang (Historic Deerhurst), Richard Nylander (SPNEA), Scott Braznell, Curator of the American Silver Museum, and his wife Pat Kane (Yale University Art Gallery), together with Cecie Clement (British Art Center, Yale) came into this category. They gave *gravitas* when it was needed but led the laughter when it wasn't. Scott Burrell, the Estate Manager at Virginia House, discovered Rosemary Lomax-Simpson could also sing songs from 'Oklahoma' as well as (both) having great horticultural knowledge. Paul Caffrey from Ireland's great mansion of Castletown told no Irish jokes, Robert Mehlman asked ever-perceptive questions, and David Wood had mastered the art of taking all his photographs from a tripod. Joan Binder found Annabel Westman's 'embroidery explanations' compulsive listening at Hardwick, but why did David Mees like the sunset better than the lecturer one evening? Our East European colleagues were Szilvia Maros from the Museum of Applied Arts in Budapest and Dr Ladislav Kesner, now Director of the National Gallery in Prague. I shall ever remember Ladislav's moving vote of thanks, expressing thanks on behalf of East European scholars for what experiences like Attingham had meant to them in darker years.

Twenty-five of the thirty-four American places allotted went to curators or those in similar posts. Lee Ellen Griffith, Secretary to the Regional Furniture Society in America, but a member of the Philadelphia Museum of Art staff, was alphabetically before Becky Hammell, from the Rockwood Museum. As her husband Peter had gone through the course in 1987 the Hammell breakfast table conversation is now equal. David Johnson from the Taft Museum in Cincinnati never failed to recognize Oriental ceramics, while Ann Kohls had worked on the important Minneapolis Institute of Arts exhibition 'The American Craftsman and the European Tradition, 1620–1820' arranged by Michael Conforti and Bill Puig (Att. '78). Susan Borchardt was delighted to join us to help her work at

Gunston Hall and Lisa Krieger, like David Johnson, joined us from the Taft Museum. Melodye Moore was the first Kaplan scholar for many years, a scholarship given by Joan Davidson in honour of her mother Alice Kaplan (Att. '70). Pam Parmal, Assistant Curator of Costume and Textiles at the Rhode Island School of Design Museum of Art left her colleagues Christopher Monkhouse (Att. '66) and Tom Michie (Att. '81) to make their own coffee and Janine Skerry, (who gave a splendid moustached perform-ance at the final party), told me I had to come to Historic Deerfield, which I have yet to do. Jayne Stokes was the Helen Lowenthal Scholar from the Milwaukee Art Museum whom I met walking in Bath after the course was over — she didn't shriek that she couldn't get rid of me, even after three weeks. Perhaps I even envied John Tschirch, for to my shame I have also never seen 'The Breakers', but I do see Charles Venable from Dallas when I go there in the Fall of 1991. George Yetter and Clyde Kestner joined the long list of those coming to us from Colonial Williamsburg. I use the diary Clyde gave all the staff to plot my 1991 dates.

Of course there were others, important others. Rick Kearns now knows why Sarah (Att. '78) said he had to go to Attingham. Jayne Kuchna wanted to come to escape proofs of *The American Art Journal* — she is Managing Editor, and she didn't — and Karl Kusserow has perhaps never quite finished the Yale catalogue he was working on. Jim Hennessy was reading law at Columbia and Gordon Frey had worked as an intern on the Met's forthcoming American Rococo exhibition. I'm sure I don't have the right title for that in any case but Philip Hayden was titled precisely enough as the 'Coordinator of Education at the Historical Society of Princeton'.

I'm sure to have forgotten someone, rendering my longer wait in the US immigration queues at JFK as punishment almost certain. What of the European 'mix'? The National Trust scholar was John McVerry from the Wessex Region, based at Stourhead. English Heritage sent a senior architect, Robin Wyatt, who was concerned with work at Kenwood, Marble Hill and Chiswick. The Victoria and Albert Museum improved its selection process and sent us Clare Graham from the Collection of Furniture and Woodwork. In provincial museum terms Annette Carruthers had just left Cheltenham to live in Edinburgh, where her expertise on the Cotswold school of wood craftsmen was viewed through the right blend of Scottish mist. Christine Boydell, as an experienced Polytechnic lecturer, nobly coped with all our projector problems without a single moan (at least audibly). Peter Boughton from the Grosvenor Museum at Chester was on a scholarship jointly funded by the Ariel Grant, made to us by Pauli McClanahan (Att. '79), and by the Attingham Trust. Manchester sent us Miles Lambert from its Gallery of English Costume and Catherine Milburn came from the London dealers Carlton Hobbs — she was its research consultant. Letitia Stevens from the Wallace Collection (but now on a Getty Conservation Fellowship at the Boston MFA) was in the under-furniture, flash-lamp contingent as a 'leading light' (sorry). We were hastened on to

the coach by the subtle wiles of Robyn Asleson (Att. '87) as Administrative
Assistant to Catherine Norman. She forgot no one: I may have done.
Indeed, almost: the interior designer from Atlanta, delightful Carolyn
Clark, and the Australian on her way home from America, Desley
Campbell-Stewart.

At the final party I contrasted two verses from poems I had composed
in 1989 and for 1990. That of 1989 was a mammoth saga of several pages
(which Kasey Grier subseqently distributed to the American members of
the Class). Its final verse was still too sad, even when partly amended:

> Fleeting shadows on the grass
> Upturned faces etched on the mind.
> Fading fingers on an empty glass
> A curling guidebook with no name.
> And on my final ending of the year
> When the newest diary lies beneath the tree
> A single silent searing tear
> For ships that passed that can't be near.

As for 1990:

> When I think of the Class
> Of the symmetrical year,
> Proportioned Ionic in strangest gear,
> When at the hottest of the year
> Draining every glass that's near
> Never downhearted, all owners should fear,
> Whilst quartered and now impaled,
> Crenellated for those who failed,
> Those at the year's end can be
>   'Merë' and 'worth'
> Gathered at the Bruel-tide log
>   As in so much
>   It's journey's end,
> Thank goodness I can call, all of you, always —
>   'My friend'.

Hardwick Hall remains for many *alumni* the most cherished memory.
The 1990 Class had the High Great Chamber etched on the mind even more
so, for we arranged a forty-five minute concert of Elizabethan music there.
Performed in costume by the trio 'Grynwode' it was very successful and by
the kindness of our National Trust colleagues we have repeated it for the
Class of 1991. There is nothing better than gazing at a room for a long time,
lulled by music, to appreciate its ever-changing decoration as shadow and
light race across the relief plasterwork of Diana's court.

For other *alumni* memory is aroused by the meetings arranged by The
American Friends or The Attingham Society. In October 1989 a *Special Tours*
visit to Bohemia was opened to 'Attingham' with Lucy Knox as organizer.
So successful was the visit, with many *alumni* based in Prague, that the
group collected money to finance a student on the 1991 School. In the

autumn also there was an Attingham Society 'Yorkshire Study Weekend' arranged by Sarah Nichols (Att. '84) and James Lomax (Att. '81). Then, in March 1990 a splendid Study Weekend in Gwent arranged with customary efficiency by David Freeman, the Society's chairman, with a very memorable dinner on a windy smoking log-fire night at Penhow Castle. In the autumn a Study Day focused attention on Sir John Soane with visits to the Soane Museum, the Picture Gallery in Dulwich, St Peter's, Walworth and Pitshanger Manor.

The American Friends had planned a trip to Charleston in October 1989 but 'Hurricane Hugo' was no observer of such niceties: the postponed trip was eventually undertaken, still in stormy weather, in March 1991. As the first event in 1990 there was a trip to Newark, NJ, to see the recently completed additions to the Museum by the architect Michael Graves and the restored areas of the Newark Public Library. There was also time for encountering brief organ recitals going on in two churches and praise for the organizational skills of Bill Dane (Att. '67) and Ulysses Dietz (Att. '83) in arranging it all. As for other shorter events, there was a November 1989 day visit to Long Island with stops at Raynham Hall, Coe Hall and Old Westbury Gardens. In distant California a reception was held at the home of Bill Whitney (Att. '73) and reports given on the Study Week, the Winter Week and views on reorganization and new acquisitions at the Fine Arts Museums of San Francisco. Then I'm quite sure Karin Peterson (Att. '78) was cheerful when she and Paul Parvis (Att. '85) arranged a garden party

Helena Hayward and Geoffrey Beard at the final party, Class of 1989, at Woburn Abbey.

Photograph: Geraldine Prince

on 10 June to welcome the Class of 1990 and to give Connecticut *alumni*
chance for an informal get-together.

During the last half of 1990 I set myself the task of raising money for a
scholarship in honour of Attingham's second Director, Helena Hayward. I
was mindful that the effort for the Lowenthal Scholarship had been recent
and that there were limits to the generosity of the most dedicated of *alumni*.
I decided to try as few as possible at first, to include some of Helena's
friends from other organizations and to get it all done by the date of the
Trust's Annual General Meeting on 5 December 1990. Because Helena is
well known to many younger *alumni* from the mid-1970s onwards there
was to be an eventual need to announce the fact in the Autumn 1990
Newsletters on both sides of the Atlantic. With that the scholarship was
secure, with some large, medium and smaller donations totalling about
$60,000. Before Lord Shelburne gave the Sixth Attingham Society Lecture
(the others had been given by Helena, as an inaugural meeting one, John
Wilton-Ely, me, Ros Savill, Gervase Jackson-Stops and Clive Wainwright),
a list of donors inscribed in a special booklet was given to the surprised
recipient. And at a lunch the following day Jack and Sybil Bruel,
coincidentally on a private visit to London, had arranged to walk into the
London restaurant with the gift of an inscribed silver salver from the
American Friends. It was all a fitting tribute to an inspired teacher, a fact
further recognized in April 1991 by the honour of being selected for an
Achievement Award from the National Art Collections Fund, as Helen
Lowenthal had been in 1988.

The memory of Phelps Warren continued to be observed by the
American *alumni*. In December 1988 the fourth Memorial Event was to view
the William and Mary exhibition at the Cooper-Hewitt Museum and hold a
party there. Then in March 1989 John Wilton-Ely gave the Warren
Memorial Lecture at the Winter Reunion held at Sotheby's. It is good on
such occasions to shake away the reality in arranging such events. When
writing her first President's letter in October 1990 Elaine Evans Dee noted
that Attingham's main support for operating funds was through once-a-
year donations from the *alumni*. In the five years, 1985 to 1990,
undesignated annual gifts had increased only 15.3 per cent: in the same
period operating expenses had increased 48.5 per cent. She repeated the
statement that 'the Attingham by-laws describe *alumni* in good standing as
those who have made a contribution in the last five years'. Perhaps if you
are reading this you have, and generously. A contribution of $75 would
also secure the updated directory of Attingham *alumni*. Elaine was right to
stress this, as every President of the American Friends has done. In autumn
1984 it had been pointed out that in the thirty-three years Attingham had
been in operation, records indicated that 1,300 people had attended the
School and/or the Special Week. For that fiscal year only 181 *alumni* made
'undesignated' gifts, and 28 'designated', or about 16 per cent of all
graduates. A $25 dollar gift from each of 500 members would still raise

$12,500 for the year. Twenty-five dollars is about the price of one of the *New York Times* best-sellers, discounted by you know who.

Any knowledgeable person who examines any Attingham accounts can see everything geared towards scholarship provision. But of course the reorganization has to operate, hence the President's annual plea. The operating income of the American Friends to 31 October 1989, was $23,423 and for 1990 $28,539. Expenditure in these years totalled, respectively, $21,897 (a balance of $1,526), and for 1990 $23,719 (a balance of $4,830).

To give English figures is not comparable, as operating funds are taken from fees for the course, topped up by investment income. In 1989 the expenses of the Summer School were estimated at £60,250, of which £41,400 would come from fees and £12,000 from external contributions to scholarships. So the School was already forecast to end in deficit. The expenses of the Study Week were estimated at £21,300 and Fees at £22,000, a surplus of only £700. The actual expenditure resulted in a deficit overall for both courses of £746, so the controls seemed adequate. At the fiscal year end of 1989, 31 August, the Accumulated Fund stood at £199,347, or at, say, $1.70 to the pound, $338,889. By the same period in 1990, with a deficit on the operating fund of £7,936, investment income and interest allowed the Accumulated Fund to stand at £240,846, or (at the same dollar conversion point) $409,438. It is the sort of back-up which allows us to operate (when external scholarship funding is available) by absorbing a deficit, however unwise, in principle, that is. The loss of significant scholarship income would alter the situation at once, necessitating the drive towards good reserves to counter this.

A final word on finances based, as I write, on estimated expenditure and income for 1991. A deficit of £3,245 is expected, and at the conversion of $1.80 to the pound (in a period which was volatile) this amounts to $5,840. Fees for the Study Week were set to produce no profit, the deficit being again on the Summer School. An improvement in the dollar to pound ratio below 1.80 helps to produce a little more to offset any deficit, and, as I write, that is happening.

Work across the winter of 1990 and the spring of 1991 by Helena Hayward and Judith Goodison as Joint Directors was concentrated on the first venture by Attingham abroad — the 1991 'Study Week in Paris'. There was need to alter for a short time any publicity which implied that the 'Study Week on the Country House in Britain' was in Paris, so 'The Attingham Study Week in Paris' it became on the brochure. The graphic image was changed to a view of François Mansart's Château de Maisons-Lafitte. The aim of the Study Week was to increase understanding of the French contribution to English taste. Staying in two small hotels in the area of the Marais visits were planned to both private *hôtels* in the city and *châteaux* in the surrounding countryside.

In April Helena and Judith made the usual reconnaissance visit, checking each venue and excitedly, each menu! There was difficulty in persuading any restaurant to commit in advance to thirty-five or more diners at one time, their hired car was almost towed away, but a beaming *gendarme* fined them on the spot and gave an obscure receipt which on subsequent examination was for some two hundred francs less than he was paid. The announcement of the Study Week in Paris led to a heavy over-subscription and, despite the Gulf War, very few backed down. Considerable help on the spot was given by Mrs Jane Pumphrey Nes (1982, Special Week) and by Betty Starr Cummin (Att. '81).

Of the thirty participants from America twenty-one were *alumni* of the Summer School. The American Friends scholar was Betsy Lahikainen, the Head Upholstery Conservator at SPNEA a most delightful member of the 1990 Summer School. From England the textile historian Mary Schoeser (Att. '87) was awarded the Monument Trust Scholarship. Christopher Wilk (Att. '78), Curator of the Furniture and Woodwork Collection at the Victoria and Albert Museum and an Attingham Trust Council Member, made a welcome addition to the group. Due to writing this history against the pressures of other work I did not go — obviously I regretted not meeting so many friends, including those like Richard Milhender who joined for a day or two, through being already in Paris.

Before the Paris event took place Helena had been giving thought to the eventual succession in the Directorship of the Study Week. For 1991 she and Lady Goodison (Judith), her Tutor and Administrator, had agreed to act as Joint Directors. At a future point Helena will move to a Consultant Director's position (a post she already holds for the Summer School). Then it will be sensible for Judith to assume a greater responsibility. At this stage some of her administrative duties will be assumed by Caroline Rimell, an American married to an Englishman, Tony Rimell. Caroline Rimell became a Trust Council Member in

Caroline Rimell, Adminstrator and Tutor, The Attingham Study Week, 1991 to date.

May 1991. She too has long experience not only of teaching art history but of organizing foreign tours for the Furniture History Society. She is Chairman of its busy Activities Committee and also much involved as Secretary to the committee concerned with fund-raising activities in America for The Georgian Group.

It is the job of any chronicler to try to keep a record precise. In consequence I own to the unaccountable lapse of re-numbering the

Summer Schools in 1987. My non-Pythagorean mind had thought '1952 plus 40 = 1992', overlooking the fact that it is, to many keener minds, '1991'. Others assume we will look back over forty years completed in 1992. So, the Class of '87 was really the thirty-sixth (not, as the programme announced, the thirty-fifth). So, 1988 = 37, 1989 =38, 1990 = 39 and 1991 = 40. So, that straightened out, what had been going on in America. From 5 February to 2 March, Will Gwilliam and Kent Brinkley (Att. '89), an architect and landscape architect respectively with the Colonial Williamsburg Foundation, exhibited their pen and ink drawings of English country houses and landscapes they had made while attending the Summer School. Proceeds from the sales of originals and prints were donated to the American Friends. Elaine Dee and Sybil Bruel planned the Annual Meeting on 29 May at the Museum of the City of New York. After the business Molly Seiler, who had been guest curator of the Museum's current show on Tiffany, spoke on 'The Artistic New York of Louis Comfort Tiffany'. Molly works in the Prints and Drawings Department of the Cooper-Hewitt Museum. As Molly Moreno she had been on the Class of '87. Phelps Warren events are planned for the Autumn and a commemorative event at Old Westbury Gardens in May 1992. The Friends were founded in 1962, ten years after the Summer School, so you can take your pick again — the rhythm is certainly better, '1952 to 1992', '1962 to 1992'.

The 40th Class took place fom 5 to 23 July 1991. In the first week at West Dean, the American Friends' President, Elaine Evans Dee, was present and we had the pleasure of having her at the Trust's Dinner on 6 July. For once, no evening lecture on Day Two! Who would prefer that to lots of wine, food and heady conversation (and, subsequently, heady aches)? The various committees in New York and London had difficult tasks — in New York because there were more requests for scholarships than could be satisfied and, in London, thirty-four applications for the eight places not already allocated. The age-range from the American side had been widened with some six members aged between fifty and sixty-nine. It is, however, a truism that you are as young as you feel and the energy output was, as usual, in overdrive. The Helena Hayward scholarship was awarded, for the first time, and went to Stefanie Walker, a research assistant at the Metropolitan Museum's Department of European Sculpture and Decorative Arts.

The curatorial emphasis apparent in 1990 was redressed a little in 1991 by the presence of several architects, led by the distinguished Yale graduate, Jared Edwards, who has an equally distinguished nineteenth century collection. Jared was joined by his wife Clare, the Chairman of the Austin House of the Wadsworth Athenæum in Hartford. I had the pleasure of being at a party given by them for the Connecticut *alumni*, arranged in March 1990 by Dr Fred Nichols, a frequent attender of Attingham Study Weeks in recent years. Charlie Evers was an architect from the Tony Atkins office in Philadelphia, supported by *alumni* such as

Tony himself (Att. '77) and Simon Tickell (Att. '87). He came with the reputation, which he lived up to, of being 'a late night raconteur'. John Tackett had qualified in both architecture and landscape and had his own firm. Kevin Wolfe was a draftsman to a firm of New York architects and Rick Redlon was an architectural historian working for the Greater Portland Landmarks, with his own firm specializing in historic reservation. Jeffrey Bostetter represented the Williamsburg tradition in recent years of sending us good artists. He was joined by his colleague there, Gordon Chappell, the Director of Landscape and Facilities, who had qualified in landscape architecture at the University of Georgia. Finally, but not least, there was Hilary Irvin, the Senior Architectural Historian to the Vieux Carré Commission in New Orleans, maintaining this district of the eighteenth-century French city.

Let me turn to the curators. Alphabetically I will again be perverse and go to the other end of the alphabet. Megan Smith was a curatorial assistant in the Department of Prints and Drawings at the Cooper-Hewitt Museum. And certainly the staff or former staff of the Rosenbach Library in Philadelphia, including Kim Rorschach (Att. '80) and Leslie Morris (Att. '87) were able to tell Susan Shifrin what to expect. I have laughed with Carl Salmons of the Saugus Iron Works in the National Park Service in a crowded car down to Boston, driven at great speed by Bill Sargent (Att. '84), with Jeff Pond (Att. '85) the other irreverent passenger. We laughed again with the Class of '91.

Kenmore is a splended house at Frederiksburg with fine plasterwork of the 1770s. We had Betsy Panhorst from there in 1987. 1991 gave us Stacia Norman, who had gone, like so many *alumni*, through the Winterthur Masters' Programme. Jessica Nicoll and Deborah Kraak delighted with their textile knowledge, shared and improved in equal measure with our Course Tutor in Textiles, Annabel Westman. Jessica was Curator of Textiles at Old Sturbridge Village and Deborah, the Assistant Curator of Textiles and Costume at the Boston MFA. Jeff Munger (Att. '79) said Debby had a 'wonderful sense of humor' and she had, as well as a fine singing voice. Elizabeth Laurent, who with Marisa Morra and Peggy Fogelman had her birthday whilst on the course, was Curator of Cliveden in Pennsylvania, based in the 1760s on English patterns. She had likewise been on the Winterthur programme and I won't say who said there was in her a 'combination of beauty and openness'.

Apart from the professional involvement of Jessica Nicoll and Deborah Kraak in textiles, Marisa Morra had worked at Brunschwig's and at the Rhode Island School of Design, and was keen on the use of textiles in upholstery. Peggy Fogelman travelled from California where she is Assistant Curator at the Getty Museum's Department of Sculpture. She had the support of three *alumni*, Peter Fusco (Att. '82), Linda Strauss (Att. '85) and Gillian Wilson (Att. '67), and was fascinated by the richness of English neo-classical sculptures. Maureen Devine, Curator of the Edsel and

Eleanor Ford House in Detroit, was anxious to expand her architectural and social history knowledge, and Mary Butler, Curator of the Homewood Museum at Johns Hopkins University, wanted to see the context which had influenced that house of *c.* 1800. We were able to announce to a delighted class that Mary had been appointed Director of Homewood from 1 July. Finally, Jim Abbott, Assistant Curator at Historic Hudson Valley, and ever-perceptive questioner — I gathered from Joe Butler (Att. '67) a little of how the delightfully named 'Sleepy Hollow Restorations' fitted into that — was researching the French interior designs of Stephan Boudin, who had worked at Leeds Castle. Oh! that we had Jim in 1990 when we visited Leeds Castle, but due to a meeting of the Trustees there I'm not sure we ever encountered the Boudin interiors for Lady Baillie anyway!

Why not start a new paragraph with Gretchen Townsend, a PhD, candidate at Yale working with Pat Kane (Att. '90) on Massachusetts silversmiths? Her fellow Yale colleague, Kathleen O'Connor, was interested in the nineteenth-century rococo revival, Janet Stewart had a Yale involvement through being Assistant to the distinguished collector, Paul Mellon. Chris Miele was taking his PhD at New York University and had already spent over two years in England as a Kress Fellow. George Glazer from the New York antiques firm of W. Graham Arader III had been previously on Study Weeks and the Winter Week. His passionate interest in furniture was shared by Mary Bergquist, a practising craftsman turning towards a career in historic and preservation architecture. The active educationalists included Kay Allaire, the Acting Coordinator of the Cooper-Hewitt Masters' Programme since Henry Joyce (Att. '76) had left for the Newport City Preservation Society. Dr Ann Ashmead was a very distinguished Research Associate at the University of Pennsylvania, whilst Dr Taube Greenspan masterminds the Royal Oak Foundation's active programme. Lamar Lentz perhaps had the most unusual job, as Curator of the International Festival Institute in Texas with its historic chapel, carriage collection and large Concert Hall. Finally, Dr Davy McCall, an outstanding former financier at the World Bank and Chairman of the Department of Economics at Washington College, had turned his hand to house preservation — he was on his third, having, since his student days, been interested in architecture and the decorative arts.

I have worked on the 1991 list in some detail, not because it was the 40th Class but to show the continuance of high standards. Added to the Americans were the fourteen Europeans. From the former East Germany we welcomed Dr Burkhardt Göres, the Director of the Museum of Applied Arts in Berlin at Schloss Köpenick. He was an authority on David Roentgen's furniture. Jana Kotalikova came from the Charles University in Prague where she was specializing in nineteenth-century Czech art, but needing the wider context Attingham gives. Her husband Jiri had come to Attingham in 1979. We were also happy, as in so many earlier years, to have someone from the Museum of Applied Arts in Budapest, Agnes

Prékopa, who specialized in Baroque applied arts, particularly silver-smithing and enamelling. More textile specialization was in the hands of Helen Smith, working on projects for Warner Fabrics, Jacqueline Herald lecturing at the textile Conservation Centre at Hampton Court Palace, and Catherine Colcutt, formerly Assistant Curator of Costume and Textiles at the Museum of London, but now Keeper of Collections at the Bourne-mouth Museums.

English Heritage was represented by two candidates rather than the usual one, Steven Brindle and Gareth Hughes. Steven Brindle was an architectural historian with the London Division who had read history at Oxford and done his doctorate on 'Medieval Architecture in Spain'. Gareth Hughes had succeeded Ruth Guilding (Att. '88) as an Assistant Curator with day-to-day responsibility for Osborne House and Walmer Castle. The Victoria and Albert Museum appointed Clare Browne, a Curatorial Assistant in the Textiles and Dress Collection, who had worked with Natalie Rothstein on the important 'Flowered Silks' exhibition. Finally, in the places allotted to such major organizations, the National Trust scholar was Simon Murray, the Historic Buildings Representative for the East Midlands Region. Simon, who had catalogued the ceramics at Upton House, was also invaluable on visits to houses in his region such as Hardwick, Kedleston, Calke and Belton.

Alastair Clarke, who was working in the furniture department at Christie's, had been keen to expand his knowledge of the fine and decorative arts. The inter-relationship of design and form can be studied well enough on any Attingham class. The administration of a house we can perhaps help less with, except to show a myriad examples. Maggie McKean was House Manager at Tatton Park but in concentrating on financial and administrative management she had felt it all too easy to lose sight of the broader historical and aesthetic foundations of the country house.

The Keeper of Art Galleries in the National Museums and Galleries on Merseyside, Julian Treuherz (Att. '84) had had three applications from his staff to try for Attingham. He had supported the Assistant Curator of Fine Art, Joseph Sharples, (who had won the 1984 Essay Medal of the Society of Architectural Historians), because he was involved in a project to restore period redecorations and colour schemes at Sudley, a Victorian house in Liverpool. Finally, a 'West European' place was given to Pieter Jongbloed from Amsterdam, the General Manager of the Teylers Museum in Haarlem, an eighteenth-century building with nineteenth-century addi-tions, and one of the oldest museums in The Netherlands.

The programme had its usual heady mix of instruction combined with unashamed pleasure. To hear, as we did, Alec Cobbe playing his fine collection of musical instruments at Hatchlands was an occasion heard by many tearful members. Chopin and Mozart have rarely sounded so fine. The trio 'Grynwode' delighted with Elizabethan music at Hardwick, and who better than David Bostwick, master of the 'pause' in description, to

Sir George Trevelyan, talking to the Class of 1991 — 'Forty Years On', at
The Old Rectory, Quenington, home of David and Lucy Abel-Smith.
Lucy is President of The Attingham Society.

evoke the architectural eccentricities of Bolsover Castle? We had an
awe-inspiring time in the Welbeck plate room, gazed in wonder at
Chatsworth's Huguenot silver and listened in rapt silence to the experiences of our Czech, Hungarian and 'East' German members. Jana's quiet
reply to one member 'but you were so far away' rendered all comment
superfluous. Finally the moated mirage of Madresfield, swans on the
water, sun on upturned picnic faces: riches within amid the bright colour of
Morris fabrics and stained glass. And on, suitably accoutred, to Hanbury
Hall for a final party. A party so distinguished by the quality of the singing
voices and Maggie McKean's violin accompaniment. Even the sing-song
satire of George Glazer's words seemed more appropriate beneath

Thornhill's 1711 ceiling paintings, recording the impeachment of Henry Sacheverell for seditious preaching.

At breakfast on the final morning, 23 July, by popular acclaim, that 'well-known Shakespearean actor, Mr Steven Brindle' recited his brilliant seven-page satire in the style of Alexander Pope, entitled, 'Epistle to Doctor Beard'. And then away for a final hour to Pershore Abbey and the long-drawn sadness of many partings, waving hands at a diminishing pattern of the blue and white coach, London bound. There was so much to recall in each mind not least the heart-felt message from our joint-Founder, Sir George Trevelyan, as he addressed the school at Quenington, and referred to in Steven's poem, of which I only have space for the final lines.*

> Now final days, and desperate grew the quest
> Remoter still we motor, south and west
> And land could hold the key, they understand
> Land made the house, the truth lies in the land.
> And ANNETTE tells of Art-and Crafty lore
> SIR GEORGE relates of ATTINGHAMS of yore
> In RODMARTON and MADRESFIELD at last
> Wee see the unity of land and past
> And present, holistic whole of work and life
> Where master, servant, craftsman, husband, wife
> Conjoin'd themselves with 'Spirit of the Place'
> No one man's work, one generation's space
> But many hands and many years combined,
> Collective work, communal toil. We find
> The mason equal to the Architect
> The humblest gardener sharing BROWN's respect,
> The Butler, Footman, Housemaid, Chaplain, Groom
> All equal with their Lord, all made the room.
> All made the house, the garden, England, all,
> And for their labours place us in their thrall;
> TREVELYAN shows the History of the land
> Is written in these stones, we understand
> Their happy witness of another day
> And equal happiness find upon the way
> And ATTINGHAM salute, with mighty cheers
> And wishes for another FORTY YEARS.

It is not the historian's job, at least here, to speculate on Attingham's future. I feel it is more or less secure, although there is always a need for vigilance over finance and over the correct succession of qualified staff — 'qualified' as much in humanity and compassion as in *academe*. For me 'Attingham' should be concerned always about the development of friendships and happiness, in the pursuit of useful knowledge. But let the

---

* The full text is given in The Attingham Society's 'Occasional Newsletter', No. 17, September 1991.

last words, on a similar theme, be those of Helen Lowenthal, when speaking to the Class of '87 at West Dean College:

> We will keep it so that it is always a party, it is always genial, it is always companionable – that you can have the lecturers, not just standing on a platform, but in amongst you, staying on for meals, travelling with you and so forth. This is one of our principles, that we would try and make everyone happy, and I don't really think there is much more that I can say . . .

I would but echo this, with Ben Jonson's words, exemplified so often by all that is 'Attingham':

> *True happiness*
> *Consists not in the multitude of friends,*
> *But in the worth and choice*

It is here with George and Helen: it is here with all of you, for this is *your* story . . .

George Trevelyan and Helen Lowenthal at Wallington,
1985.
Photograph: Nancy Hirst

APPENDIX
THE ATTINGHAM SUMMER SCHOOL
ALUMNI, 1952 to 1991

Whenever possible, a member's affiliation or address is given *at the time of Summer School attendance*. These details are taken from the annual lists. However, there is not a complete set of these available, and attendance or non-attendance after their issue renders immediate mistakes. Some of these have been eliminated by use of the invaluable 1984 *Alumni Directory*, and the 1991 computerized list (New York). Please draw attention to these shortcomings. *Third, Special and Study Week attendance is not listed.*

Nancy Aakre
Asst Editor, Publications
Minneapolis Institute of Arts
1979

James Archer Abbott
Asst Curator
Historic Hudson Valley
1991

Helen Abell
Regent, Locust Grove
Louisville, KY
1968

Betsy Ache
Docent, Bayou Bend
Collection
Houston, TX
1983

Michael Adams
President 'Progress
through Preservation';
Part-time, Cleveland
Museum of Art, OH
1985

Mrs S. Adams
Harpenden, Herts.
1952

Wendy Adler (Jordan)
Assoc Editor,
Historic Preservation,
National Trust for
Historic Preservation
Washington, DC
1977

Tracy Albainy
Assistant to the Director,
Cooper-Hewitt Museum,
New York
1990

Miss Zafie Alber
National Museum
Cracow, Poland
1977

Ellenor Alcorn
Curatorial Assistant
European Decorative Arts
Museum of Fine Arts, Boston
1983

Mrs J. McF. Alexander
Dept of Art
Memphis State Univ.
1966

Maryjean Alexander
Decorator; Designer
New York
1977

Kathleen Allaire
Coordinator, Master of Art
Programme, Cooper-Hewitt
Museum,
New York
1991

Alice Wiley Allen
1958

Christopher Allen
Hunterian Art Gallery
Univ. of Glasgow
1977

Gloria Allen
Associate Curator
D.A.R. Museum
Washington DC
1983

Mary Link Allen
Asst Director,
Gunston Hall
Lorton, VA
1986

Phyllis Allen
Chairman, Dept of
Interior Environment
Brigham Young Univ., Utah
1975

Mrs Wendell D. Allen
1958

Mary Allis
Fairfield, Conn.
1954

Dr Allmayer-Beck
Vienna
1964

Miss M. Allthorpe-Guyton
Castle Museum, Norwich
1974

Hope Alswang (Joyce)
Dept of Decorative Arts
The Brooklyn Museum
1976

Henry Alvarez
Manager, New York
Graphic Society
1967

Mrs M. Alvarez
1958

Louise Todd Ambler
Curator, Harvard Univ.
Portrait Collection
Fogg Art Museum
1976

Leonard Amico
Asst to the Director
Krannert Art Museum
Univ. of Illinois
1980

Copley Amory
1961

Jørgen Andersen
Radio and Education
Copenhagen
1953

Charles Anderson
Prof. American Lit.,
John Hopkins Univ., MD.
1964

Mrs C. Anderson
1964

Jan Anderson
Municipal Art Society of
New York, Brooklyn, NY
1978

Jennie Tate Anderson
1962

Lee Anderson
Art Teacher, Collector
New York
1968

Mary P. Anderson
1964

Patricia Anderson
Curatorial Asst
Smith College Museum of Art
Northampton, MA
1982

Susan Anderson
Curatorial Asst
Philadelphia Museum of Art
1977

Jan Anderssen
Riksantilsvariatet
Oslo, Norway
1968

George Andreve
Graduate Student
(Architecture)
Univ. of Virginia
1972

Gail Andrews
Curator of Decorative Arts
Birmingham Museum of Art
Birmingham, AL
1981

Ronald Andrews
Historic Preservation
Consultant
City of Hagerstown, MD
1976

Stephenson Andrews
Curator of Collections
Assoc. for Preservation of
Virginia Antiquities
1985

Miss L. M. Antonsen
Copenhagen Univ.,
Denmark
1952

Thomas Appelquist
Senior Designer,
Philadelphia
1987

Judith Applegate
Assistant Curator
European Decorative Arts
Boston Museum of Fine Arts
1977

Pamela K. Armour
Museum and College Trustee
Chicago, IL
1983

Andrew Arrol
Architect,
Shrewsbury
1978

Ann Ashmead
Research Associate
Univ. of Pennsylvania
1991

Norman Askins
Graduate Student
(Architecture)
Univ. of Virginia
1967

Robyn Asleson
Graduate Student
(Art History), Yale Univ.
1987

Anthony J. Atkin
Architect
Utah and Philadelphia
1977

John C. Austin
Colonial Williamsburg
Department of Collections
1958

Barbara Bacot
Grants Administrator
Louisiana State
Hist. Preservation Office
1982

Henry Parrott Bacot
Assistant to Curator
Anglo-American Art
Museum
Louisiana State Museum
1966

Joseph A. Baird
Univ. of California at Davis
1959

Carol Baker
Senior Guide
H. F. Du Pont Museum
Winterthur, DE
1988

Mrs J. H. Baker
New York
1956

Richard Brown Baker
New York
1964

Mrs T. W. Balch
Baltimore, MD
1956

Mrs W. S. Baldinger
Museum of Art
Univ. of Oregon
1964

Jane Ball
Administrator
Edmonston-Alston House
Historic Charleston Fdn.
1984

Mrs F. S. Ballard
Fairmount Park Comm.
Philadelphia
1964

Anneke Bambery
Keeper, Bramall Hall
Stockport
1989

Stephen Banigan
Architect, Washington DC
1983

Andrew Barber
Asst Hist. Bldgs Rep.
The National Trust
(E. Midlands Region)
1988

Pamela Pierrepont Bardo
Curator of Collections
New Orleans Museum of Art
1974

Deborah Barker
Asst Instructor
Dept of Art History
Univ. of Kansas
1979

Dr Barkoczi
Fine Arts Museum
Budapest, Hungary
1981

Isabel Barmore
Park Avenue, NY
1955

Jairus Barnes
Western Reserve Historical
Society, Cleveland, OH
1982

Lavonia Barnes
Preservationist
Waco, TX
1972

David Barquist
Asst Curator
Yale Univ. Art Gallery
1986

Miss M. J. Barry
Interior Designer,
New York
1964

Judith Barter
Curatorial Intern
St Louis Art Museum
1975

Wilmot Bartle
Author
Caldwell, N.J.
1987

Jean Bartlett
Preservationist
Bronxville, N.Y.
1975

Louisa Bartlett
Asst to Curator
American Art
Philadelphia Museum of Art
1975

Richard Bartlett
Dept of Textiles
Victoria & Albert Museum
London
1974

P. Russell Bastedo
Graduate Student
Univ. of Delaware
1969

Dr Ferenc Batári
Keeper of Furniture
Decorative Arts Museum
Budapest, Hungary
1986

Barbara Batson
Asst Director for Collections
The Valentine Museum
Richmond, VA
1989

Blanche Batson (Desmond)
Artist
1963

Whaley Batson
Guide, MESDA
Winston-Salem, N.C.
1982

Prof. James Baughman
Ohio State Univ.,
Columbus
1965

Ronald Bauman
Landscape Architect
Wilmington, DE
1972

Atherton Bean
Trustee, Institute of Arts
Minneapolis
1970

Mrs A. Bean
1970

David Beevers
Assistant Curator
Tredegar House
Newport, S. Wales
1978

Christopher Beharrell
The National Trust, London
1979

Frederick Belden
Landscape Architect,
Colonial
Williamsburg, VA
1971

G. C. Belden
President, Wilmington
Board of Education, DE
1964

Louise Belden
Curatorial Asst
H. F. Du Pont Museum
Winterthur, DE
1964

Miss H. R. Belknap
H. F. Du Pont Museum
Winterthur, DE
1965

Michael Bellamy
Inspector of Ancient
Monuments, Historic
Buildings Commission
London
1984

Isabel H. Benham
Financial Researcher
New York
1954

Reed Benhamou
Assoc. Prof.,
Interior Design
Indiana Univ.
1986

Charles S. P. Bergen
Master's Degree Student
Yale School of Architecture
1989

Mary Bergquist
Preservation Carpentry
Student,
Cornish, N.H.
1991

Roger Berkowitz
Assistant Curator
Decorative Arts
The Toledo Museum of Art
Toledo, OH
1977

Sarah Bevan (Meschutt)
Keeper of Edged Weapons
The Tower Armouries
London
1988

James Biddle
Metropolitan Museum
New York
1958

Deborah Binder
Dept of Decorative Arts
St. Louis Art Museum, MD
1984

Joan Binder
Docent, Mellon Centre
for British Art,
New Haven, CT
1990

Thérèse Bitter
Staff Architect
Scalamandre Silks, Inc.
New York
1988

Roderic Blackburn
Albany Inst. of History & Art
Albany, N.Y.
1976

Samuel Blaisdell
Parke-Bernet Galleries
New York
1965

Robbie Blakemore
Interior Design Historian
Univ. of Tennessee
1983

Dr W. Blauensteiner
Vienna, Austria
1957

Mrs T. R. C. Blofeld
Hoveton, Norfolk
1959

Judith Winslow Blood
Craft Programme Researcher
Colonial Williamsburg, VA
1974

Peter Blume
Museum Curator
Allentown, PA
1976

Alf Boe
Chief Curator, Kunstindustri
Museum, Oslo, Norway
1965

Paula Boghosian
Principal, Historic
Environment Consultants
Sacramento, CA
1980

Catherine Bohlen
Teacher
(Hist. & Hist. of Art)
1961

Judith Bolingbroke (Howard)
Ceramics Dept
Victoria & Albert Museum
London
1971

Stephen Bonitatibus
Architect
Philadelphia, PA
1983

Edwin T. P. Boone
Philadelphia, PA
1961

Susan Borchardt
Curator, Gunston Hall
Lorton, VA
1990

Prof. Paul Bortnovici
Bucharest, Rumania
1976

Jeffrey Bostetter
Draftsman
Colonial Williamsburg, VA
1991

David Bostwick
Keeper, Social and
Labour History
Sheffield City Museums
1986

Mary Boswell
Registrar, Assoc. for
Preservation of Virginia
Antiquities
1976

Thomas Boswell
Restoration Supervisor
Assoc. for Preservation of
Virginia Antiquities
1976

Ruth Bottomley
Bethnal Green Museum
of Childhood (V&A)
London
1989

Jack Boucher
Chief of Historic Sites
State of New Jersey
1969

Peter Boughton
Keeper of Art
Grosvenor Museum
Chester
1990

Susan Bourne
Assistant Curator
Towneley Hall Art Gallery
Burnley, Lancs
1985

René Boux
University Teacher
Bridgeport, CT
1962

Robert Bowen
Graduate Student (Art Hist)
Univ. of Texas
1974

Mr. A. Bower
London
1952

Angela Bowlin
Metropolitan Museum
New York
1963

Sterling Boyd
Instructor, Art History
Washington & Lee College,
VA
1967

Christine Boydell
Lecturer, History of Design
Lancashire Polytechnic
1990

G. U. Boyles
Fashion Inst. of Technology
New York
1966

Hilary Bracegirdle
Ceramic Dept, Victoria &
Albert Museum, London
1984

Derek Bradford
Assoc. Professor
Rhode Is., School of Design
1979

Lucille Brady
Professional Gilder
Annapolis, MD
1986

Barbara Brand
Administrator
Hammond-Harwood House
Annapolis, MD
1979

Rosemary Brandau
Mgr., Historic Area
Food Prgs.
Colonial Williamsburg, VA
1989

Beverly Brandt
Asst Professor, Art & Design
Iowa State Univ.
1987

W. Scott Braznell
Curator, American Silver
Museum, Hamden, CT
1990

Charissa Bremer-David
Asst Curator
J. Paul Getty Museum, CA
1989

The Viscountess Bridgman
Leigh Manor, Salop.
1957

Anna Brightman
Decorator; Designer
Austin, TX
1965

Steven Brindle
Architectural Historian
English Heritage
1991

Mark Kent Brinkley
Landscape Architect
Colonial Williamsburg, VA
1989

Heriberto J. Brito
Architectural Historian
National Register of
Historic Places
1979

Billie Britz
Restoration Architect,
Scarsdale, New York
1972

Bowden Broadwater
Architecture Critic, *Newsday*,
New York
1966

Harold J. Bromm
Graduate Student
Pratt Institute, New York
1971

Bradley Brooks
Curator, Willis Moody House
Galveston, TX
1989

Mary Brooks
Asst Keeper of Textiles
(Conservation) The Castle
Museum, York
1989

Barbara Brown (Lee)
Curator of Art Education
Milwaukee Art Centre
1973

Bennie Brown
Librarian and Curator of
Collections
Gunston Hall, VA
1982

C. Dudley Brown
Preservationist
Washington, DC
1978

Charlotte Brown
Assistant Prof. (Architecture)
Department of Art
Duke University
1978

Hillary Brown
Project Architect in
private practice
New York
1980

Michael K. Brown
Curatorial Asst
Dept of American Decorative
Arts
Boston Museum of Fine Arts
1979

Peter Brown
Director, Fairfax House
York
1985

Miss P. Y. Brown
Architect
Connecticut
1953

Robert Brown
New York
1963

Willard E. Brown
Willard E. Brown Investments
Waco, TX
1982

Clare Browne
Section of Textiles
Victoria & Albert Museum
London
1991

Charles Brownell
Ph.D. Candidate
(Art Hist.)
Columbia Univ.
1968

Ann Brubaker
Director of Education
Nelson Gallery of Art
Kansas City, MO
1980

William Bruning
Attorney, Kansas City
1981

Paul Buchanan
Director of Architectural
Research, Colonial
Williamsburg, VA
1969

Frances Buckland
Assistant
The Wallace Collection
London
1976

J. R. Buckler
Staff Horticulturist
Smithsonian Institution
1975

Barbara Buckley
Mellon Fellow in Painting
Cleveland Museum
1987

Denis Budke
Ph.D. Candidate
Univ. of Kansas
1969

James Buie
Architect, Austin, TX
1969

Elizabeth Bullock
Asst Dean
College of Charleston, S.C.
1974

James Bullock
Arch. Historian, Denver, CO.
1972

Mrs Hannah Burdock
Alfred Univ., N.Y.
1955

James H. Burke
Rare book dealer
New York
1963

Jean Burks
Research Asst
Decorative Arts
Cooper-Hewitt Museum
New York
1984

Scott F. Burrell
Estate Mgr., Virginia House
Mechanicsville, VA
1990

Anthony Burton
Victoria & Albert Museum
London
1968

Robert Bush
Architect
Atlanta, GA
1967

Wrenda Bush (Crain)
Graduate Student
Auburn, AL
1970

Jeanne Butler (Hodges)
Administrator
A.I.A. Foundation;
Curator, The Octagon
Washington, DC
1974

Joseph T. Butler
Curator
Sleepy Hollow Restorations
Tarrytown, NY
1967

Mary Butler
Director
Homewood Museum
Baltimore, MD
1991

William Butler
Student Fellowship
Winterthur Museum
Programme
1981

Richard Button
President
Richmondtown Restoration
Staten Island, New York
1971

Linda Cabe
Yale Graduate; Intern at
Mellon Centre for British Art
1982

Helen Cady
Assoc. Prof. Housing &
Design, Cornell Univ.
1969

Paul Caffrey
Curator, Castletown House
Ireland
1990

Fausto Calderai
Writer on Italian Furniture
Florence, Italy
1984

Carol Callahan
Instructor
Univ. of Colorado at Denver
1985

Mrs Maja Cambj
Art Historian
Split, Yugoslavia
1976

Alan L. Campbell
Associate Director
Private cultural foundation
New York
1973

Cathryn Campbell
Asst Professor
Auburn Univ., AL
1989

Louisa Dresser Campbell
1957

Tom Campbell
Textile Researcher
London
1988

Desley Campbell-Stuart
Architect
Queensland, Australia
1990

Jay E. Cantor
Researcher in Art and
Architecture
New York
1971

Alice Carkin
Univ. of California at
Berkeley
1954

Nancy Carlisle
Ph.D. Candidate
Univ. of Pennsylvania
1984

M. Allison Carll
Interior Design Educator
Univ. of Illinois
1985

Charles & Mary Grace Carpenter
Authors
New Canaan, CT
1986

John Carpenter
Art History Major
Brown Univ., R.I.
1983

Caroline Carr (Whitworth)
Asst Keeper. Dec. Arts
Bolling Hall
Bradford Museums
1986

Joseph Carr
Assistant Usher
The White House
Washington, DC
1981

Annette Carruthers
Free-lance researcher
Edinburgh
1990

Barbara Carson
Radcliffe Inst. Cataloguer
Harvard Univ. Coll. of Hist.
Scientific Instruments
1968

Cary Carson
Teaching Fellow
Ph.D. Candidate
Harvard Univ.
1968

Mrs J. Carson
Bryn Mawr, Penn
1954

Mary Frances Carter
Chm. Int. Design Dept
School of Architecture
Auburn Univ. AL.
1966

Rand Carter
Chairman, Dept of Art
Hamilton College
Clinton, NY
1975

Henry Cauthen
Exec. Director
Preservation Soc. of
Charleston, S.C.
1976

Adolpho Cavallo
Museum of Fine Arts
Boston
1959

Edward Lee Cave
Senior Vice-President
Operations, Sotheby's
New York
1974

Frederick Cawley
Assistant Director
Preservation League
New York State
1977

Elizabeth Chamberlin
Guide, H. F. Du Pont
Museum, Winterthur, DE
1971

Jeannie Chapel (Hobhouse)
Royal Holloway College
Univ. of London
1977

Lucinda Chapman
Museum Consultant
New York State Educ. Dept
1973

Martin Chapman
Dept of Prints & Drawings
Victoria & Albert Museum
London
1979

Edward Chappell
Dir. of Architectural Research
Colonial Williamsburg, VA
1986

Gordon Chappell
Director, Landscape &
Facilities
Colonial Williamsburg, VA
1991

Stuart Chase
Director
Raynham Hall Museum
Oyster Bay, N.Y.
1988

Leon Chatelain
Architect, Waterford, VA
1981

Mrs H. B. Chatfield
Cincinnati, OH
1959

Frank Cheney
Architect, Philadelphia, PA
1986

John Alan Cherol
Preservation Society
Newport County
Newport, R.I.
1979

John Chesshyre
Hist. Bldgs. Rep.
The National Trust
(E. Midlands Region)
1987

Timothy Chester
Curator of Decorative Arts
Louisiana State Museum
1982

Charles Chevalier
College Professor
Mt. Clemens, MI
1967

Eloise Mackie Childs
Interior Designer
Baltimore, MD
1975

Marie Chiles
Historic Waco
Foundation, TX
1991

Miss L. H. Chisholm
1958

Virginia Chisholm
1962

Hermine Chivian
Research Cataloguer
Metropolitan Museum
New York
1967

Deborah Chotner
Curatorial Assistant
Smith College Museum of Art
1976

Marian Christie
Chairman of Decatur
Washington, DC
1958

Dorian Church
Asst Keeper, Decorative Arts
Bolling Hall, Bradford
1983

Margaret Civetta
Associate
Rosenberg & Stiebel, Inc.
New York
1989

Charles Clapper
Landscape Architect
U.S. National Park Service
Colorado
1974

Carolyn Clark
Interior Designer
Atlanta, GA
1990

Deborah Clark
Asst Keeper, Decorative Arts
Manchester City Art Gallery
1982

Mark A. Clark
Curator of Decorative Arts
The Dayton Art Institute, OH
1970

Alistair Clarke
Dept of Furniture
Christie's,
London
1991

Constance Clement
Deputy Director
British Art Centre, Yale Univ.
New Haven, CT
1990

Lisa Clinton (Lady White)
Dept of Furniture &
Woodwork
Victoria & Albert Museum
London
1978

Mrs G. B. Coale
New York
1959

Olivia Coan
Collector,
Minneapolis
1956

Sarah Coffin (Klebinov)
Student (Art History)
Yale Univ.
1972

Kimble A. Cohn
Architect
St Louis, MO
1977

Elizabeth Ann Coleman
Apprentice Trainee
Newark Museum, N.J.
1964

Catherine Colcutt
Keeper of Collections
Bournemouth Museums
Service
1991

Susie Collingridge (Gore)
Asst Hist. Bldgs. Rep.
The National Trust
Cornwall
1981

Caroline Colt
Rochester, New York
1963

James Connelly
Dept of Art History
Univ. of Kansas
1965

Suzanne Conway
Asst Prof. Art History
Chestnut Hall College
Philadelphia
1986

Peter Whigman Cook
Chief Curator
Bennington and Tepping
Tavern Museums
Bennington, VT
1975

Edward S. Cooke
Winterthur,
Masters' Programme
1979

Mrs Cole Coolidge
Wilmington, DE
1963

Shirley Cooper
Berkeley, CA
1958

Wendy Cooper
Mellon Research Fellow
The Brooklyn Museum
1972

Patricia Corbett
Graduate Student
Univ. of Maryland
1972

Mrs J. K. Corbin
New Haven
Preservation Trust
1966

Rosemary Corroon
Assistant Decorative
Arts Dept, Cooper-Hewitt
Museum,
New York
1985

Christina Corsiglia
Curatorial Asst
Boston Museum of Fine Arts
1980

Giorgiana Corsini
Curator of the Corsini Coll.
Florence;
Vice-Presdt. Hist.
Houses Assoc. of Tuscany
1988

Simon Cottle
Deputy Keeper
Glasgow Museums &
Art Galleries
1988

Belinda Cousens
Asst Hist. Bldgs Rep.
National Trust
Attingham Park
1981

Howard Coutts
Research Fellow
Royal Museum of Scotland
1988

Prof. Donald Covington
Department of Art
California State Univ.
San Diego, CA
1973

Mildred Cowan
Preservationist
Nashville, TN
1973

Ellen Coxe
Architectural Historian
Marian Hist. Trust
1979

Judy Coyne (Becker)
Volunteer Asst
American Wing
Metropolitan Museum
New York
1978

John Craib-Cox
Univ. Student
St Louis, MO
1965

Robert Craig
Graduate Student
(Architecture)
Cornell Univ.
1971

Miss E. Crane/Miss K. Crane
1961

Morna Crawford
Senior Lecturer
Boston Museum of Fine Arts
1975

Greer Crawley
Bolling Hall Museum
Bradford,
Yorks.
1979

Richard Crisson
Historical Architect
N. Atlantic Centre
U.S. National Parks Service
1980

Susan Crosier
Director,
Oneida Hist. Soc.
1969

Marjorie Cross
Wilmington, DE
1961

Frederick Crowell
Architectural Historian
New York
1977

Mrs B. Cubbedge
Savannah, GA
1963

Elizabeth Starr Cummin
Asst to Curator
Univ. of Penn. S.E. Asia
Museum
1981

Abbott Lowell Cummings
Metropolitan Museum
New York
1953

Kathleen Cummings
Chicago, IL
1979

P. E. Curnow
Ministry of Works, London
1956

David Curry
Asst to the Director
Univ. of Kansas
Museum of Art
1975

Dewey Curtis
Curator, Pennsbury Manor
Morrisville, PA
1968

Philip Curtis
Curator,
Decorative Arts
The Newark Museum, N.J.
1974

John Cushion
Victoria & Albert Museum
London
1961

Herbert Cutler
Superintendent,
Senate House
Kingston, N.Y.
1973

Countess Loredano Da Schio
Palladian Institute
Vicenza, Italy
1960

William J. Dane
Newark Public Library
Art & Music Dept
Newark, N.J.
1967

David Dangremond
Graduate Fellow
H. F. Du Pont Museum
Winterthur, DE
1976

B. Danzinger
Columbia School of
Architecture Student
1965

Michael Darby
Victoria & Albert Museum
London
1968

Wendy Darby
Master's Candidate
(Hist. Preservation)
Columbia Univ.
1986

Alan Darr
Curator of Decorative Arts
Detroit Institute of Arts
Detroit, MI
1982

Carl Dauterman
Associate Curator
Decorative Arts
Metropolitan Museum
New York
1957

Mrs C. Dauterman
1957

Miss G. D. Dauterman
Student, Connecticut College
New London
1965

Charity Davidson
Maryland Historical Trust
Annapolis, MD
1982

Barbara Ann Davies
Teacher
1958

Louise Davies
Woodside, CA
1960

Karen Davis
National Museum Act Fellow
Yale Univ. Art Gallery
1982

Julia Davis
Research Associate
(Garden History)
Colonial Williamsburg, VA
1973

Marylou Davis
Furniture Restorer
Southbridge, MA
1983

Nancy K. Davis (Brian)
Dept of Interior Design
Southern Illinois Univ.
1978

Peter Day
Assistant Keeper of
Collections, Chatsworth
1974

Vera Day
Denver, CO
1954

Robert Dean
Student,
New York School of
Interior Design
1969

John M. DeHaas
Design and History Dept,
Montana State Univ.
1971

Vonny de Mist
Dept of Coins and Medals
Rijksmuseum,
Amsterdam

Mrs J. L. R. De Morrini
Pine Manor Junior College
Wellesley, Mass.
1952

N. J. T. de Sousa
Porto, Portugal
1966

Dan Deibler
Florida Division of Archives
Historic Sites specialist
1981

Miss L. F. Delehanty
Dept of History of Art
Univ. of Pennsylvania
1965

Eleanor P. Delorme
Lecturer,
Museum of Fine Arts,
Boston
1971

Faith Dennis
Dept of Renaissance and
Modern Art,
Metropolitan Museum,
New York
1957

Mrs F. L. Dennis
Washington DC
1963

Miss E. Densmore
Worcester Art Museum
Mass.
1964

Walter Densmore
Mount Vernon, VA
1954

Susan Denyer
Hist. Bldgs. Representative
The National Trust
(Lake District)
1982

John Desmond
Architect,
Hammond, LA
1963

Peter Deveikis
Student,
Marlboro College, Mass.
1971

Maureen Devine
Curator,
E & E Ford House
Detroit, MI
1991

Richard Dexter
Decorator; Designer
New York
1959

Professor Desa Diana
Town Museum
Split, Yugoslavia
1969

Edward Diestelkamp
Graduate, Univ. of
S. California;
Postgraduate Student
Univ. of London
1978

Ulysses Dietz
Curator, Decorative Arts
The Newark Museum
Newark, N.J.
1983

Gaylord Dillingham
Dillingham & Co.
Antique Dealers
San Francisco, CA
1981

J. E. Dillon
US National Park Service
Washington, DC
1975

Robert Dimit
Director
Stan Hywet Hall
Akron, OH
1971

Stephanie Dinkins
Writer and photographer
New York
1967

Elaine Dodge
Nova Scotia, Canada
1961

Professor Philip Dole
School of Architecture
University of Oregon
Eugene, OR
1981

Joan Dolmetsch
Curator of Maps and Prints
Colonial Williamsburg, VA
1973

Robert F. Domergue
Antiques dealer
San Francisco, CA
1987

Miss F. V. Doneghy
Cataloguer,
Univ. Library
Univ. of Minnesota
1966

William Doneghy
Architect
Washington, DC
1966

Ernest Donnelly
Architectural illustrator
1958

Laura Donnelly
Graduate Student
George Washington Univ.
1977

Marian Donnelly
Dept of Art History
Univ. of Oregon
Eugene, OR
1972

Catherine-Mary Donovan
Boston, Mass
1952

Charles Dorman
Documentary designer
US National Park Service
1967

Samuel J. Dornsife
Director,
Lycoming Hist. Soc.
Williamsport, PA
1966

Diana Dorrance
1977

Ed. Polk Douglas
Univ. of Virginia
Graduate Programme
1976

Murray Douglas
Vice-President,
Brunschwig & Fils
New York
1979

William Lake Douglas
Asst Prof. School of
Architecture
Univ. of Arkansas
1981

Robin Dowden
Graduate Student and
Teaching Assistant
Univ. of California at Davis
1980

Frances Downing
Instructor,
Univ. of Oregon
1976

Mrs Brent Drane
Chapel Hill, NC
1955

Louisa Dresser
Worcester Museum,
Mass.
1957

Robert Drew
Instructor,
New York School
of Interior Design
1971

Lois Drewer
Asst Professor
Herbert & William Smith
College, Geneva
New York
1978

Diana Dripps
President,
Women's Committee
Philadelphia Museum of Art
1977

John H. Dryfhout
Museum Curator
US National Park Service
Saint-Gaudens National
Historic Site
1971

Alan DuBois
Assistant Director
Museum of Fine Arts
St Petersburg, FL
1984

Prof. Alastair Duckworth
Dept of English
Univ. of Florida
1985

Philip Duckworth
Furniture Dept
Phillips, London
1984

Philip Dunbar
Student,
Rutland, Mass.
1953

Eleanor Duncan
Assistant Curator
Colonial Williamsburg, VA
1957

Diane Dunkley
Manager,
Governor's Palace
Colonial Williamsburg, VA
1983

Hank Dunlop
Associate Professor
California College of Arts and
Crafts
1980

Deborah Dunning
Exec. Director, The
Providence R.I. Preservation
Society
1980

Charles DuPont
Graduating Senior (B.Arch)
Illinois Inst. of Technology
1973

**Pierre De L. Ruffiniere
DuPrey**
Architecture Student
Westbury, L.I.
1965

Donald H. Dwyer
Arch. Historian
New York
1963

Clare Eames (Le Corbeiller)
Metropolitan Museum
New York
1956

Stephen Earle
Student
(Textile Major)
Rhode Is. School of Design
1980

Mrs T. Eaton
Toronto, Canada
1959

Anne Eatwell
Dept of Ceramics
Victoria & Albert Museum
London
1979

Allison Eckardt (Ledes)
Assistant to the Editor
Antiques Magazine,
New York
1979

Richard Edgcumbe
Asst Curator
Peterborough City Museum
1984

Frances Edmunds
Historic Charleston
Foundation
Charleston, S.C.
1977

Clare Edwards
Trustee
The Wadsworth Atheneum
1991

Jared Edwards
Architect,
West Hartford, CT
1991

Mark Richardson Edwards
Historic Site Survey
Coordinator
Maryland Historical Trust
1976

Betty Eggert
Acting Curator
Clermont Museum
1971

Miss Prentiss Eley
Asst to Director
The Royal Dale Foundation
New York
1979

Dorothy Ellesin (Janus)
Asst Editor
Antiques Magazine
New York
1974

Virginia Eley
Graduate Student
Winterthur, Univ. of
Delaware
1964

Anita Ellis
Curator, Decorative Arts
Cincinnati Art Museum
1983

Martin Ellis
Deputy Keeper
Applied Art
Birmingham City Art Gallery
1989

Linda Ellsworth
Director, Mid-Atlantic
Region
Nat'l Trust for Historic
Presvt., Philadelphia, PA
1989

Virginia Elverson
Docent
Bayou Bend Collection
Houston, TX
1974

Ruth Emery
University Professor
1961

Robert Emlen
Exec. Director
John Nicholas Brown Centre
Providence, R.I.
1991

Arthur Emperatori
Toronto, Canada
1975

Mrs. J. R. English
Trustee,
Mount Vernon, VA
1953

Irene Eno
Art Dept,
The American Univ.
Washington DC
1964

Geza Entz
Art Hist. Inst. of the Academy
Budapest, Hungary
1985

Jennifer Esler
Exec. Director,
Cliveden, PA
1988

Robert Eurich
Asst Curator
Nassau Co. Hist. Museum
1972

Richard Carl Eustice
M.A. Candidate
(History of Art)
Univ. of Kansas
1979

Barbara Evans
Staff Member
Whitney Museum of
American Art, New York
1971

Mrs D. W. Evans
Marion, OH.
1957

Miss E. A. Evans
Victoria & Albert Museum
London
1965

Elaine Evans (Dee)
Curator of Drawings & Prints
Cooper-Hewitt Museum
New York
1980

Grace Evans
Art Historian
1962

John M. Evans
Washington & Lee University
Lexington, VA
1979

Laura Evans
Programme Co-ordinator
Cooper-Hewitt Museum
New York
1989

Charles Evers
Resource Manager
Project Architect
Philadelphia, PA
1991

Sister Mary Ewens
Chairman,
American Studies
Rosary College, IL
1973

Hilarie Faberman
Curator of Western Art
Univ. of Michigan Art Gallery
1985

Marsha Lee Fader
Historical Architect
N. Atlantic Region
US National Park Service
Nantucket, MA
1976

Betsy Fahlman
Guest Curator
Corcoran Gallery
Washington, DC
1980

Oliver Fairclough
Deputy Keeper of Applied
Art
Birmingham Museum & Art
Gallery
1983

John George Fanelli
Promotion Director
N.Y. Convention & Visitors
Bureau, New York
1974

Anne Farnam
Curator, Essex Institute
Salem, MA
1983

Jane Farrington
Asst Keeper of Fine Art
Manchester City Art Gallery
1985

Alan Fausel
Curatorial Asst
Fine Arts Museums of
San Francisco
1988

Eleanor Fayerweather
Curator, Costume Centre
Rhode Island Sch. of Design
Providence, R.I.
1966

Mary Louise Fazzano
Asst to Curator of
Decorative Arts
Museum of Art
Rhode Is. School of Design
1981

Deborah Federhen
Instructor
H. F. Du Pont Museum
Winterthur, DE
1986

Richard Fee
Cataloguer
Parke-Bernet Galleries
New York
1971

Hortense Feldblum
Preservationist
New York
1966

Arthur M. Feldman
Assoc. Curator
Renwick Gallery
Smithsonian Institution
1973

Mrs T. Felton
Antiques Center,
New York
1964

Katherine Fennelly
Old Sturbridge Village,
Mass.
1956

Donald Fennimore
Associate Curator
H. F. Du Pont Museum
Winterthur, DE
1986

John C. Ferguson
Architectural Historian
Historic District Commission
New Orleans, LA
1980

Sheila ffolliott
Asst Professor
George Mason Univ., VA
1979

J. Wesley Fields
Assistant Curator
Old Salem Inc. N.C.
1977

Debra Fillos
Asst Director
Florence Griswold Museum
Deep River, CT
1988

Anne-Sophie Fischer-Hansen
Student, Univ. of Copenhagen
1987

Richard C. Fisher
Architect, Texas
1953

James Fitch
School of Architecture
Columbia University
1966

Desmond Fitzgerald
(Knight of Glin), Dept of
Furn. & Woodwork
Victoria & Albert Museum
London
1965

Lucy Fitzgerald
Reference Librarian
Montclair, N.J.
1968

Charles Fleischmann
Collector; Manager of
Trust Investments
Cincinnati, OH
1982

E. McClung Fleming
H. F. Du Pont Museum,
Winterthur, DE
1959

Mrs E. McC. Fleming
1959

Ronald L. Fleming
Alumnus, Harvard Graduate
School of Design
1968

Patricia Fletcher
Cataloguer
Frick Art Reference Library
New York
1967

Henry N. Flynt
New York
1954

Peggy Fogelman
Asst Curator
The J. Paul Getty Museum,
Malibu, CA
1991

H. A. Crosby Forbes
Founder and Curator
Museum of American China
Trade, Salem, MA
1980

Alastair Forsyth
Research Asst
Southampton Art Gallery
1989

Charles Foss
Curator, King's Landing
Historic Village
Fredericton, Canada
1972

Helen Foster
New York & Paris
1960

Marion Foster
Preservationist, New York
1969

Mrs E. McSherry Fowble
Curatorial Asst
H. F. Du Pont Museum
Winterthur, DE
1968

Mrs C. E. Fox
Dept of History
Univ. of Pennsylvania
1966

Frances Fox-Robinson
(Collard)
Dept of Furniture & Woodwork
Victoria & Albert Museum
London
1979

Ross Francis
Vice-President, Development
Brunschwig & Fils, New York
1987

Catherine Frangiamore
(Lynn)
Cooper-Hewitt Museum
New York
1969

Margaret Frankenburg
Guide specialist
H. F. Du Pont Museum
Winterthur, DE
1981

Dr Gyorgy Frankl
Hungarian Academy
Budapest,
Hungary
1984

Robert Frankl
Curator
Phoenix Art Museum
Arizona
1972

Anthony Frederick
Architect
Houston, TX
1989

Gregory Free
Architectural Historian
Mississippi Dept of Archives
& History
1977

David Freeman
Keeper, Tredegar House
Newport, Wales
1983

Mrs E. L. Frelinghuysen
Holmder, N.J.
1963

Gordon Frey
Intern, Metropolitan Museum
New York
1990

Arnold Friedman
Assoc. Prof.,
Pratt Institute, New York
1965

Stephen Frith
Ph.D. Student
Columbia Univ.
1988

John H. Fritz
Assoc. Prof., History and
Liberal Arts Farleigh Dickinson
Univ., N.J.
1969

John Fuggles
Libraries Adviser
The National Trust
London
1983

Professor Ruth Funk
Dept of Interior Design
Russell Sage College
Delmar, N.Y.
1983

Mrs Furman
The National Trust
London
1953

Laurie Fusco
Head of Academic Affairs
J. Paul Getty Museum
Malibu, CA
1982

Peter Fusco
Curator, Dec. Arts &
European Sculpture
County Museum of Art
Los Angeles, CA
1982

Catherine Futter (Scoggin)
Graduate Student
Yale Univ.
1988

David Gallager
Furniture Specialist
Sotheby's Arcade Auctions
New York
1984

Nigel Galliers-Pratt
Mawley Hall, Salop.
1971

Aaron Gallup
Architectural Historian
State Office for Hist.
Preservation
Sacramento, CA
1980

Mrs K. Gambrill
Peafrack, N.J.
1956

John F. Gane
Architect
Hoosick, New York
1978

Sally Gant
Education Co-ordinator
MESDA, Winston-Salem,
N.C.
1987

William Garbo
Landscape Architect
Jackson, MS
1979

Jane Gardner
Victoria & Albert Museum
London
1975

Paul Gardner
Curator of Ceramics and
Glass
Smithsonian Institution
Washington, DC
1977

Irvin (Terry) Garfield
Architect, Philadelphia
1985

Cliff Garten
Teaching Fellow
Rhode Island School
of Design
1978

Grace Gary
Director, Mid-Atlantic
Region, National Trust for
Historic Preservation
1985

S. P. Gasparez
Lecturer,
New York
School of Design
1965

Alexandre Gaudieri
Graduate Student
New York Univ.
1974

Margot Gayle
Deputy Director
Public Affairs
City Planning Commission
New York
1965

Edith Gecker
Decorator; Designer
New York
1978

Mrs W. M. Geer
New York
1957

Maureen Cassidy Geiger
Master's Degree Candidate
Cooper-Hewitt Museum
Programme, New York
1985

Andrea George
Assoc. Curator
Cusworth Hall Museum
Doncaster, Yorks
1982

Ronald Geraci
Architect, Silver Spring, MA
1983

Mrs John Gerdes
New York
1955

Scott Gerloff
Survey Coordinator
Univ. of S. Dakota
1977

Elizabeth Gerry
Metropolitan Museum
New York
1967

Cdr. Roger Gerry
US Naval Hospital
St Albans, LI
1953

Mrs R. G. Gerry
1953

Joseph Getty
Field Historian
Maryland Historical Trust
1976

Anne L. Gibbs
Northwestern Univ.
Evanston
1960

Julian Gibbs
The National Trust
(East Anglia Region)
1978

Patricia Gibbs
Research Associate
Colonial Williamsburg, VA.
1984

Jane Giffen (Nylander)
Curator of Ceramics and
Textiles
Old Sturbridge Village
1970

Ann Gilkerson
Ph.D. Candidate (Fine Arts)
Harvard Univ.
1981

Mrs Robert Gillie
Eye, NY
1955

Lorraine Gilligan
Curator, Operating Officer
Coe Hall at Planting Fields
Oyster Bay, N.Y.
1985

Prof. Hope Gladding
Univ. of California at
Berkeley
1954

Vaughn Glasgow
Ph.D. Candidate (Art
History)
Penn. State Univ.
1969

George Glazer
Director of Furniture Dept
W. Graham Arader III
New York, N.Y.   .
1991

Larry Gleeson
Assoc. Prof. of Art History
North Texas State University
1983

Michael Glynn
Architect, Cambridge, Mass.
1977

Abby Goell
Appraiser, New York
1963

Ellen Goheen
Asst Curator
Nelson-Atkins Museum,
Kansas City
1973

Mr & Mrs J. C. Goodbody
Colonial Williamsburg, VA
1956

James Goode
Curator, Building
Smithsonian Institution
Washington, DC
1974

Mary Goodwin
Paper Conservator
The National Trust,
London
1985

Burkhardt Göres
Director, Museum of
Applied Art, Berlin, Germany
1991

Clorinda Gorman
East Hampton, N.Y.
1960

Joan Gorman
Assoc. Curator
Brandywine River Museum
1978

Peter Goss
Asst Prof. Architectural
History, Univ. of Utah
1974

Mrs W. F. Gossett
Evanston, IL
1963

Nancy Goyne (Evans)
H. F. Du Pont Museum
Winterthur, DE
1965

Dr Irene Grabowska
Cracow, Poland
1973

Priscilla Grace
Trustee, Philadelphia
Museum of Art
1972

Clare Graham
Furniture & Woodwork
Collection
Victoria & Albert Museum
London
1990

Frank Graham
Division of Education
Philadelphia Museum of Art
1963

John N. Graham II
Curator of Collections
Colonial Williamsburg, VA
1952

Richard Graham
Assoc. Professor of Interior
Design
Michigan State Univ.
1977

Roy Graham
Architect, Univ. of Virginia
1966

William Graham
Architectural Research Fellow
Colonial Williamsburg, VA
1983

Barbara Gratkowska-Ratynska
Keeper of Furniture
The Royal Castle,
Warsaw
Poland
1986

Nancy Gray
Washington, DC
1965

Richard Gray
Senior Keeper of
Decorative Arts,
Manchester City Art Gallery
1983

Robert J. Gray
Restorer, Architect
Washington, DC
1968

Sabele Gray
Graduate Student
Cooper-Hewitt, Parsons
Program, New York
1989

Paul Green
Professor of Sociology
Salem State College
1982

Barry Greenlaw
Assoc. Curator of Collections
Colonial Williamsburg, VA
1970

Taube Greenspan
Director of Programmes
The Royal Oak Foundation
New York
1991

Andrew Greg
Keeper of Fine Art
Laing Art Gallery
Newcastle-upon-Tyne
1985

Irene Gregg
Fashion Inst. of Technology
New York
1968

Richard Gregg
Paine Art Centre
Oshkosh, WI
1962

Harry D. Gremillion
Student (Art History)
L'Ecole du Louvre
1973

H. D. M. Grier
Asst Director
The Frick Collection
New York
1957

Katherine C. Grier
Historian
The Strong Museum
New York
1989

Lee Ellen Griffith
Assistant Curator for Loans
Philadelphia Museum
1990

Barbara Grigg
City Museum & Art Gallery
Birmingham (England)
1966

Amy Gristede
Lecturer, New York
1968

Tracy Haight Griswold
Interior Designer
New York
1975

Sally Groff
Preservationist
Owing Mills, MD
1975

Sibyl McCormac Groff
Student (Restoration,
Preservation)
Columbia Univ.; Author
1973

Suzy Wetzel Grote
Curatorial Trainee
The Brooklyn Museum
1974

Dorothy Grotz
Guide, H. F. Du Pont
Museum, Winterthur, DE
1964

Stephen Grout
Prof. Design & Art History
Philadelphia Coll. of Textiles
& Science
1988

Frances M. Grube
American Wing
Metropolitan Museum
New York
1967

Robert Guffin
McNeil Fellow
H. F. Du Pont Museum
Winterthur, DE
1988

Ruth Guilding
Asst Curator
Osborne House
English Heritage
1988

The Hon. Desmond Guinness
Irish Georgian Society
1970

Elizabeth Gusler
Teaching Curator
Colonial Williamsburg, VA
1985

Alfred Gustave
Interior Architecture and
Design,
Scottsdale, Arizona
1976

Mrs Peggy Gustave
Interior Designer
1976

Miss M. A. Guyton
The Castle Museum,
Norwich
1974

Willard Gwilliam
Dir., Architecture &
Engineering
Colonial Williamsburg, VA
1988

Martha Hackley
The Frick Collection
New York
1970

Winifred Hadsel
Preservationist
Lexington, VA
1978

Kenneth Hafertepe
Doctoral Candidate
Univ. of Texas
1984

John Haggard
Architectural Designer
Winchester, Kentucky
1971

Elizabeth Hall
Historic Buildings Council
London
1955

Dennis Halloran
Student, Teaching Asst
Manitowoc., WI
1970

**Mrs Roger Hallowell and
Beatrice Hallowell**
Westwood, MA
1956

Carolyn Halpin-Healy
Graduate Student
Art History
Williamstown, MA
1986

Gus C. Hamblett
Professor of Architectural
History and Design
Texas A&M University
College Station, TX
1978

Chloë Hamilton (Young)
Curator,
Art Museum,
Oberlin, OH
1960

Helen Hamilton
Administrator, Historical
Society of Princeton, N.J.
1975

Jean D. Hamilton
Victoria & Albert Museum
London
1963

Miriam Hamilton
Old Government House
Parramatta,
Australia
1986

Suzanne Hamilton
Graduate Student
Univ. of Delaware
1967

Elizabeth Hamlin
Graduate Student
Univ. of Delaware
1967

Peter Hammell
Head Division of Education
& Public Programmes
H. F. Du Pont Museum
Winterthur, DE
1987

Rebecca Hammell
Curator,
Rockwood Museum
1990

Barbara Hammond
Asst Director
Lyndhurst, N.Y.
1987

Charles Hammond
Curator
Gore Place Society
1977

Mrs M. C. Hammond
Guide
H. F. Du Pont Museum
Winterthur, DE
1965

Mrs R. Hamran
Curator
Aust-Agder Museet
Arendal,
Norway
1967

David Hanks
Interior Designer
St Louis, MI
1965

Mrs B. Hardin
Elmira, N.Y.
1954

Deirdre Hardy
Asst Professor
Univ. of Oklahoma
1985

John Hardy
Dept of Furn. & Woodwork
Victoria & Albert Museum,
London
1966

June E. Hargrove
Prof., Univ. of Maryland
Washington, DC
1990

Virginia Harker
Interior Designer
Ontario,
Canada
1968

M. J. Harkins
Springman School
Glenview, Ill.
1975

James Harrington
Professor of Art
Univ. of Georgia
1976

Susan Harris
Archivist with Architectural
firm, New York
1981

Avril Hart
Textiles Dept
Victoria & Albert Museum
London
1970

Emma Hart
Collector
1958

Christopher Hartley
Assistant Curator
The National Trust for
Scotland
1985

Kathryn Hartman
Architectural Historian
Washington, DC
1968

Joy Hartshorn
Senior Guide
H. F. Du Pont Museum
Winterthur, DE
1986

Marcia Harty
Librarian
1960

Ralph Harvard
Design Assistant to
Mario Buatta
New York
1986

Elain Harwood
Research Asst
English Heritage, London
1987

Charles Hasbrouck
Preservation Planner
San Francisco
1978

James Haskett
Chief, Interpretation Services
US National Park Service
1973

Mrs C. Norwood Hastie
Charleston, S.C.
1957

Lynne Hastings
Curator, Hampton National
Historic Site
Cockeysville, MD
1988

John Davis Hatch
Norfolk Museum, VA
1956

Mrs J. D. Hatch
1956

Robert Hatch
Architect, National Trust for
Historic Preservation,
Washington, DC
1971

Frederick Haupt, III
Director of Public Affairs
National Trust for Historic
Preservation
Washington, DC
1970

Judith Hawk
Architectural Instructor
Northern Virginia
Community College
1976

Harriette Hawkins
Fellow, Winterthur Museum
Programme
1982

Jeffrey Haworth
Hist. Bldgs Representative
The National Trust
(Severn Region)
1982

Malcolm Hay
Asst Curator
Palace of Westminster,
English Heritage
1986

Philip Hayden
Coordinator of Education
Princeton Historical Soc.
1990

S. Hayden
Wooster College
Wooster, OH
1980

Joanna Hecht
Cataloguer of Western Art
Metropolitan Museum
New York
1970

Morrison H. Heckscher
Graduate Student in Art
History,
Columbia University,
New York
1966

Barbara Heiberger
Textile Conservation Officer
Council of Museums in Wales
1985

Harvey B. Heider
Architect
South Orange, N.Y.
1953

Patricia Heintzelman
Graduate Student (Art
History)
Univ. of Delaware
1972

Robert Helbig
Interior Designer,
New York
1964

Huyler C. Held
Presdt. S.P.L.I.A.;
Preservationist
1979

Mary Heming
Consultant on Textiles
Metropolitan Museum
New York
1969

Mrs M Henderson
Southampton
1961

Robert Hendrick
Winterthur Student
1960

Jack and James Hendrix
Interior designers,
New York
1970

James Hennessy
Student
Columbia Univ. Law School
1990

Hanley Henoch
Architect
New York
1952

Anita Henry
President of her own
fabric business
New York
1966

Jacqueline Herald
Free-lance Textile Historian
London
1991

Mrs G. C. Hering Jr.
Wilmington, DE
1963

John Hermanson
Furnishings Consultant
Shirley-Eustis House
Cambridge, MA
1989

Mary Ellen Hern
Curator of Art
Staten Island Inst. of Arts and
Sciences
1987

Lady Hervey-Bathurst
Rumson, N.J.
1955

John Herzan
Connecticut Historical
Comm., Hartford, CT
1981

R. F. Hester
Chm., Dept of Int. Design
Richmond Professional Inst.
1965

Benjamin Hewitt
Post-doctoral student in
American Arts, Yale Univ.
1972

Mark Hewitt
Architectural Designer in
private practice, New York
1980

William Hickman
Restorer
Metropolitan Museum,
New York
1987

Kathryn Hiesinger
Dept of Decorative Arts
Philadelphia Museum of Art
1973

Jean Hildreth
Curator, Costume Institute
Phoenix Art Museum
1973

Robin Hildyard
Victoria & Albert Museum,
London
1980

Ernest Hillman, Jr.
Fairfield, CT
1956

Jane Hirschkowitz
Curator of Toys
Museum of the City of
New York
1988

Lillian Hirschmann
Dealer; Collector
New York
1954

Nancy Hirst
Preservationist; Chairman,
Council, The Woodlawn Fdn.
1979

Gunnar Hjeld
Asst Keeper
The Royal Palace
Oslo, Norway
1974

Alison Hoagland
Architectural Historian
Hist. Amer. Bldgs. Survey
1986

Libby Orme Hodges (Oliver)
Historical flower arranger
Colonial Williamsburg, VA
1978

William Hodges
Furniture Consultant
1978

Gerhard Hojer
Bayerisches Nationalmuseum
Munich
1965

Hillman Holland
Decorator; Designer
Atlanta, GA
1982

Thomas Holleman
Architect, Rochester, Mich.
1978

David Hollenberg
Architect
Philadelphia, PA
1977

Peter Holliday
Asst Professor
Univ. of Houston
1984

Nancy Holmes
Preservationist
Mobile, AL
1970

John Holverson
Director
Portland Museum of Art, ME
1982

Abigail Homer
Chief of Programmes and
Budget
US National Park Service
Boston
1984

Daniel Hopping
Architect, Bronxville
1952

Carsten Hopstock
Norsk Folkmuseum, Oslo
1960

Elizabeth Horne
Wadesboro',
N.C.
1957

Virginia Horne
Wadesboro',
N.C.
1957

Linda Horvitz
Assistant Curator
European Art
Wadsworth Atheneum
1984

Charles Hosmer
College Professor, History
Principia Coll. Elsah. IL
1964

Mrs J. Hosmer
Museum Curator
1964

Ann Shepard Houston
Architect
Philadelphia, PA
1984

Professor & Mrs Lewin
Houston
1961

David Howarth
The National Trust
1977

Gertrude D. Howe (Newton)
Metropolitan Museum
New York
1956

Katherine Howe
Assoc. Curator
Bayou Bend Collection
Museum of Fine Arts,
Houston
1975

Josephine Howell
New York
1956

Margize Howell
Art Curator
Donaldson, Lufkin & Jenrette
New York
1985

Wilbur Hubbard
Architectural Historian
Chestertown, MD
1960

Richard Hudgens
Architect
Linden, AL
1982

Gareth Hughes
Architect
English Heritage
1991

Octavia Hughes
Dept of Textiles
Boston Museum of Fine Arts
1969

Mark Hulla
Decorator; Designer
New York
1978

R. Carole Humberman
(Bierman)
Historian, Office of
Archaeology
US National Park Service
1973

E. Ray Humiston
Preservationist
New York
1967

Miss M. C. Humphrey
Glenview, Kentucky
1954

Tiffany Hunt
Deputy Curator
Salisbury & S. Wiltshire
Museum, Salisbury
1981

Patricia Hurley
Curatorial Assistant
Rhode Island School of
Design, Museum of Art
1978

Ronald Hurst
Curator of Furniture
Colonial Williamsburg, VA
1986

Jethro Hurt III
Assistant Director & Curator
Old Westbury Gardens
Old Westbury, N.Y.
1983

Suzanne Hutton
Asst Librarian
H. F. Du Pont Museum
Winterthur, DE
1974

William Hutton
The Toledo Museum of Art
1954

Bryden Bordley Hyde
Museum Board Member
Baltimore, MD
1979

Douglas Hyland
Curator,
Western Art
Spencer Museum
Univ. of Kansas
1981

John J. Ide
Architect
Park Avenue, New York
1953

Mrs J. Ide
1953

Elizabeth Igleheart
Architectural Historian
Maine Historic Pres. Comm.
Portland, ME
1988

Nancy Iliff
Antiques dealer
Lexington, KY
1988

Hilary Irvin
Senior Archtl. Historian
Vieux Carré Commission
New Orleans
1991

Robert Grant Irving
Ph.D. Candidate
(Hist. of Architecture)
Yale Univ.
1968

Richard Iverson
Asst Prof. Ornamental
Horticulture
State Univ. of New York
1989

Miss E. Jackson
Boston School of Fine Art
1953

Lesley Jackson
Asst Keeper,
Decorative Art
Manchester City Art Gallery
1989

Ruth Jackson
Curator of Decorative Arts
Montreal Museum of Fine
Arts, Canada
1972

Anthony James
Division, Archives & History
Raleigh, N.C.
1978

Steven Janke
Asst Professor Art History
State Univ. of New York
College
1974

Clare Janinck
The National Trust for
Scotland
1964

Jan Jasik
Furniture Conservator
S.P.N.E.A., Boston
1988

Frances Jay
New York
1963

Thomas Jayne
Student (Archt. and Art Hist.)
Univ. of Oregon
1981

Wm. J. Jedlick
Graduate Student
New York Hist. Assoc.
1967

Kevin Jenness
Dept of Interpretation
Old Sturbridge Village
1976

J. L. Sibley Jennings Jr.
Architect, Macon, GA
1969

David T. Johnson
Asst Director, Taft Museum
Cincinnati, OH
1990

J. Stewart Johnson
Curator of Decorative Arts
The Newark Museum, N.J.
1965

Marilynn Johnson
Museum Staff Member
New York
1965

Susan Johnson
Curatorial Assistant
Carnegie Museum of Art
Pittsburgh, PA
1978

Phillip Johnston
Associate Curator
Decorative Arts Dept
The Wadsworth Atheneum
Hartford, CT
1975

Mrs C. W. Jones
Minneapolis
1957

Mrs James B. Jones
Williamsburg, VA
1956

Josephine Jones
Ossining, N.Y.
1956

Lawrence Jones
President, Intarsia, Ltd.
Ellicott City, MD
1987

T. Ruben Jones
Atlanta, GA
1964

Mrs Wilmot Jones
Guide
H. F. DuPont Museum
Winterthur, DE
1972

Pieter Jongbloed
Teylers Museum
Haarlem, Holland
1991

Harriet Jordan
Student, Garden History
Beaconsfield, Bucks
1985

James Jordan
Exec. Director
Greensboro Presvt. Soc.
1986

Henry Joyce
Curator, Woburn Abbey
England
1976

Robert Joyce
Master's Candidate
(Architecture),
Yale Univ.
1988

Vera Kaden
Victoria & Albert Museum,
Library, London
1972

Peter Kaellgren
Asst Curator
Royal Ontario Museum,
Toronto, Canada
1988

Margaret Kahn
Assistant to the Director
The Frick Collection
New York
1968

Rosalind Kahn
Collector
1961

Patricia Kane
Curator
American Decorative Arts
Yale Univ. Art Gallery
1990

Alice Kaplan
President
American Federation of Arts
New York
1970

Elizabeth Kaplan (Boas)
Fellow, Training Programme
Metropolitan Museum
New York
1974

Wendy Kaplan
Dept of American Arts
Boston Museum of Fine Arts
1981

Nedra Karrer
Guide
H. F. Du Pont Museum
Winterthur, DE
1971

Prof. C. Bud Kaufmann
University of Missouri
Columbia, MO
1973

Richard Kavesh
Alfred University
Art Department
Alfred, N.Y.
1975

G. Kavli
Kunst Industrie Museum
Oslo
1955

H. L. Kealy
Dept of Architecture
Univ. of Illinois
1973

Richard Kearns
Preservationist, New York
1990

Ann Keenan
Director of English
Braintree Public School
Braintree, MA
1971

John Keene
Historian
Illinois Historical Society
1973

Graeme Keith
M. H. de Young Memorial
Museum, San Francisco
1965

Dr George Kelenyi
Univ. of Budapest
1972

Mr & Mrs John Kellenberger
Greensboro', N.C.
1957

Donald Kelley
Boston Athenaeum
Boston, MA
1975

Dr. W. Graf Kelnein
Markgraflich Badische
Verwaltung
Salem/Baden, Germany
1956

Robert C. Kennedy
Preservationist, New York
1963

Winifred Kennedy
Museum Registrar
1962

Myrtle L. Kerr
State Supervisor for Art
Louisiana Board of Educ.
1967

Ladislav Kesner
Keeper
Medieval Bohemian Painting
National Gallery,
Prague
1990

Barry Kessler
Winterthur Museum
Programme
1983

Clyde Kestner
Director of Engineering
Colonial Williamsburg, VA
1990

Barbara Keyser
Intermuseum Conservation
Assoc., Oberlin, OH
1972

Thomas Kheel
Graduate Student
(Art History)
Cornell Univ.
1974

Juliet Kinchin
Asst Keeper
Pollok Hall,
City of Glasgow
Museums
1981

Caroline King
Education Coordinator
Williams College Museum of
Art
1989

Prof. Grace King
Chairman, Art Dept
Mary Washington College
Fredericksburg, VA
1976

John King
Yorktown Heights,
New York
1974

Jonathan Kinghorn
Pollok Hall, City of Glasgow
Museums
1987

Pamela Kingsbury
Curator of Prints & Drawings
Univ. of Kansas Museum of
Art
1972

Barbara Louise Kirschten
Ph.D. Candidate
Harvard Univ.
1976

Prof. John Kiser
Dept of Fine Arts
Univ. of Tennessee
1972

Wanda Reed Kiskinen
(Radcliffe)
Preservationist; Archivist
Washington, DC
1966

Daniella Kisluk-Grosheide
Curatoral Assistant
Metropolitan Museum
New York
1986

Johan Knap
Sandefjord Sjofartsmuseum
Sandefjord,
Norway
1967

Gwendolyn Koch
Master's Candidate
Univ. of Evansville
1974

Vance Koehler
Intern. Photo-Archives
J. Paul Getty Museum, CA
1985

H. F. Koeper
School of Architecture
Univ. of Minnesota
1952

Ann Kohls
Asst Curator
Minneapolis Institute of Arts
1990

Drs Eloy Koldeweij
Leiden Univ.
The Netherlands
1989

Jaroslava Kopecna
(Dobrincic)
National Gallery, Prague
1983

Jiri Kotalik
National Gallery, Prague
1979

Jana Kotalikova
Charles Univ., Prague
1991

Paula Kozol
Intern, Boston Museum of
Fine Arts
1983

Deborah Kraak
Asst Curator
Textiles & Costume
Boston Museum of Fine Arts
1991

Donna Krawczyk (Berry)
Curatorial Asst
Colonial Williamsburg, VA
1974

Janet Laurel Kreger
Graduate Student
School of Architecture
Columbia Univ.
1976

Lisa Krieger
Adjunct Curator, Consultant
Taft Museum, Cincinnati
1990

Nancy Kruger
Sales Consultant
New York
1983

Dr Vera Kruzio-Uchytil
Zagreb Museum, Yugoslavia
1983

Cynthia Kryston
Park Historian
US National Park Service
Concord, MA
1971

Jayne Kuchna
Managing Editor
American Art Journal
New York
1990

Karl Kusserow
Student,
Yale Univ.
1990

Natasha Kuzmanovic
Ph.D. Candidate
Univ. of Michigan
1984

Nancy Kwallek
Assoc. Professor
Division of Interior Design
University of Texas at Austin
1982

F. C. Kyle
Board Member
Columbus Museum, GA
1964

Mrs Vanda Ladovic
Zagreb, Yugoslavia
1970

Dean T. Lahikainen
Research Curator
Essex Institute, Salem
1990

Elizabeth Lahikainen
Head Upholstery Conservator
SPNEA, Boston
1990

Aileen Laing
Assoc. Prof. Art History
Sweet Briar College, VA
1980

Bonita LaMarche
Asst Curator
Detroit Institute of Arts
1989

Miles Lambert
Asst Keeper (Costume &
Textiles)
Manchester City Art Gallery
1990

Mildred Lamm
Professor of Interior Design
Alexandria, VA
1984

Joshua Lane
Graduate Student
Yale Univ.; Intern Yale Univ.
Art Gallery
1988

Michael Lane
Director
Glensheen Hist. House
Museum, Duluth, MN
1984

Mills B. Lane
Publisher
The Beehive Press,
Savannah, GA
1988

Terry Lane
National Gallery of Victoria
Melbourne,
Australia
1975

Diane Langwith
Docent Chairman,
Bayou Bend Collection
Houston TX
1985

Mildrid Lanier
Conservator
Williamsburg, VA
1964

Lorraine Lanmon
Corning Museum of Glass
Corning, N.Y.
1962

Carter Larsen
Preservationist
San Francisco
1984

Diana Larsen
Intern
Boston Museum of Fine Arts
1987

John C. Larsen
Asst Professor of
Library Service School
Columbia Univ.
1973

John Larson
Architectural Historian
Detroit Institute of Arts
1989

Sarah T. Latham (Kearns)
Researcher,
Community Development
Department
Landmarks Preservation
Commission
New York City
1978

Clare Latimer (Taylor)
Asst Keeper. Dec. Arts
Manchester City Art Gallery
1986

Elizabeth Laurent
Curator of Collections
Cliveden, PA
1991

Kedrun Laurie
Assistant,
Geffrye Museum
London
1982

Mrs James Lawrence
1956

Elizabeth Lawson
Architect; Asst Prof. Dept of
Architecture,
Drexel Univ., PA
1988

Major Nicholas Lawson
House Owner,
Shropshire
1984

Emmeline Leary
Museums Officer
London Borough of Ealing
1988

Antoinette Lee
Ph.D. Candidate (American
Studies)
George Washington Univ.
1973

Mrs Newbold Legendre
1958

Jane Legget
Dept of Museum Studies
Univ. of Leicester
1980

Lamar Lentz
Curator
International Festival
Institute, Texas
1991

Philip Leonard
Curator, Lecturer
National Gallery of Art
Washington, DC
1985

W. Neil Letson
On staff of the Architect of
the Capitol, Washington, DC
1966

Arline Popper Leven
Assistant to the Director
Washington Univ.
Gallery of Art
1977

Betty Leviner (Hyman)
Curator of Exhibition
Buildings
Colonial Williamsburg, VA
1987

Sarah Levitt (Allen)
Asst Curator, Applied Art
Bristol City Art Gallery
1986

Alice Levkoff
Historic Charleston
Foundation
1977

Prof. Raymond Levra
Art & Humanities Dept,
Cochise College, AR
1971

Carolyn Lewis
Student, Univ. of Delaware
1966

John Lewis
Solicitor
Attingham Trust Council
Member
1981

Robert Lewis
Architect, President
Robert K. Lewis, Inc.
Cold Spring Harbour
1986

Jan H. Lexow
Stavanger Museum
Oslo, Norway
1959

Valencia Libby
Longwood Programme
Fellow
Univ. of Delaware
1983

Jack Lindsey
American Dept
Philadelphia Museum
1987

Catherine Lippert
Assoc. Curator
Indianapolis
Museum of Art
1978

Helene Lipstadt
Gradate Student
(Architecture)
Columbia Univ.
1969

Bertram Little
Director, Soc. for Pres.
New England Antiquities
Boston
1953

Mrs Bertram Little
Mr Jon B. Little
Miss Selina F. Little
1953

Charles L. Livingston
Brooklyn, N.Y.
1965.

Mrs A. S. Locke
Cambridge, Mass.
1955

Christopher Loeblein
Curator of History
Charleston Museum, S.C.
1988

Mildred Loftus
Senior Interior Designer
B. Altman & Co.
New York
1969

James Lomax
Asst Keeper
Manchester City Art
Gallery
1981

Jo Anne Lonam
California State Univ.,
Environmental Design
Sacramento, CA
1976

E. LoNano
New York
1952

Paul Lougeay
Prof. of Architecture &
Design
Southern Illinois Univ.
1981

R. H. R. Loughborough Jr.
Coudersport, Penn
1959

Carl Lounsbury
Architectural Historian
Raleigh, N.C.
1981

John Lovell
Regional Supervisor
(Historic Presvt.)
NYS Off. of Parks,
Recreation & Historic
Preservation
1987

Linda Lovell
Staff Lecturer
Metropolitan Museum
New York
1970

David Lowe
Arch. Historian
New York
1982

Mrs J. Lowe
New York
1956

Clive Lucas
Architect
Sydney, Australia
1983

Barbara Rose Luck
Registrar
A. A. Rockefeller Folk Art
Center
Williamsburg, VA
1973

Robert Luck
Cooper-Hewitt Museum
New York, NY
1962

Karl Lunde
Instructor,
Dept of Art History
Columbia Univ.
1970

Danuta Luniewicz-Koper
Curator,
Art Centre
The Royal Castle
Warsaw,
Poland
1988

Nadine Luporini
(Rondinella)
Graduate Student
Univ. of Delaware
1967

Charles Thomas Lyle
Director,
Monmouth County
Historical Association
1977

James Lyle
Cambridge, MA
1961

Robert Lym
Architect; Senior Associate
I.M. Pei & Partners
New York
1983

Stanton Lyman
Architect
Brookline, MA
1966

Susan J. Storey Lyman
Trustee of S.P.N.E.A.,
Boston
1966

Sarah Lytle
Director,
Museum Activities
Middletown Place
Foundation
Charleston, S.C.
1989

Rodolfo Machado
Head, Dept of Architecture
Rhode Island School of
Design
Providence, R.I.
1981

Margaret Schuyler Machell
Keeper of The Grange
Art Gallery of Ontario,
Canada
1976

Carol Macht
Senior Curator
Decorative Arts
Cincinnati Art Museum, OH
1974

Kathleen MacIntyre
Guide Specialist
H. F. Du Pont Museum
Winterthur, DE
1985

William MacIntyre
Research Fellow
Colonial Williamsburg, VA
1987

Prof. Maynard Mack
Dept of English Lit.
Yale Univ.
1969

Mrs Florence Mack
Member, Exec Ctte
Yale Univ. Art Gallery
1969

Robert MacKay
Director, S.P.L.I.A.
Long Island, N.Y.
1975

Barry Mackintosh
Staff Historian
U.S. National Park Service
Washington, DC
1975

Susan MacMillan
Department of Textiles
Boston Museum of Fine Arts
1974

Marion MacRae
Instructor
Ontario College of Art
1970

Paula Madden
Appraiser
Portland, OR
1984

John Maddison
Asst Hist. Bldgs Rep.
National Trust (East Anglia
Region)
1984

Mary Jean Madigan
Curator, American History
Hudson River Museum
Yonkers, N.Y.
1975

Dr Stephan Tschudi Madsen
Riksantikvaren
Oslo, Norway
1970

Margot Magee (Sackett)
King's Landing Historical
Settlement, Fredericton,
Canada
1977

Jean Elizabeth Mailey
Assoc. Curator
Textile Study Room,
Metropolitan Museum,
New York
1974

**Bozenna Majewska-
Maszkowska**
Warsaw Museum, Poland
1971

Debra Mancoff
Ph.D. Candidate
(Art History),
Northwestern Univ.
1980

**Anne Manningham-Buller
(Parsons)**
Dept of Furniture &
Woodwork
Victoria & Albert Museum,
London
1980

Michele Marincola
Dept Assistant
Boston Museum of Fine Arts
1985

Gertrude Markell
JFK Library & Museum
Columbia Pt. on Dorchester
Bay
Boston, MA
1962

Szilvia Maros
Museum of Applied Arts
Budapest,
Hungary
1990

Christopher Marsden
West Yorkshire Archive
Service
Leeds
1989

Melissa Marsh
Vice-Presdt. Museum
Facilities
Historic Annapolis Inc.
1987

Eliza Marshall
Student,
Parsons School of Design
New York
1968

Edward Martin Jr.
Dept of Landscape
Architecture
Mississippi State Univ.
1985

Floyd Martin
Visiting Lecturer,
Art and Design,
Univ. of Illinois
1982

Lyman L. Martin
New York
1954

Dr. Anna Masarykova
National Gallery,
Prague
1969

Edward Masek Jr.
Projects Administrator
Maryland Historical Trust
1980

Mary Anne Massie (Hunting)
Curatoral Assistant
(free-lance)
New York
1989

Barbara C. Massey (Bailey)
Docent, Bayou Bend
Collection
Houston, TX
1978

Ann Merritt Masson
Curator of Exhibitions,
Gallier House Museum
New Orleans
1976

Frank Walker Masson
Staff Architect in private
practice
New Orleans, LA
1978

Frank Matero
Asst Prof. (Architecture)
Columbia Univ.
1984

Christine Matheu
Architect; Lecturer
Univ. of Pennsylvania
1989

Oliver Maurice
Asst Regional Agent
National Trust (Lake District)
1974

Edward Maverick
Architect,
New York
1952

Prof. E. de N. Mayhew
Connecticut College
New London, CT
1953

David Maxfield
Editor,
Smithsonian Inst.
News Service
1985

Miss C. C. Mayer
Cooper Union Museum
New York
1965

Alfred Mayor
Cambridge, Mass.
1959

Bruce McAlpin
New Year Botanical Garden
Snuff Mill
Bronx, N.Y.
1976

Davy H. McCall
Chair,
Dept of Economics
Washington College
1991

Rita McCarthy
Independent Researcher
Cincinnati, OH
1984

Pauli McClanahan
Secretary to The American
Friends of the Attingham
Summer School
Washington, DC
1979

David McCullough
Student
Savannah College of Art
1985

Cathryn McElroy
Curator, Flagler Museum
Palm Beach, FL
1972

Edgar McElroy
Interior Designer, New York
1968

David McFadden
M.A. Candidate, Univ. of
Minnesota; Research Asst,
Minneapolis Institute of Arts
1973

Dennis McFadden
Graduate Student
(Architecture) Columbia
Univ.
1976

Milly McGehee
Winterthur Museum
Graduate Programme
1975

Anne McGrath
U.S. Foreign Service School
Georgetown Univ.
1958

Jack McGregor
Metropolitan Museum
New York
1959

Flora McInnes
Senior Guide, H. F. Du Pont
Museum, Winterthur, DE
1982

Elizabeth McIntire
Assistant Prof. of Fine Arts
Principia College, Elsah, IL
1991

Maggie McKean
House Manager
Tatton Park, Cheshire
1991

Margaret McKellar
Whitney Mus. of Amer. Art.
New York
1958

Ruby Mae McKelvie
Guide, H. F. Du Pont
Museum, Winterthur, DE
1970

Jennifer McKendry
Ph.D. Student (Art History)
Univ. of Toronto, Canada
1988

David D. McKinney
Ph.D. Student (Architecture)
Univ. of Virginia
1988

Kristan McKinsey
Acting Asst Curator
St. Louis Art Museum, MO
1989

Mary A. McLaughan
Docent and Museum Lecturer
Bayou Bend Collection
Houston, TX
1974

Elizabeth McLane
Student (Hist. Preservation)
Columbia Univ.
1973

Charles McMurray
Architect in private practice
Charlotte, N.C.
1980

William P. McNaught
Graduate Student
Portland, Oregon
1970

John McVerry
Asst Hist. Bldgs. Rep.
The National Trust (Wessex
Region)
1990

Christine Meadows
Curator
Mount Vernon Restoration
1967

Sarah Medlam
The Bowes Museum
Barnard Castle, Durham
1979

Kathryn Meehan
Horticultural Consultant
Smithsonian Institution
Washington, DC
1984

Prof. Carroll Meeks
Architectural Historian
1962

Mrs C. Meeks
1962

David Mees
Student (Art History)
Leiden Univ.
The Netherlands
1990

Ferris Megarity
Merchandise Director
B. Altman & Co.
New York
1968

Robert Mehlman
Instructor (Arts)
New York Univ.
1990

Richard Mehring
Chief, Preservation Projects
U.S. National Park Service
1972

Melissa Meighan
Asst Curator
Decorative Arts
Philadelphia Museum
1986

Hugh Mellor
The National Trust
London
1980

Elinor Merrell
Antiques dealer,
New York
1954

Agnes Merrick
Baltimore, MD
1963

David Meschutt
Student (Museum Studies)
Cooperstown, N.Y.
1988

Pauline Metcalf
Decorator; Designer
Associate of Richard A.
Nelson Inc.
New York
1966

Grace Meyer
New York
1960

Susan Meyer
Curator
Salisbury Mansion
Worcester Historical
Museum, MA
1986

Robin Michel
Historic Site Manager
New York State Division for
Historic Preservation
1976

Elizabeth Michelson
Free-lance writer
Southbury, CT
1989

Audrey Michie
Lecturer,
M.E.S.D.A.,
Winston-Salem, N.C.
1979

Thomas Michie
Student (History of Art)
Yale Univ.
1981

Judith Middleton
Administrator
Nathaniel Russell House
Historic Charleston Fdn
1983

Christopher Miele
Fellow,
New York Univ.
1991

Catherine Milburn
Research Consultant
Carlton Hobbs Antiques
London
1990

Richard Milhender
Director & Vice-Presdt.
SMD Industries,
Boston MA
1981

Arthur Miller
Architect
Philadelphia, PA
1985

John F. Miller
Graduate Student
(Art History)
Univ. of Maryland
1972

Lee Hunt Miller
Asst Curator. Amer.
Decorative Arts
M. H. de Young Museum
San Francisco
1985

Prof. Maxine Miller
Housing & Int. Design Dept
California State College at
Los Angeles
1968

Nancy S. Miller
Historian
The Maryland Historical
Trust
1970

V. Isabelle Miller
Curator
Museum of the City of New
York
1957

William Miller
Assoc. Professor
Colby College
Waterville, ME
1970

John Milley
Curator
Independence Nat'l Hist.Park
Philadelphia, PA
1972

G. Cory Millican
Assoc. Professor
Dept of Design
Cornell Univ.
1972

Claire Mills (Timings)
Conservation Student
London
1984

Dorothy Miner
Legal Counsel
New York Landmarks
Preservation Commission
1977

John Miners
Historical Rep.
Pallu & Lake Furnishings
London
1986

Louise Mitchell
Power House Museum
Sydney, Australia
1989

William Mitchell
Georgia Historical
Commission, Atlanta, GA
1968

Miss Dubravka Mladinov
Zagreb Museum, Poland
1969

Miklos Mojzer
Dept of European Art
Hungarian National Museum
Budapest
1977

Mary Alice Molloy
Author
Chicago, IL
1986

Mark Moloney
Graduate Student
School of Fine Art
Rosary College, Florence
Italy
1976

Mr & Mrs C. T. Monahon
Providence, R.I.
1957

Gilbert P. Monet
Student
(Architecture and the Arts)
Wilmington, DE
1976

Christopher Monkhouse
Student (Architecture)
Univ. of Pennsylvania
1966

Charles F. Montgomery
H. F. Du Pont Museum,
Winterthur, DE
1952

Florence Montgomery
Textile Historian
H. F. Du Pont Museum,
Winterthur, DE
1952

Duke Moody
Landscape Architect
Memphis, TN
1953

Margaret Moore
Asst Curator
Decorative Arts, Clarke
Institute, Williamstown, MA
1989

Melodye Moore
Historic Site Manager
Mills Mansion
Rhinebeck, N.Y.
1990

Robert Moore
College Professor
Univ. of Minnesota
Minneapolis
1964

Thurston Moore
Assoc. Prof. of English
Univ. of Kansas
1980

Marjorie Morehous
Instructor, Continuing
Education
Univ. of Tennessee
1981

Melissa Moreno (Seiler)
Graduate Student
Cooper-Hewitt Museum
New York
1987

William Morgan
Graduate, 1966
Dartmouth College, N.H.
1966

Marisa Morra
Student
Winterthur Museum
Programme
1991

Mrs C. M. Morris
Washington D.C.
1957

Leslie Morris
Curator, History &
Bibliography, Rosenbach
Museum & Library
Philadelphia, PA
1987

Lindsay Morrison
Bowhill, Scotland
1978

Sheila Morrison
Asst Teacher
Textiles, Cornell Univ.
1974

Eb. B. Morrow
Preservationist
Waco, TX
1973

Samuel Morrow
Preservationist
Washington, D.C.
1963

Caroline Mortimer
Student, Cooper-Hewitt
Masters' Programme
New York
1984

Sarah Mortimer
Philadelphia
1955

Mrs Terry B. Morton
Editor, *Preservation News*
National Trust for Historic
Preservation
Washington, D.C.
1968

Matthew Mosca
Architectural Technician
Office of Historic Properties
National Trust for Historic
Preservation
Washington, D.C.
1978

Roger Moss
Graduate Teaching Asst
Univ. of Delaware
1966

Roy Moyer
Director
American Federation of Arts
New York
1970

Mary B. W. Munford
The Baltimore Museum of Art
Baltimore, MD
1975

Jeffrey Munger
Asst Curator, European
Decorative Arts,
Boston Museum of Fine Arts
1979

Miss E. Murdoch
Victoria & Albert Museum
London
1959

Joan Murphy
Chairman Docent
Organization
Bayou Bend Collection
1982

Simon Murray
Historic Buildings
Representative
The National Trust
(E. Midlands Region)
1991

Mrs W. D. Murray
1958

William Murtagh
National Trust for Historic
Preservation
Washington, D.C.
1963

Milo Naeve
Assistant Director
Dept of Collections
Colonial Williamsburg, VA
1969

Charles Nagel
Director
St Louis City Museum, MO
1957

Mrs C. Nagel
1957

David Nathans
Fellow
Winterthur Programme
1974

Miss H. M. Nebelthau
Librarian
Minneapolis Inst. of Arts
1966

Gwendolyn B. Needham
College Professor
Davis, CA
1969

Judith Neiswander
Ph.D. Candidate
Westfield College
Univ. of London
1986

Christina Nelson
Graduate Student
Univ. of Illinois
1971

Richard Nelson
Interior Designer
New York
1967

William Neudorfer
Architect
Rockville, MD
1984

Susan Newell
Museum Asst
The Wallace Collection
London
1987

Mrs F. C. Newkirk
New York
1963

Edward Nickels
Director
Collections & Exhibits
Shakertown at Pleasant Hill
Danville, KY
1988

Sarah Nichols
Asst Curator
Museum of Art
Carnegie Inst.
Pittsburgh, PA
1984

Jessica Nicoll
Curator of Textiles
Old Sturbridge Village
1991

Nina Nightingale
1958

Florence Guild Nixon
Decorator; Designer
New York
1965

Stacia Norman
Curator
Kenmore,
Fredericksburg, VA
1991

Percy North
Asst Professor, Art History
George Mason
University, MD
1981

Thomas Norton
Author
New York
1961

Thomas Nothaft
Prof. History of Design
Wayne State Univ.
1979

Prentiss Eley Nottebohm
Mount Pleasant
Spring Grove, VA
1979

Clarabel Noyes
Senior Guide, H. F. Du Pont
Museum, Winterthur, DE
1984

Penelope Noyes
Soc. Pres. New England
Antiquities, Boston
1958

Richard Nylander
Curator of Collections
Soc. Pres. New England
Antiquities, Boston
1990

Barbara O'Brien
History Dept,
Shipley School
Bryn Mawr, PA
1980

Maureen O'Brien
Curator of Collections
Mountclair Art Museum, N.J.
1979

Kathleeen O'Connor
Graduate Intern
Mellon Centre,
Yale
1991

Susan Odell (Walker)
Conservation Technician
Boston Museum of Fine Arts
1989

Caroline Odgers
Public Relations Dept
Victoria & Albert Museum
London
1972

Jane Ohly
Curatorial Assistant
Museum of Art
Rhode Island School of
Design
1984

Mrs C. O'Malley (Collins)
Education Dept
Victoria & Albert Museum
London
1970

Jack Ordeman
Westport, CT
1955

Mrs Evelyn Francis Ortner
Interior Designer
Brooklyn, New York
1974

David Osborn
Member, Board of Directors
California Heritage Council
1967

Judy Osborne
Canada,
National Trust
1953

Vals Osborne
Vice-President &
Director of Education
Sotheby's, New York
1987

Derek E. Ostergard
Adjunct Professor
Parsons/Cooper-Hewitt
Program, New York
1986

Lydia Jo Owen
Graduate Student
Tulane Univ.
1977

David Owsley
Victoria & Albert Museum
London
1966

Nancy Packer
Curator of Collections
Association for Preservation
of Virginia Antiquities
1989

Marion Page
Associate Editor
Interiors Magazine
New York
1967

Roberta Paine
Metropolitan Museum
New York
1959

Stephen Pallrand
Student (Art History)
Oberlin College, N.J.
1981

The Hon. Anthea Palmer
Asst Hist. Bldgs. Rep
The National Trust
(Thames & Chilterns Region)
1986

Arlene Palmer (Schwind)
Asst Curator, Glass and
Ceramics
H. F. Du Pont Museum
Winterthur, DE
1974

George Palmer
Associate Director
(N. E. Region)
US National Park Service
1972

A. H. B. Paneyko
Antique Dealer, New York
1964

Elizabeth Panhorst
Curator
Kenmore
Fredericksburg, VA
1987

Emma Papert
Librarian
Metropolitan Museum
New York
1965

William Papp
Antiques Dealer
New York
1983

Nicholas Pappas
Architect, Preservationist
Washington, D.C.
1975

Catherine L. Parker
Intern, Metropolitan Museum
New York
1982

James Parker
Metropolitan Museum
New York
1955

Jean Parker (Murphy)
Student (History of Art)
Yale Univ.
1973

Thomas Parker
Director
The Boston Society
1977

Pamela Parmal
Asst Curator
Textiles & Costume
Rhode Island School of
Design, Museum of Art
1990

Ruth Parmly
1958

Mary Parry
London
1959

Merribell Parsons
Curator of Decorative Arts
Minneapolis Institute of Arts
1969

Miss N. Paterson
London
1952

Paul Parvis
Teacher (Historic Interiors)
Univ. of Delaware
1985

Herbert Paston
University of Massachusetts
Fine Art Center
1971

John Newton Pearce
Curator (Dept of Properties)
National Trust for Historic
Preservation
1966

Lorraine Pearce
Museum Teacher
Washington, D.C.
1965

Michael Pearman
Asst Librarian,
Chatsworth
1979

Jeremy Pearson
Curator of Applied Art
Royal Albert Memorial
Museum, Exeter
1983

Marjorie Pearson
Director of Research
Landmarks Preservation
Commission,
New York
1983

Amelia Peck
Curatorial Assistant
Metropolitan Museum
New York
1985

B. S. Pedersen
Oslo,
Norway
1963

Donald Peirce
Librarian Asst; Curatorial
Intern,
St Louis Art Museum
1973

Eldridge Pendleton
Director
Old Gaol Museum
York, Maine
1981

Isabel Perkins (Roberts)
Assistant to the Director
Shreve, Crump & Low,
Boston
1985

John Perkins
Graduate Student
(Architecture)
Yale Univ.
1983

Shelley Perlove
Instructor, Art History
Wayne State Univ., Detroit
1978

Peter F. Perreten
Asst Prof. of English
Ursinus Coll. PA
1978

Rosalind Peters (Simon)
London
1973

Carl Peterson
Oberlin College
Department of English
1976

Karin Peterson
Curator; Director of
Interpretation
Historic Annapolis Inc.
1978

Dr P. Petrescu
Institute of Art History
Bucharest, Rumania
1974

David Pettigrew
New York State Hist. Assoc.
Cooperstown, N.Y.
1970

Morgan Peyton
Curator, Glenwood
Charleston, WV
1980

Candace Pezzera
Head Tour Guide
John Brown House, MA
1984

Harry Pfanz
Chief, Park History Office
US National Park Service
Rockville, MD
1973

Ruth Philbrick
1958

Stephanie Phillips
Admin. Assistant,
Cliveden, PA
1977

Mary Pierpont
Librarian,
Ossining, New York
1959

Robert Pierpont
Chief Restoration Officer
State of New York
1979

William Pierson
College Professor
Williamstown, MA
1954

Martha Pike
History Curator, The Museums
at Stony Brook, N.Y.
1981

William Pillsbury
Graduate Student
Univ. of Delaware
1969

Roger Pinkham
Victoria & Albert Museum,
London
1970

Sue Pittman
Decorator; Designer
Houston, TX
1987

H. G. Place
National Trust for Historic
Preservation
Washington, DC
1958

Mrs H. G. Place
1958

Tamara Plakins (Thornton)
Graduate Student
Yale Univ.
1983

Joanne Platou
Chief Curator
Historic New Orleans Coll.
1980

Mrs H. N. Platt
Philadelphia
1963

Stuart L. Platts
Asst Keeper, Heaton Hall
Manchester City Art Gallery
1980

Russell A. Plimpton
Minneapolis Institute of Arts
1954

Mlle Renée Plouin
Paris
1959

Kathleen Plummer
California State Univ.
Sacramento, CA
1980

Michael Podmaniczky
Associate Furniture
Conservator, H. F. Du Pont
Museum, Winterthur, DE
1989

William Julius Polk Jr.
St. Louis, MO
1957

Jeffry Pond
Architect
Boston, MA
1985

Jonathan Poston
Director of Programmes
Historic Charleston
Foundation
1986

Lydia Bond Powel
Keeper of the American Wing
Metropolitan Museum
New York
1952

Mrs T. I. Hare Powel
Regent, Mount Vernon
1952

Miss N. Powell
Chester
1952

Emma Lou Powers
Research Associate
Dept of Historical Research
Colonial Williamsburg, VA
1989

Alexis Praus
Director of Public Museum
Kalamazoo, MI
1967

Pavel Preiss
Research Curator
National Gallery, Prague
1987

Agnes Prékopa
Museum of Applied Arts
Budapest, Hungary
1991

Anne Preston
Guide
H. F. Du Pont Museum
Winterthur, DE
1971

Mrs. Walter Price
Gunston Hall Plantation
Lorton, VA
1977

Sumpter Priddy
Art Consultant
Richmond, VA
1986

E. J. Priestley
Assistant Curator
City of Liverpool Museum
1974

Geraldine Prince
Lecturer, Dept of Fine Art
Edinburgh Univ., Scotland
1989

Deborah Prosser
Ph.D. Candidate
Univ. of Pennsylvania
1989

Francis Puig
Graduate Student
(American Studies)
Yale Univ.
1978

Olga Pulmanova
National Gallery,
Prague
1967

Mildred Putnam
Cleveland, OH
1959

Mrs David H. M. Pyle
Far Hills, N.J.
1955

Robert Pyle
Investor & Collector
Greenville, DE
1982

Mrs Florence Pyne
Far Hills, N.J.
1956

Miriam Rabb
Administrator
Oaklands, VA
1974

Marc Rabun
Curatorial Assistant
David Hanks & Associates
New York
1989

Ronald Raetzman
Asst Prof. of Art
Colorado State Univ.
1967

Martha Rainbolt
Instructor in English,
Stephens College
Columbia, MO
1979

Ronald Ramsay
Graduate Student
(Architecture)
Columbia Univ.
1971

Mrs Stuart Rand
1958

Richard Rankin
Dept of Human
Environment
Univ. of Kentucky
1980

Frederick Rath
National Trust for Historic
Preservation
Washington, DC
1954

Mrs F. Rath
Preservationist
1954

Selma Rattner
Graduate Student
(Architecture)
Columbia Univ.
1967

Deborah Fulton Rau
Architectural Historian
New York
1988

Gloria Ravitch
Curatorial Asst
M. H. de Young Museum
San Francisco
1981

Anna Rawa-Szubert
Textile Conservation Dept
The Royal Castle, Warsaw
Poland
1989

Charles Rawson
Woodbury, CT
1956

Prof. Lawrence Ray
Lambuth College
Jackson, TN
1975

Julia Raynesford (Boyd)
Dept of Furn. and
Woodwork
Victoria & Albert Museum
London
1971

Mrs L. B. Rediker
Interior Designer
Birmingham, AL
1964

Richard Redlon
Architectural Historian
Greater Portland Landmarks
1991

John Redmill
Architect,
London
1978

Peter Rees
Historical Areas Conservation
Division
London
1979

David Reese
Director
Abigail Adams Smith
Museum,
New York
1983

Mrs Reeves
Charleston, S.C.
1960

Michael Regan
Whitworth Art Gallery
Univ. of Manchester
1973

Dorothy Regnery
Arch. Historian,
Author
Portola Valley, CA
1978

Donald Reichert
Assoc. Director
George W. V. Smith Art
Museum,
Springfield,
Mass.
1970

Bernard J. Reilly
Interior Designer
Detroit
1969

Dr. John Reinhard
Surgeon
1958

Mrs J. Reinhard
1958

Elizabeth Reynolds
Architectural Historian
Dept of History
State of Mississippi
1975

Mary Reynolds
Asst Curator
Rhode Island Historical
Society
1976

Elizabeth Rhoades
Curator
New Haven Colony
Historical Society
1974

Nancy Richards
Assoc. Curator
(Historic Properties)
National Trust for Historic
Preservation
Washington, DC
1979

Nancy E. Richards
Curatorial Asst
H. F. Du Pont Museum
Winterthur, DE
1966

Nancy G. Richards
Museum Board Member
Annapolis MD
1986

Thom Richardson
Research Asst
The Tower Armouries
London
1986

Nan Rickey
Interpretative Planner
US National Park Service
Hagerstown, MD
1972

Sheila Rideout
Director,
Wilton Museum
Ridgefield, CT
1969

Mrs John Riker
Rumson, NJ
1955

Patricia Riley
Master's Candidate
Cooper-Hewitt Museum
New York
1986

Graeme Rimer
Research Asst
The Tower Armouries
London
1987

Michael Ripton
Director
Historic Sites & Properties
Pennsylvania Historic
Commission
1982

Nancy Rivard (Shaw)
Acting Curator, American Art
The Detroit Institute of Arts
1977

David Robb
Curator
Kimbell Art Museum
Fort Worth TX
1977

Samuel A. Roberson
Herron School of Art
Indianapolis, IN
1962

Barbara Roberts
Dept of Furniture &
Woodwork
Victoria & Albert Museum
London
1970

Annette Robertson
Administrator
Milwaukee Art Centre
Museum
1978

Cheryl Robertson
Asst Prof.
Winterthur & Univ. of
Delaware
1988

Niente Robertson (Smith)
Partner, Antiques Business
Washington, DC
1980

Camille Robinson
President
Historic Petersburg
Foundation
Petersburg, VA
1976

Mrs R. G. Robinson, OBE
New Orleans
1959

Laura Roe
Ph.D. Candidate
Yale Univ.
1982

Ellen Rogers
Chief Curator
Jekyll Island Museum
1986

Phillis Rogers (Sharpe)
Research Assistant
National Monuments Record
London
1975

Mrs P. Rogers
Berryville, VA
1954

Joseph L. Roman
Teacher, New York School
of Int. Design
1965

Daru Rooke
Research Assistant
Leeds City Art Galleries
1989

Priscilla Roosevelt
Assistant Professor
Catholic University of
America, Washington, DC
1989

Kimerly Rorschach
Ph.D. Candidate (Art
History)
Yale Univ.
1980

Allen Rosenbaum
Staff Lecturer
Metropolitan Museum
New York
1966

Harvey Rosenberg
Assistant Professor
Fashion Institute of
Technology,
New York
1988

Martin Jay Rosenblum
Restoration Architect
Philadelphia, PA
1976

Stewart Rosenblum
Attorney,
New York
1984

David Rosenthal
Architect
Alexandria, VA
1973

Treve Rosoman
Curator, Study Collections
English Heritage,
London
1987

Catherine Ross
Clifton Park Museum
Rotherham, Yorks
1984

John Drake Ross
Boston, MA
1956

Marion Dean Ross
School of Architecture
Univ. of Oregon
1955

Marjorie Ross
Boston, MA
1956

Dr G. Rotter
Kunsthistoriches Museum,
Vienna
1964

Christopher Rowell
Historic Buildings Rep.,
The National Trust
(N. Wales)
1977

Margaret Rowlett
H. F. Du Pont Museum
Winterthur, DE
1964

Kathleen Roy
Lecturer
Chicago Art Institute
1979

Beatrix Rumford
Assistant Curator
Department of Collections
Colonial Williamsburg, VA
1970

Mrs J. C. Russell
Restoration Architect
Philadelphia
1953

David Rust
Ph.D. Student
Institute of Fine Arts
New York Univ.
1960

Anna Rutledge
Museum Curator
Charleston, S.C.
1953

Mrs K. W. Ryder
New Brunswick, Canada
1961

Anne Ryland
Asst Prof. Interior Des.
Richmond Professional
Institute
1964

Julius Sadler
Architect
Litchfield, CT
1970

Frances Safford
Curator
Metropolitan Museum
New York
1967

Ruth Sagar
National Trust
London
1973

Stephen Saitas
Stephen Saitas Design
New York
1988

Prof. Carl A. Saladino
Dept of Architectural Design
Univ. of Cincinnati
1968

Virginia Saladino
Decorator; Designer
New York
1965

David L. Salay
Graduate Student (History)
Univ. of Delaware
1972

Larry Salmon
Asst Curator of Textiles
Boston Museum of Fine Arts
1969

Carl Salmons
Saugus Iron Works
US National Park Service
1991

Mark Sammons
Lead Interpreter
Old Sturbridge Village
1984

Linda Samter (Hollenberg)
Art Historian,
Cataloguer
New York
1977

Miss W. Graham Samuel
Cheyne House
London
1952

Frank Sanchis
Administrative Architect
New York City
Landmarks Preservation
Committee
1980

Theodore Sande
Vice-Presdt. Historic
Properties
National Trust for Historic
Preservation
1980

Penny Sander
Asst Curator
S.P.N.E.A.,
Boston
1985

Gordon Sands
Ph.D. Candidate
Yale Univ.
1982

Patricia Sands
President,
S.P.L.I.A.
Oyster Bay, L.I.
1984

William R. Sargent
Assoc. Curator
China Trade Museum
Salem, MA
1984

Ilona Sarmany (Parsons)
Budapest
1975

Caroline Sartor
Landscape Architect
Nashville, TN
1982

Adrian Sassoon
Research Scholar
18th Century French
Decorative Arts; formerly J.
Paul Getty Museum, CA
1985

Richard Saunders
Ph.D. Candidate
Yale Univ.
1975

Charles C. Savage
Curator of Education
St Louis Art Museum
1972

J. Thomas Savage
M.A. Candidate
Cooperstown
Programme in Museum
Studies
1980

**Catherine Savedge
(Schlesinger)**
Architectural Researcher
Colonial Williamsburg
1972

Rosalind Savill
Museum Assistant
The Wallace Collection
London
1975

Earl Joseph Savoie
Interior Design
Baton Rouge, LA
1977

Charles Sawyer
Division of Arts
Yale Univ.
1955

Mrs Charles Sawyer
1955

Carole Scanlon
Guide and Historian
Independence Hall
Philadelphia
1970

Margaret Scarborough
Austin, TX
1954

Mrs M. D. Schaak
Interior Designer
Southport, CT
1966

Roger Scharmer
Landscape Architect
Sacramento, CA
1973

Miss V. J. Scheidemantel
Art Institute of Chicago
1959

W. A. Hayden Schilling
Prof. of History
Wooster College
Wooster, OH
1979

Janice Schimmelman
Graduate Student
(Art History)
Univ. of Michigan
1972

Mary Schoeser
Archivist
Warner (Fabrics)
Braintree, Essex
1987

Hardinge Scholle
National Trust for Historic
Preservation, Washington
DC
1952

Louis Schreider
Architecture Student
Houston, TX
1966

Max Schulz
Univ. of Southern California
Department of English
Los Angeles, CA
1977

Marvin Schwartz
Brooklyn Museum, N.Y.
1957

Mrs M. Schwartz
1957

Gary Scott
Architectural Historian
U.S. National Park Service
Washington, DC
1981

Janet Scovill (Wilkins)
Lord & Taylor
New York
1975

Joellen Secondo
Dept Assistant
Boston Museum of Fine Arts
1988

Melvin Seiden
Museum Trustee,
New York
1975

Dr Hana Seifertova
Keeper of Flemish Paintings
National Gallery,
Prague
1989

Mary Glaze Seiler
Silver Springs, MD
1960

J. Daniel Selig
Lecturer
Museum of Fine Arts
Boston
1967

Tsune Sesoko
Journalist and Exhibition
Organizer
Tokyo,
Japan
1978

Darrell Sewell
Curator of American Art
Philadelphia Museum
1978

George Green
Shackelford
History Dept
Virginia Polytechnic
1958

George T. M. Shackelford
Graduate Student
(History of Art)
Yale Univ.
1978

Jane Shadel (Spillman)
Research Asst
Corning Museum of Glass
1967

Sandra Shaffer (Tinkham)
Instructor,
Educ. Dept Museum,
City of New York
1969

Wendy Shah
Consultant Textile
Conservation,
Museum of Art
Rhode Island School
of Design,
Providence, R.I.
1979

Margaret Shanks
Chairman of Docents
The Bayou Bend Collection,
Houston, TX
1976

Anne Sharkey
Executive Assistant to
Director
American Federation of Arts
1971

Lewis Sharp
Graduate Student
Univ. of Delaware
1968

Joseph Sharples
Asst Curator,
Fine Arts
National Museums and
Galleries on Merseyside
1991

Louise E. Shaw
Asst Curator
Atlanta Hist. Society
1981

John Sheeran
Keeper,
Dulwich Picture Gallery,
London
1984

Mrs. Edwin Sheldon
New York
1957

Barbara Shellenberger
Guide & Teaching Specialist,
H. F. Du Pont Museum
Winterthur, DE
1987

Feay Shellman
Curator of Collections
Telfair Academy
Savannah, GA
1979

Mary Shenkir
Virginia Historical
Landmarks Comm.,
Charlottesville, VA
1968

Anna Shepard
New York
1957

Raymond Shepherd
Administrator of
Cliveden, PA
1979

Judy Sheridan
Decorator; Designer
New York
1983

Curt Sherman
Asst Prof. Interior Design
Washington State Univ.
1974

Sarah Sherrill
Associate Editor
Antiques Magazine
New York
1980

Bruce Sherwood
Associate
Museum Education
H. F. Du Pont Museum
Winterthur, DE
1971

Susan Shifrin
Curatorial Asst
Rosenbach Museum &
Library, Philadelphia
1991

Deborah Shinn
M.A. Candidate
Inst. of Fine Arts
New York Univ.
1979

Michael Shipperbottom
Architect, London
1981

Ruth Shrigley
Asst Keeper, Dec. Arts
Manchester City Art Gallery
1987

Mrs John Shissler (Nasanow)
Editor of Publications
Minneapolis Institute of Arts
1972

Natalie Shivers
Project Architect
Los Angeles, CA
1987

Derek Shrub
Dept of Furn. & Woodwork
Victoria & Albert Museum
London
1965

Philip Siebert
Graduate Student
History of Art
Univ. of Michigan
1969

John Sigle
Architect
Baton Rouge, LA
1970

Nathan Silver
Asst Prof., Architecture
Columbia Univ.
1964

14*

Dr. Gabriela Simkova
National Gallery, Prague
1985

Marc Simpson
Ph.D. Candidate (Art
History)
Yale Univ.
1980

Pamela Simpson
Asst Professor
Art History
Washington & Lee Univ.
Lexington, VA
1977

Jozsef Sisa
Department of Ancient
Buildings
Budapest,
Hungary
1983

Janine Skerry
Asst Curator
Historic Deerfield
Deerfield, MA
1990

John D. Skilton
Fairfield, CT
1956

Mabel R. Skjelver
Assoc. Professor
Textiles
Univ. of Nebraska
1974

Thomas Slade
Architectural Historian
National Trust for
Historic Preservation
Washington, DC
1975

Luboš Slavíček
National Gallery
Prague
1982

Richard Slavin
Manager
Olana Historic Site
New York State Division for
Historic Preservation
1975

Mary Sloane
Assoc. Prof. of English
Florida Atlantic Univ.
1981

Elizabeth Sly
Guide
H. F. Du Pont Museum
Winterthur, DE
1964

Ann Webster Smith
Executive Vice-President
Historic Annapolis, Inc.
1984

Arthur Smith
Chatham College
Department of History
Pittsburgh, PA
1970

C. W. Smith
Architect
Fairfield, CT
1965

George M. Smith
Administrator
Belle Grove
Middletown, VA
1973

Helen Smith
Weave Design Manager
Warner Fabrics, Braintree
Essex
1991

Mrs James Smith
Interior Designer
Baton Rouge, LA
1971

Janet Smith
Washington State Univ.
1963

L. E. Smith
New York
1957

Margaret Smith
Curatorial Asst
Cooper-Hewitt Museum
New York
1991

Molly K. Smith
Vice-President
Dillingham & Co.
San Francisco, CA
1986

Murphy Smith
American Philosophical
Society
Philadelphia, PA
1960

Nancy A. Smith
Student, Author
Carlisle, MA
1969

Ruth Smith
Teacher
Toledo Art Museum, OH
1960

Miss S. B. Smith
Baltimore, MD
1963

Victor Porter Smith
Coordinator, Art Educ.
Missouri Public Schools
1969

Barbara Snow (Delaney)
Antiques Magazine
New York
1952

Clyde C. Snyder Jr.
Student (Fine Arts)
New York Univ.
1967

William Snyder
Stan Hywet Hall Foundation
Akron, OH
1975

Philip Solomon
Curator of Decorative Arts
Indianapolis Museum of Arts
1970

Prof. Frank Sommer
University of Delaware
1952

Selesett Somorjay
Ancient Monuments Dept
Budapest, Hungary
1987

James C. Sorber
Restorer, Craftsman
West Chester, PA
1974

Lauren Soth
Dept of Art History
Carleton College
Northfield, MN
1973

Miss M. Souther
Jamaica Plain
MA
1954

J. Peter Spang
Special Projects
Historic Deerfield, MA
1990

Scott Spence
Architect
Collonial Williamsburg, VA
1977

Katherine Spencer
Dept of Furniture &
Woodwork
Victoria & Albert Museum
London
1982

Dr Anna Spitzmuller
Kunsthistorisches Museum
Vienna
1963

Waldo Sprague
1958

June Sprigg
Freelance Writer; Guest
Curator,
Whitney Museum
1986

Lynn E. Springer (Roberts)
Curatorial Assistant
City Museum of St Louis
1970

Betty Spurgeon
Graduate Student
(Architecture) Columbia
Univ.
1971

Edith Standen
Keeper of Textile Dept
Metropolitan Museum
New York
1956

Stanislav Stanicic
Museum Curator
Zagreb,
Yugoslavia
1967

Ian Stapleton
Architect
Sydney, Australia
1985

Ralph Stark
Director
Interior Design Programme
Indiana Univ.
1976

Kevin Stayton
Asst Curator
Decorative Arts
The Brooklyn Museum
Brooklyn, N.Y.
1983

Anna Stearns
Preservationist
Nashua, N.H.
1970

Margaret Stearns
Asst Curator
Costumes & Dec. Art
Museum of the City of
New York
1960

Roger Stearns
Decorative Painter
Boston, MA
1982

Romaine Stec (Somerville)
Baltimore, MD
1962

Prof. Martin Steinmann
Dept of English
Univ. of Minnesota
1966

Mrs M. Steinmann
1966

Carl. Stepan
Restorer & Conservator of
Furniture
Graz,
Austria
1989

Mrs S. Walter Stern
New Orleans, LA
1959

Letitia Stevens
Furniture Conservation Dept
The Wallace Collection
London
1990

Janet Stewart
Assistant to Mr Paul Mellon
(Virginia)
1991

Susan Stitt
Administrator,
M.E.S.D.A.
Winston-Salem, NC
1971

David Stockwell
David Stockwell, Inc.
(Antique Dealers)
Wilmington
1952

Mrs E. Stockwell
1952

Jane Stokes
Asst Curator,
Dec. Arts
Milwaukee Art Museum
1990

Jarek Stoklasa
National Gallery
Prague
1981

Marilyn Stokstad
Dept of Art History
University of Kansas
1968

May N. Stone
Graduate Student
(Architecture, Restoration
and Preservation)
Columbia Univ.
1976

Mrs C. Lawson Stote;
Sally Stote
Shrewsbury
1959 and (both) 1971

Donald Stover
Fine Arts Museums of
San Francisco, CA
1977

W. D. Stowell
Baldwinville, Mass.
1963

Judith Straeten
Archivist & Curator
Brunschwig & Fils
New York
1988

Betty Strauss (Kosco)
Graduate Student
Univ. of Delaware
1966

Jane Strauss
Escort Training Supervisor
Colonial Williamsburg
Williamsburg, VA
1979

Linda Strauss
Conservation Assistant
J. Paul Getty Museum
Malibu, CA
1985

Monica Strauss
Assoc. Prof.
Cooper-Hewitt Museum
1985

Peter L. L. Strickland
Graduate Student
Philadelphia
1970

Susan Strickler
Curator of American Art
Worcester Art Museum
Worcester, MA
1982

Nina Stritzer
Adjunct Prof.
Parsons School of Design
New York
1987

Carola Stuart
The National Trust
(Wessex Region)
1979

Jane Stubbs
Rare book dealer
J. H. Stubbs Rare Books &
Prints,
New York
1988

John Stubbs
Architect; Instructor
Louisiana State Univ.
1976

Sue S. Studebaker
Teacher/Lecturer
Warren County Museum
Dayton, OH
1987

Mary Sullivan
H. F. Du Pont Museum
Winterthur, DE
1965

James Susman
Graduate Student
(Architecture)
Univ. of Texas
1978

Miss S. Sutcliffe
Mount Vernon, VA
1958

Helen Sutherland
Providence, R.I.
1957

Susan Swan
Curator of Textiles
H. F. Du Pont Museum
Winterthur, DE
1982

Scott. T. Swank
Deputy Director for
Interpretation
H. F. Du Pont Museum
Winterthur, DE
1989

John Sweeney
Winterthur Museum
Winterthur, DE
1960

Lucy Sydnor
Arch. Historian; President
Women's Council
Virginia Museum of Fine Arts
1969

Philip Sykas
Asst Keeper, Conservation
(Costume & Textiles)
Manchester City Art Gallery
1988

Meredith Sykes
Director of Survey
Landmarks Preservation
Comm., New York
1979

Dr. Hedvig Szabolsci
Hungarian Academy
Budapest, Hungary
1973

Maria Tabb
First Regent
Gunston Hall, VA
1976

John Tackett
Principal
John Tackett Design
New York
1991

Ross Taggart
Senior Curator
Nelson-Atkins Museum
of Art
Kansas City, MO
1972

Mrs J. C. Talinferro Jr.
Baltimore, MD
1956

Vernon Tancil
Museum Curator
Independence National
Historical Park
Philadelphia
1964

Susan Douglas Tate
College of Architecture
University of Florida
Gainesville, FL
1977

Hugh Holloway Taylor
Assoc. Prof. Art History
Washington and Jefferson
College, PA
1978

Margaret Taylor
Lecturer to Schools
Boston Museum of Fine Arts
1968

Nancy Taylor (Vineburgh)
Graduate Student
(Architecture)
Columbia Univ.
1972

Thomas Hart Taylor
Architectural Historian
US National Park Service
1974

Nancy Teagarden
Guide
H. F. Du Pont Museum
Winterthur, DE
1970

Carole Teller
Art History Teacher
New York
1970

Lisa Terrace (Koch)
Res. Asst, Dept of Textiles
Boston Museum of Fine Arts
1965

Allen Terrell
1962

Marcia Terzo
Graduate Student
(Archt) Columbia Univ.
1969

Charlton M. Theus Jr.
Estate Appraiser
New York
1967

Mrs Will H. Theus
Author
Savannah, GA
1956

Judith Thieme
Graduate Student
(Museology)
Univ. of Connecticut
1972

Curtis Ray Thomas
Research Asst
The Wallace Collection
London
1975

Marie Thomas
Charlotte, N.C.
1955

Minor Wine Thomas
Colonial Williamsburg, VA
1955

Mrs M. W. Thomas
1955

Lydia Thomen
Senior Guide
H. F. Du Pont Museum
Winterthur, DE
1985

Eleanor Thompson
Asst to the Avery Librarian
Columbia Univ.
1975

Mrs. M. Fraser Thompson
Williamsburg, VA
1956

Glenn Thompson
Director of Education
National Trust for Historic
Preservation, Washington
DC
1969

Nicholas Thompson
Architect,
London
1980

Jonathan Thornton
Asst Prof. Objects
Conservation
Cooperstown
1983

Mrs. B. D. Thorsen
Portland, Oregon
1963

Christa Thurman
The Art Institute of Chicago
1965

Anthony Tibbles
Curator, Speke Hall
Merseyside County Museums
Dept
1982

Charles Tichy
Architectural Restoration
Consultant
State of New Jersey
1974

Simon Tickell
Project Architect
Philadelphia, PA
1987

Christine Tindale
Asst to the Librarian
Chatsworth
1980

William Tishler
Prof. of Landscape
Architecture
Univ. of Wisconsin
1980

Francis J. Tolford
Evanston, IL
1953

Maurice Tomlin
Dept of Furn. & Woodwork
Victoria & Albert Museum
London
1965

Gretchen Townsend
Ph.D. Candidate
Yale Univ.
1991

Roberta Townsend
Museum Guide
1962

Ann Toy
Curator, Vaucluse House
Sydney, Australia
1983

Berry Tracy
Iowa City, Iowa
1955

Kenneth Trapp
Curatorial Assistant
Decorative Arts
Cincinnati Museum
1983

Dorothy Travis
Interior Designer
Atlanta, GA
1983

Julian Treuherz
Deputy Director
Manchester City Art Gallery
1984

Catriona Trevelyan
Attingham Park, Salop
1963

Mildred Trimble
Chief Colour Design Division
US Govt. Washington, DC
1968

Sergei Troubetzkoy
Chairman, Help Encourage
Landmark Preservation Inc.
Richmond, VA
1981

B. Allen Trousdale, III
Graduate Student
(Architecture)
Columbia Univ.
1967

Charles Truman
Dept of Metalwork
Victoria & Albert Museum
London
1977

Robert T. Trump
Antiques dealer
Whitemarsh, PA
1953

Mrs R. W. Trump
(mother of R. T. Trump)
1953

Marjorie Trusted
Dept of Sculpture
Victoria & Albert Museum
London
1987

John Tschirch
Education Coordinator
'The Breakers'
Newport, R.I.
1990

Elizabeth Tucker
Cooper River Plantation
Tours
Charleston, S.C.
1981

Margaret Tuft
Student (Restoration and
Historic Preservation)
Columbia Univ.
1968

Edward Turberg
Restoration Consultant
Wilmington, N.C.
1980

Penelope Turle
New York
1954

Louise B. Turner
Regent,
Gunston Hall, VA
1982

Suzanne Turner
Prof. of Landscape
Architecture,
Louisiana State Univ.
Baton Rouge, LA
1979

John W. Tyler
History Teacher
Groton School, MA
1981

Mrs M. S. Valk
Charleston, S.C.
1955

Mrs Georgie Van de Kamp
Chairman
Descanso Gardens Building
Fund
Pasadena, CA
1980

Professor James G. Van
Derpool
Avery Librarian,
Columbia Univ.
1952

Miss Peggy Van Derpool
1952

Anne Van Ingen
Programme Associate
NYS Council on the Arts
New York
1986

Anna Van Meter
Architect
Lexington, KY
1971

Margaret Van Schaack
1966

Isabelle Van Tichelen
Research Asst (Textiles)
Musées Royaux, Brussels
1990

John Varian
Attorney, Park Ave.
New York
1961

John Vaughan
Sotheby's, London
1972

Constance Vecchione
(Hershey)
Instructor in History
Immaculate College,
Philadelphia
1968

Charles Venable
Assoc. Curator
Dallas Museum, TX
1990

Jeanne Vibert (Sloane)
Assistant Director
American Decorative Arts
Christie's, New York
1983

Dr Milada Vilimkova
National Gallery,
Prague
1970

Clare Vincent
Curatorial Assistant
Metropolitan Museum
New York
1964

Gilbert Vincent
College Professor
Cooperstown Graduate
Programme
1985

Giles Newby Vincent
Architect
London
1986

Nancy Vineburgh
1972

Vicki Vinson
Curatorial Asst, Reves
Collection
Dallas Museum of Art, TX
1988

Daniela Voith
Architect
Philadelphia, PA
1982

Burkard Von Roda
Keeper, History of Art
Basel Museum, Switzerland
1988

Mrs James Wagenvoord
Cataloguer
Metropolitan Museum
New York
1964

Susan Wagg
Art Historian
Montreal, Quebec
1983

Clive Wainwright
Museum Library
Victoria & Albert Museum
London
1967

James Waite
Asst to the Director of
Architectural Research,
Colonial Williamsburg, VA
1970

Alexandra Walker
Harris Museum & Art Gallery
Preston,
Lancs
1983

Stefanie Walker
Research Asst
Metropolitan Museum
New York
1991

Charles Wall
Superintendent
Mount Vernon, VA
1953

Patricia Wall
Mount Vernon, VA
1955

Susan Wallace-Reiling
Curator of Collections
Vizcaya Museum & Gardens,
FL
1979

Breffny Walsh
Director
Rensselaer County Hist.
Society
1985

Anne Wardwell
Special Assistant
Massachusetts Historical
Commission
1969

David Warren
Curator, Bayou Bend
Collection
The Museum of Fine Arts
Houston, TX
1969

Phelps Warren
President, American Friends
of Attingham 1962–79
1959

Howard Washburn
New York Univ.
1959

Giles Waterfield
Assistant Curator
Art Gallery & Royal Pavilion
Brighton
1978

Deborah Dependahl Waters
Librarian, Decorative Arts
Photo Coll.
H. F. Du Pont Museum
Winterthur, DE
1975

Nancy Waters
Curator
Staten Island Historical
Society
1987

Gerald R. W. Watland
Architect and preservationist
New York
1958

Louise Watson
New York
1963

Elizabeth Wattles
Park Avenue, New York
1955

Melvin Watts
Curator, Currier Gallery
Manchester, N.H.
1975

Mary Jo Weale
Florida State University
Dept of Interior Design
Tallahassee, FL
1970

O. J. Weaver
Ministry of Works
London
1955

Annabel Webb (Westman)
Research Assistant
Cawdor Castle
Nr. Nairn, Scotland
1977

Mrs Frankie Webb
The Charleston Museum
Charleston, S.C.
1969

John W. Webber
Boston
1953

Anne Weber
Architect
Natchez, MS
1986

Marian Weeks
Chesterton, MD
1957

Beth Wees
Asst Curator
Clark Art Institute
Williamstown, MA
1981

Martin Weil
Architect
Wilmington, DE
1967

Robert Weis
Curator
The Carroll Museum, MD
1983

Norman Weiss
Undergraduate
New York Univ.
New York
1967

Lavinia Wellicome
Curator
Woburn Abbey,
Bedfordshire
1986

Mark J. Wenger
Architect
Colonial Williamsburg Fdn,
Williamsburg, VA
1980

Mark R. Wenger
Research Architect
Colonial Williamsburg Fdn
Williamsburg, VA
1984

J. Gilbert Werle
New York School of Interior
Design
1963

Constance Werner (Ramirez)
Preservationist
Arlington, VA
1962

Robert Weston
Graphic Designer
Portland, Oregon
1971

Rosalind Westwood
Asst Curator,
Oakwell Hall
Yorks
1988

Mrs Clayton E. Whipple
Clinton, MD
1955

Mrs C. Whitcomb
New York Times
1960

Kirk White
New York
1965

Louise White
Curator
E. Martello Gallery
Key West, FL
1967

Patti Foos Whitelaw
Decorative Arts Consultant
Historic Charleston
Foundation
1965

Susanna Whitman
(Kinghorn)
Appraiser; Student
Cooper-Hewitt Museum
New York
1987

William Whitney
Instructor, Art History
Chabot College
San Francisco
1973

Donald Whitton
Librarian; Lecturer
Maria Co. CA
1974

William Whitwell
Asst Prof. (Art History)
Hollins College
Roanoke, VA
1971

Roger Whitworth
Historic Buildings Rep
The National Trust
(Yorkshire Region)
1989

Barbara Wilbur
Lecturer at Colonial
Williamsburg
1967

Christopher Wilk
Design Collection Researcher
& Cataloguer
The Museum of Modern Art
New York
1978

Mrs Earle Kress Williams
New York
1954

Margaret Williams
Chairman
Art Dept
St Mary's College,
Raleigh, N.C.
1979

Page Williams (Dwyer)
New York
1963

Patricia Eileen Williams
Education Coordinator
National Trust for Historic
Preservation
1976

Elizabeth Wilson
Sotheby's, London
1973

Gillian Wilson
Dept of Furniture &
Woodwork
Victoria & Albert Museum
London
1967

Gordon Bernard Wilson
Architectural Designer
Ontario,
Canada
1965

Mrs H. V. F. Wilson
Hudson Advertising Co.
New York
1959

John Wilson
Master's Candidate
Inst. of Fine Arts
New York Univ.
1980

Mary M. B. Wilson
Ph.D. Candidate (Univ. of
Delaware)
1975

Michael Wilson
Victoria & Albert Museum
London
1970

Timothy Wilson
Land Agent (Severn Region)
National Trust
1987

Enid Winslow
Staff Member
The American Federation of
Arts, New York
1971

Susan Winther
Interior Designer
Colonial Williamsburg
Williamsburg, VA
1981

Nora Downs Wiseman
St. Louis Art Museum
Forest Park
St. Louis, MO
1982

Phillip Wisley
Student
(Architectural History)
Ball State Univ. Indiana
1972

Dr Franz Sayn Wittgenstein
Munich
1955

Leila Wittler
Knoedler & Co.
New York
1959

Otto Wittmann
Director
Toledo Museum of Art
1960

Mrs Margaret Wittman
1960

C. Cameron Wolfe
Curator, European Art
Denver Art Museum
1984

Kevin Wolfe
Designer in firm of Architects
New York
1991

Ann Wood
Curatorial Assistant
Museum of Fine Arts
Houston, TX
1989

Charles B. Wood, III
H. F. Du Pont Museum
Library
Winterthur, DE
1966

David Wood
Curator, Concord Museum
Concord, MA
1990

Elizabeth Wood
Librarian, Joseph Downs
Coll., H. F. Du Pont Museum
Library, Winterthur, DE
1966

Josephine Wood
Preservationist
St Louis, MO
1970

Karen McK. Wood
Architectural Designer
Chevy Chase, MD
1987

Lucy Wood
Asst Keeper
Lady Lever Art Gallery
Port Sunlight,
Wirral
1988

Margaretta Wood
Preservationist
Baltimore Pike
Wawa, PA
1977

Pamela Wood
Senior Keeper
Nottingham Castle Museum
1985

Anne F. Woodhouse
Fellow, H. F. Du Pont
Museum
Winterthur, DE
1978

Charles Woods
Member,
Board of Directors
California Heritage Council
San Francisco
1967

Marianne Woods
Former Director
Rogers Hist. Museum, PA
1987

William Woolfenden
Detroit Institute of Arts, MI
1959

Robert Works
Graduate Student
(Architecture)
Yale Univ.
1982

Jeffrey Wortman
Graduate Student
School of Fine Arts
New York Univ.
1971

Caroline Wright
Princeton, N.J.
1963

Jane P. Wright
Senior Guide
H. F. Du Pont Museum
Winterthur, DE
1981

Mrs Lois Wright
New York
1955

Barbara Wriston
Museum of Fine Arts
Boston
1953

Lois Wyatt
Baton Rouge, LA
1963

Robin Wyatt
Architect
English Heritage
1990

George Yetter
Architectural Archivist
Colonial Williamsburg, VA
1990

Charles York
Interior Design Division
Univ. of Texas at Austin
1973

Patrick Youngblood
Ph.D. Student
Courtauld Institute
Univ. of London
1981

Dr Anna Zador
Art History Professor
Budapest
1964

Nikita Zaitzevsky
Graduate Student
(Fine Arts)
Harvard Univ.
1969

János Zakariás
Dept of Ancient Monuments
Budapest, Hungary
1988

Ronnie L. Zakon (Siegel)
Curator of Education
Museum of Art
Rhode Is. School of Design
1982

Ghenete Zelleke
Graduate Student
Cooper-Hewitt Master's
Programme
1983

Ruth Ziegler
Sotheby's, London
1975

Eva Zikova
National Gallery, Prague
1980

Henry Zimet
Vice-President
French & Company,
New York
1984

Philip Zimmerman
Ph.D. Student, Boston Univ.
1977

Alice Zrebiec
Associate Curator
Metropolitan Museum
New York
1987

Personal cartouche (Elizabeth Shrewsbury)
- on tower parapets

Hardwick Hall

Kent Brinkley

GENERAL INDEX

Figures in *italics* denote illustrations. Names in the foregoing alphabetically arranged Appendix of *Alumni* are not included here. Several persons who have been married, subsequent to their attendance, are noted under their maiden names.

Abbott, James Archer *136, 167*
Ackerman, Mary 145
Adams, Michael 107
Adams, Mrs. S. 4, *4 facing*
Albainy, Tracey 158
Alber, Zafie 69
Allaire, Kathleen 167
Allan, Christopher 69
Allen, Mary Link 119
Allmayer-Beck, Dr 28
Alswang (Joyce), Hope 66, 155
Ambler, Louise Todd 66
American Federation of Arts 33, 46, 52, 57, 71
American Friends of Attingham Inc. 23, 25–7;
    administrative arrangements, (American Federation of Arts) 33, 46, 52, 71, (National Trust) 72, 76, 93–4; finances ('62–3) 25–6, ('71) 53, ('79–81) 76, 79, 80, 83, 84, ('82) 89, 93–4, 96, ('84–5) 103, 104, 105, 109, 163, ('87–8) 128, 134–5, 141, 142, ('89–90) 154–5, 163; Mid–Atlantic Chapter 112; name 60; (*Newsletter*) 17, 103, 110, 145, 154; officers, ('60s) 25, 27, 28, 33, 37–8, ('70s) 52, 59, 60, 73, 76–7, 81, ('80s) 84, 88, 90, 99, 109, 115, ('90) 155; Phelps Warren Memorial Lecture 109, 127–8, 135, 162; professional ethos 68; regional activities 59, 98–9, 105, 111–12, 161–2, 165
American National Trust 1, 4, 66, 73; and American Friends 72, 76, 93–4
Andrews, Stephenson 107, 111
Antonsen, Inge 'Lucy' 4, *4 facing*, 5
Armour, Pamela K. 98
Arrol, Andrew 74, 101
Ashmead, Ann 167
Asleson, Robyn 131, 158, 160
Atkin, A. J. 69, 98, 99, 103, 111, 165–6
Attingham Alumni Directory (1984) 74, 81, 98, 104–5, 110, 128
Attingham Park, Shropshire *ii, 16, 50, 55;* accommodation 9–10, 54, 55, 56, 70; Adult College 11, 12, 14, 15, 17–18, 21, 35, 47, 65; Concord College 89, 98
Attingham Society 108, 109–10, 113, 126, 160–1; Lectures 110, 162

Attingham Summer School Trust: establishment 42–3, 44–5, 47; Members of the Association 101, 105; name 45, 152; officers 47–8, 52–3, 86, 88, 89, 90, 96; Patrons 73, 84, 85, 88; planning reviews 88–90, 96–7, 124–7: *see also* finances

Baker, Carol 139
Bambery, Anneke 151
Barber, Andrew 140
Bardo, Pamela Pierrepont 59
Barker, Deborah 78
Barkoczi, Dr Stephen 88
Barquist, David 119
Bartle, Wilmot 131
Batári, Dr Ferenc 119
Batson, Barbara 148
Batson, Whaley 94
Baumgarten, Linda 145
Bean, Atherton and Winifred 46
Beard, Dr Geoffrey vii, *106, 123, 161;* and American Friends 135, 154, 155; Attingham Society Lecture 162; and Hayward Scholarship 162; Phelps Warren Lecture 127–8; and review of plans, ('86) 125, 126; and Summer School 30–1, 94, 95, 97, 102, (Principal Tutor) 105, 110, 113, 114, 118–19, 120–2, (Director) 32, 123, 130, 137, 146, 157, 160: Trust offices 101, 152
Beevers, David 74
Beharrell, Christopher 78
Belknap, Helen R. 29
Bell, Frank 68, 98
Bell, Ruth 31
Bellamy, Michael 103
Benham, Isabel 11, 84, 96, 99, 103, 104
Bergen, Charles S. P. 148
Bergquist, Mary 167
Berkowitz, Roger 69
Berwick, Lady 4, 7, 8, 10, 14, 23, 32, 56–7
Bevan (Meschutt), Sarah 66, 140
Biddle, James 27, 33, 37, 60, 73, 76
Biddle, Louisa 22
Binder, Deborah 102

Binder, Joan 158
Bitter, Thérèse 139
Blackburn, Roderic 142
Blauensteiner, Dr W. 17
Bliss, Mr and Mrs Robert Woods 1
Blofeld, Mr and Mrs T. R. C. 31
Blunt, Anthony 3, 6, 35
Boe, Alf 29
Bohlen, Catherine 23, 81
Boone, Edwin T. P. 23
Borchardt, Susan 158–9
Bostetter, Jeffrey 166
Bostwick, David 119, 168–9
Boughton, Peter 159
Bourne, Susan 108
Bower, A. 4
Boydell, Christine 159
Bracegirdle, Hilary 103
Brady, Lucille 119
Brand, Barbara 78
Brandau, Rosemary 148
Brandt, Beverly 131
Braznell, W. Scott 158
Bremer-David, Charissa 145, 148
Bridgman, Viscountess 17
Brindle, Steven 168, 170
Brinkley, Mark Kent 148, 151, 165; drawings 77, 82,
    150, 208
Britz, Billie 56
Brooks, Bradley 148
Brooks, Mary 148, 151
Brown, Hilary 103
Brown, Michael K. 78
Brown, Peter 108, 139
Browne, Clare 168
Brubaker, Ann 81
Brudenell, Marian 86, 147
Bruel, Sybil 103, 104, 108, 113, 128, 141, 158, 162,
    165
Buchanan, Paul 39
Buckler, James R. 75
Buckley, Yvonne 30
Burgin, Angela 145
Burks, Jean 102
Burrell, Scott F. 158
Burrow, Hugo 9, 22
Burton, Anthony 34
Butler, Joseph T. 33, 167
Butler, Mary 167
Butler, William 87, 98
Button, Richard 48–9

Caffrey, Paul 158
Calderai, Fausto 102–3
Campbell, Alan L. 59, 75, 86, 128, 154, 155
Campbell, Cathryn 148
Campbell, Tom 140
Campbell-Stewart, Desley 160
Cantor, Jay E. 49, 153, 154

Carpenter, Charles and Mary Grace 119
Carr (Whitworth), Caroline 119
Carruthers, Annette 159
Carson, Cary and Barbara 34
Cave, Edward Lee 58–9
Chapel (Hobhouse), Jeannie 69, 83, 94–5
Chapman, Martin 78
Chappell, Edward 119
Chappell, Gordon 166
Chase, Stuart 139
Cherol, John Alan 78
Chesshyre, John 132
Chevalier, Charles 33, 34, 56, 98, 108
Childs, Eloise Mackie ('Missy') 63, 81
Church, Dorian 98, 145
Civetta, Margaret 151
Clark, Carolyn 160
Clark, Deborah 94
Clark, Mark A. 46
Clarke, Alistair 168
Clement, Constance ('Cecie') 158
Clifton Taylor, Alec 19, 22, 28, 52, 69, 86
Clinton, Lisa (Lady White) 74
Coan, Olivia 17
Colcutt, Catherine 168
Collingridge (Gore), Susie 87–8
Colvin, Michael 51
Cooke, Edward S. 78
Cooper, Wendy 56, 145
Cornforth, John L.: offices held 48, 85, 101; and
    Summer School 52, 73, 79, 80, 85
Corsiglia, Christina 81
Corsini, Giorgiana 141
Cottle, Simon 140
Cousens, Belinda 87, 157
Coutts, Howard 140
Cox, Sir Trenchard 31, 32, 47, 48, 85, 87
Crawley, Greer 78
Crowell, Frederick 70, 72, 73, 75
Cummin, Betty Starr 87, 108, 155, 164
Cushion, John 35; and Special Weeks 86, 91, 92–3,
    95; at Summer School 25, 29, 34, 36, 39, 81, 88,
    102
Czechoslovakia, ('89) visit to 160

Da Schio, Contessa Loredano 22, 28, 56, 75, 88
Dane, William J. 78, 161
Dangremond, David 66
Darby, Michael 34
Darr, Alan 94
Dauterman, Carl 17, 37
Davis, Julia 75
Day, Peter 82, 145
de Morini, Mrs J. L. R. 4, 4 facing
Dee, Elaine Evans 81–2, Amer. Friends' Presdt 155,
    162, 165
Dennis, Faith 17
Densmore, Walter 12
Denyer, Susan 94

Desmond, John 37
Devine, Maureen 166–7
Devonshire, Deborah, Duchess of 7, 59, 82, 84, 130, 147
Diana, Prof Desa 39–40
Diestelkamp, Edward 74
Dietz, Ulysses 98, 161
Dillingham, Gaylord 87, 109
Dodge, Elaine 23
Domergue, Robert F. 131, 145
Doneghy, William 31, 59, 86
Donovan, Catherine-Mary 4 facing
Dornsife, Samuel J. 31
Douglas, Mrs Murray 78, 103, 131
Drayton, Cynthia 145
Drury, Martin 88, 90, 116–17, 137, 143, 144
Duckworth, Philip 103
Duncan, Willard 17
Dunkley, Diane 98
Dunlop, Hank 82, 145
Dyson, Mrs D. M. 4

Earle K. Williams, Mrs 51
East European students 28, 33, 56, 59–60, 158
Eatwell, Anne 78
Eckardt (Ledes), Allison M. 78, 155
Edgcumbe, Dr Richard 103, 117, 152
Edwards, Clare 165
Edwards, Jared 165
Ellis, Martin 149, 151
Ellsworth, Linda 150
Elsdon, Judith 147
Elverson, Virginia 59, 60–1
Emery, Ruth 65
Entz, Geza 108
Esler, Jennifer 139
Evans, Laura 150
Evers, Charles 165

Faberman, Hilarie 107
Farrington, Jane 108
Fausel, Alan 139
Fawcett, Jane 30
Fazzano, Mary Louise 87
Federhen, Deborah 119
Feldblum, Hortense 31, 34, 39, 56, 63, 86; funds scholarships 32, 72
Fennimore, Donald 119
Fillos, Debra 139
finances: ('50s) 14–16, 17–18, 21; ('60s) 22, 32, 33, 35–6; ('69–70) discussions leading to setting up of Trust 41–2, 42–3, 44–5; ('70s) 47, 52, 53, 57, 73, 79, 80, 83; ('80s) 84, 88–90, 99–101, 105, 122, 124, 129, 134–5, 136, 141–2; ('89–90) 154–5, 163; ('91) 163; American Friends and 79, 96, 141, 154–5; capital fund 90, 124, 141, 143, 163; exchange rates 96, 99, 100, 141–2, 163; fees to staff 33, 67, 84, 88, 89–90, 99, 100, 124, 141; see also under: Special Weeks; Study Weeks

Fischer-Hansen, Anne-Sophie 132
Fitch, James 31, 60
Fitzgerald, Desmond (Knight of Glin) 30
Fleischmann, Charles 94
Flynt, Henry N. 12
Fogelman, Peggy 166
Forbes, H. A. Crosby 82
Ford, Sir Brinsley 85, 105–6, 116, 137
Forsyth, Alastair 151
Forsyth, George H, Jr. 4
Fox-Robinson (Collard), Frances 78
Francis, Ross 131
Frankl, Dr. Gyorgy 103
Frederick, Anthony 85, 148
Freeman, David 98, 109, 142, 161
Frelinghuysen, Mrs Frederick 34, 37, 72
Frey, Gordon 159
Frith, Stephen 139
Fuggles, John 98, 109, 117, 124, 152
Fusco, Laurie 94
Fusco, Peter 94, 166
Futter (Scoggin), Catherine 139

Gage, Deborah 102, 135
Galliers-Pratt, Anthony M. G. 41; appointed Trust Chm 43, 79, 88; and finance 15, 41, 44, 52, 79, 125; host to Summer Schools 51, 52, 70, 80, 88, 101; setting up of Trust 42, 43, 44
Galliers-Pratt, Nigel 51
Gant, Sally 131
Gardner, Paul 69, 75
Garfield, Irvin (Terry) 107
Garlick, Dr Kenneth 47, 48, 73
Gary, Grace 107
Geiger, Maureen Cassidy 107
George, Andrea 94
Gibbs, Julian 74, 87
Gibbs, Patricia 102
Giffen (Nylander), Jane 46
Gilligan, Lorraine 107
Gladding, Prof Hope 17, 21, 37
Glazer, George 145, 167, 169
Goheen, Ellen 59
Goodison, Judith, Lady 145, 146, 152, 156, joint Direc. Study Week 163–4
Goodwin, Mary 108
Gore, F. St John 33, 47, 48, 85, 101
Göres, Dr Burkhardt 167
Gorman, Joan 74
Goss, Peter 59
Goyne (Evans), Nancy 29
Grabowska, Dr Irene 59
Grafton, Hugh, Duke of 59, 84
Graham, Clare 159
Graham, John N. II 4, 4 facing
Graham, William 98
Gratkowska-Ratynska, Barbara 119
Gray, Richard 98, 151
Gray, Sabele 148

Green, Paul 109, 111
Greenlaw, Barry 46
Greenspan, Dr Taube 167
Greg, Andrew 108
Grier, Harry 17, 21, 25, 26–7, 28, 33–4, 52; death
    56; Scholarship 58, 59, 66, 72
Grier, Katherine C. ('Kasey') 148, 160
Griffith, Lee Ellen 158
Gristede, Amy 63
Griswold, Tracy Haight 63
Groff, Sibyl McCormac 58, 59, 63, 84, 96, 99, 109,
    134
Grout, Stephen 139–40
Guffin, Robert 140
Guilding, Ruth 140, 168
Guinness, Hon. Desmond 20, 46, 48
Gusler, Elizabeth 107, 111
Gwilliam, Willard 15, 20, 34, 102, 140, 165

Hackley, Martha 46
Hafertepe, Kenneth 102
Hall, Elizabeth 14
Halloran, Dennis 112
Hamilton (Young), Chloë 22
Hamilton, Helen D. 63, 88, 103
Hamilton, Miriam 119
Hammell, Peter 131, 158
Hammell, Rebecca 158
Hammond, Barbara 131
Hammond, Charles 69
Hamran, Mrs R. 33
Hanks, David 29, 56
Hardy, John 34, 46, 95, 107, 117, 122, 136
Hargrove, June E. 158
Harper Adams Agric. Coll., Salop 98, 101
Harrington, Prof James 66
Hart, Avril 46
Hartley, Christopher 108, 118
Harvard, Ralph 118, 119–20, 145
Harwood, Elain 132
Hastings, Lynne 140
Haupt, Frederick III 46
Hawk, Judith 66
Haworth, Jeffrey 94
Hayden, Philip 159
Hayward, Helena 36–7, 36, 40, 106; Attingham
    Society Lecture 110, 162; career 36–7; National
    Art Collections Fund Achievement Award 162;
    offices 33, 47, 48, 83, 87; and planning reviews 90,
    126; Scholarship 162, 165; and Sponsors' Week 83;
    directs Study Weeks 111, 113, 122, 128, 136,
    146–7, 151–2, 157, 163–4; and Summer School
    16, 18, 28, 29, 32, 34, 36, 39, 40–1, 43, 78, 80,
    102, 156, 161, (Joint Director) 37, 48, 56, 57,
    61–3, (sole Director) 32, 37, 65, 67, 74, 88, 102,
    (Consultant Director) 96, 103, 105, 110; visits to
    New York 104, 113, 154
Hayward, John 24, 36–7, 48, 59, 88, 101, 102–3; as
    tutor 18, 28, 29, 86, 95

Hecht, Joanna 46
Heckscher, Morrison H. 31, 84, 93, 103, 110, 154;
    American Friends' President 90, 98, 103, 115
Heiberger, Barbara 108
Hejdowa, Dr Dagmar 128
Held, Huyler C. 78, 81, 84, 109, 155
Hennessy, James 159
Henoch, Hanley 4, 4 facing, 8, 22
Herald, Jacqueline 168
Hermanson, John 151
Hern, Mary Ellen 131–2
Hewitt, Mark 82
Hickman, William 132
Hiesinger, Kathryn 59
Hillman, Ernest, Jr. 17, 25, 26, 27, 51, 54, 59
Hirschkowitz, Jane 140
Hirschman, Lillian 75, 86
Hirst, Nancy 78, photos by, 36, 171
Hjeld, Gunnar 59
Hodges, Jeanne Butler 67
Hojer, Gerhard 29
Holland, Hillman 94
Hollenberg, David 66
Homer, Abigail 102
Hood, Graham 128
Hopping, Daniel 4, 4 facing, 7, 8, 27
Hopstock, Carsten 22
Houston, Ann ('Shep') 102
Howard, Jeremy 147
Howe (Newton), Gertrude D. 17
Howell, Margize 107
Hughes, Gareth 168
Hunt, Tiffany 87
Hurley, Patricia 74, 98
Hurst, Ronald 119
Hurt, Jethro, III 98
Hutton, William 21

Igleheart, Elizabeth 140
Iliff, Nancy 140
Irvin, Hilary 166
Iverson, Richard 148, 151

Jackson, Lesley 151
Jackson, Ruth 56, 75
Jackson-Stops, Gervase 46, 109, 162; and Summer
    School 106, 116, 122, 145, 147
Jacobs, Miss R. M. 4
Janinck, Clare 28
Jasik, Jan 140
Jayne, Thomas 87, 98
Jennings, J. L. Sibley, Jr. 40, 102
Johnson, David T. 158
Johnson, J. Stewart 75; American Friends' offices 37,
    73, 155, (President) 76, 79, 84, 90; at Summer
    School 29, 80, 82, 147, 158
Johnston, Phillip 63
Jones, Lawrence 132

Jongbloed, Pieter 168
Jonge, Dr. C. H. De 11
Jordan, Harriet *108*
Joyce, Henry 66, 167
Joyce, Robert 140

Kaellgren, Peter 140
Kahn, Margaret ('Peggy') 27, 33, 34
Kalnein, Dr Graf 17
Kane, Patricia 158, 167
Kaplan, Alice 46; Scholarship 52, 159
Kaplan, Wendy 87
Karpinski, Miss 29
Katzenbach, William E. 27, 36
Kavli, G. 14
Kearns, Richard 159
Kearns, Sarah Latham 109, *153*, 154, 159
Keith, David 29
Kelenyi, Dr George 56
Kennan, Ann 75
Kennedy, Robert C. 28, 33, 37, 56, 59
Kesner, Dr Ladislav 158
Kestner, Clyde 159
Kinchin, Juliet 87
King, Caroline 148
Kinghorn, Jonathan 66, 132
Kisluk-Grosheide, Daniella 119
Knap, Dr Johan 46
Knox (Abel-Smith), Lucy *95*; and Summer School 83,
    88, 95, 102, 114, 117; Chairman of Attingham
    Society 109, 113, 160
Koch, Lisa 29, 75, 155, 159
Koeper, H. F. 4, *4 facing*
Kohls, Ann 158
Koldeweij, Eloy 151
Kopecna, Jaroslava 103
Kotalik, Jiri 78, 167
Kotalikova, Jana 167, 169
Kraak, Deborah 166
Krieger, Lisa 159
Kruzio-Uchytil, Dr Vera 34
Kuchna, Jayne 159
Kusserow, Karl 159

La Marche, Bonita 148
Ladovic, Vanda 46
Lahikainen, Dean 158
Lahikainen, Elizabeth 158, 164
Lambert, Miles 159
Lane, Joshua 140
Lane, Mills B. 140
Lanier, Mildred 28
Larsen, Carter 102
Larsen, Diana 132
Larson, John 63, 148
Latham (Kearns), Sarah T. 109, *153*, 154, 159
Latimer (Taylor), Clare 119
Laurent, Elizabeth 166

Laurie, Kedrun 94
Lawson, Elizabeth ('Jo') 140
Lawson, Major Nicholas, MVO 103
Le Corbeiller, Clare 17, 99, 109, 124
Leary, Emmeline 140
Ledes, Allison 78, 155
Legget, Jane 82
Leisenring, Julia 145
Lentz, Lamar 167
Leven, Arline Popper 75
Leviner (Hyman), Betty 132
Levitt (Allen), Sarah 119, 138
Levkoff, Alice 69, 75
Levra, Raymond 75
Lewis, John vii; apptd Trust Chm *143*, 144, 147; and
    finance 96, 99, 125, 141, 154; revises Rules 90;
    and scholarships 83, 87; at Summer School 82, 87,
    148
Libby, Valencia 98
Lindsey, Jack 131
Lippert, Catherine 74
Little, Bertram 21, 37, 57
Lloyd Williams, Bron 4 *facing*
Lo Nano, Ernest 4, *4 facing*
Loeblein, Christopher 140
Loftus, Mildred 39
Lomax, James 87, 139, 161
Lomax-Simpson, Rosemary 52, *58*, 59, 81, 113, 158;
    Course Administrator 52, 56, 57, 61–3, 67, 79, 88,
    95, 102, 110; retirement 113, 119–20, 135
Lounsbury, Carl 111
Lowell Cummings, Abbot 11
Lowenthal, Helen *4 facing, 13, 30, 40, 171*; and
    American Friends 70–1, 71–2, 77; on Attingham
    ethos 170–1; career 30, 31, 35, 43, 65, 87, 136–7;
    80th birthday 92; on H. Hayward 43, 57; honours
    43, 136–7; lecture recorded 2, 137; on L. Powel
    68–9; Scholarship 49, *153*, 154; and Special Weeks
    77, 80, 86, 88, 91, 95, 109; at Study Week, ('86)
    122; and Summer School ('50s) 1, 2, 4, 6, 9, 10,
    12, 14, 16, 19, 20, ('60s) 22, 33, 40, 41–2, ('70s)
    48, 52, 61–3, 65, 70, 73–4, ('80s) 2, 113, 116,
    125, 137; and Trust 42–3, 88; on P. Warren 105;
    and Winter Week 124
Lucas, Clive 108
Luck, Barbara Rose 59
Luck, Robert 33, 37, 59
Luniewicz-Koper, Danuta 141
Lytle, Sarah 148

Machell, Margaret Schuyler 75
Macht, Dr Carol 59
Mack, Prof Maynard 39
Mackay, Robert 63
Maddison, Dr John 103, 139, 157
Madsen, Dr Stephan Tschudi 46
Mailey, Jean Elizabeth 59
Majewska-Maszkowska, Dr Bozenna 50
Mancoff, Debra 82

Manningham-Buller (Parsons), Anne 82
Marincola, Michele 108
Maros, Szilvia 158
Marsden, Christopher 151
Marsh, Melissa 132
Masarykova, Dr Anna 39
Mason, Pippa 157
Massie (Hunting), Mary Anne 151
Masson, Frank Walker 74
Matero, Frank 102
Matheu, Christine 148
Maverick, Edward 4, 4 *facing*, 7, 8, 22, 24, 34;
    Scholarship 81, 87
Maxfield, David 107, 109
Mayor, Alfred 59, 73
McCall, Davy H. 167
McClanahan, Pauli 76, 78, 84, 88, 159
McFadden, David 59
McFadden, Dennis 66
McKean, Maggie 168, 169
McKendry, Jennifer 140
McKinney, David D. 140
McKinsey, Kristan 148
McNaught, William P. ('Bill') 46, 99, Amer. Friends'
    Presdt *115*, 117, 147–8, 155, 158
McVerry, John 159
Meadows, Christine 112
Medlam, Sarah 78
Meehan, Kathryn 102
Meeks, Prof Carroll 24
Mees, David 158
Megarity, Ferris 76, 84, 99, 104; at Summer School
    34, 39, 59, 63
Mehlman, Robert 158
Meighan, Melissa 119
Mellor, Hugh 82
Meschutt, David 66, 140
Metcalf, Pauline C. 31, 56, 75, *153*, 154
Michelson, Elizabeth 151
Michie, Audrey 78, 145
Michie, Thomas 87
Miele, Christopher 167
Milburn, Catherine 159
Milhender, Richard 87, 98, 109, 111, 145, 164
Miller, Lee Hunt 107
Miller, V. Isabelle 17
Miners, John 119
Mist, Vonny de 83
Mitchell, Louise 151
Mladinov, Dubravka 40
Mojzer, Miklos 69
Monkhouse, Christopher 31, 58, *153*, 154, 155; on
    Phelps Warren 27, 105, 109
Montgomery, Charles F. 4, 4 *facing*
Montgomery, Florence 4, 4 *facing*, 86, 145
Moore, Margaret 148
Moore, Melodye 159
Moore, Prof Robert 37, 59
Moreno (Seiler), Melissa ('Molly') 131, 165
Morra, Marisa 166

Morris, Leslie 132, 166
Morrison, Lindsay 74
Mortimer, Sarah 22
Mosca, Matthew 74
Moyer, Roy 46
Munger, Jeffrey 78, 166
Murray, Simon 168
Murtagh, Dr William 37, 51
Musgrave, Clifford 32, 40, 46, 101; offices 47, 48, 53,
    59

Naeve, Milo 39
Nagel, Charles 17, 21
Nathans, David 84
National Trust: and Attingham Trust 125, 126, 137;
    scholarships 69, 87, 94, 132, 140, 159, 168; and
    Summer Schools 9, 11, 14–15, 18, 31, 35–6, 73
Nelson, George A. 60, 73
Nelson, Richard 154
Nes, Jane Pumphrey 164
Neudorfer, William 102
Newell, Susan 132
Nichols, Dr Frederick 165
Nichols, Sarah 103, 139, 161
Nickels, Edward 140
Nicoll, Jessica 166
Norman, Catherine *114*, *149*, 151, 154; course
    planning 130, 145, 146, 156
Norman, Stacia 166
Norway, visits to 46–7
Noyes, Clarabel ('Chinx') 102
Nutting, Diane 106–7, 147
Nylander, Richard 158

O'Brien, Barbara 112
O'Connor, Kathleen 167
Odell (Walker), Susan 148
Osborne, Vals 132
Ostergard, Derek E. 119

Packer, Nancy 151
Pallrand, Stephen 87
Palmer, Hon. Anthea 119
Palmer (Schwind), Arlene 59
Panhorst, Elizabeth 132, 166
Papert, Emma 29
Pappas, Nicholas 63, 67, 75, 81, 98, 112
Paris Study Week 134, 152, 163–4
Parker, James 13
Parker, Thomas 69, 75
Parmal, Pamela 159
Parry, Mary 29, 34
Parsons, Merribell 39, 46, 75
Parvis, Paul 107, 161–2
Paterson, Miss N. 4, 4 *facing*
Pearce, John 37
Pearman, Michael 78, 82

Perkins (Roberts), Isabel ('Beau') 108
Peterson, Karin 74, 86, 145, 161–2
Petrescu, Dr Paul 61
Pettigrew, David 46, 73, 75, 84, 104
Pevsner, Prof Sir Nikolaus 6, 24, 48, 59, 101; at Summer Schools 6, 12, 19, 32, 43, 51–2, 56
Pierson, William 12, 21
Pittman, Sue 132
Plakins (Thornton), Tamara 66
Platou, Joanne 82
Platts, Stuart L. 81, 82, 87
Plimpton, Russell A. 12, 17, 21
Podmaniczky, Michael 148
Pond, Jeffry 108, 166
Poston, Jonathan 119
Powel, Lydia Bond 4 *facing*, 5; American Friends' offices 27, 29, 33, 34, 37; death and tributes 68–9; and summer schools 11, 14, 17, 21, 22, 23, 24, 28, 34, 46, 68
Powel, Mrs Hope Hare (*later* Harkness) 4, 4 *facing*, 7, 8, 68–9
Powell, Miss N. 4
Powers, Emma Lou 151
Preiss, Dr Pavel 132
Prékopa, Agnes 167–8
Priddy, Sumpter 119
Prince, Geraldine 148, 150
Prosser, Deborah 150
Puig, Francis ('Bill') 74, 158
Pulmanova, Olga 29, 33
Putnam, Mildred 29–30

Rabun, Marc 151
Radcliffe, Wanda 86
Radnor, Helen, Dowager Countess of 53, 58
Rath, Frederick 4, 12
Rathbone, J. F. W. 1, 6, 31
Rau, Deborah Fulton 140
Ravitch, Gloria 87, 137
Rawa-Szubert, Anna 148
Ray, Prof Lawrence 63, 145
Raynesford (Boyd), Julia 51
Redlon, Richard 166
Redmill, John 74
Reese, David 98, 128
Richards, Nancy G. 31, 119
Richardson, Thom 119
Rimell, Caroline *164*
Rimer, Graeme 132
Robb, David 69
Roberts, Barbara 46
Robertson, Barbara 11
Robertson, Cheryl 140
Roda, Dr Burkard von 141
Rogers (Sharpe), Phillis 63, 66, 69, 122
Rooke, Daru 151
Roosevelt, Priscilla 150
Rorschach, Kimerly 82, 128, 166
Rosenberg, Harvey 139, 140

Rosenblum, Martin Jay 66
Rosenblum, Stewart 102
Rosenthal, David 56
Rosoman, Treve 132, 145
Ross, Prof Marion Dean 13
Rötter, Dr G. 28
Rowell, Christopher 69, 73, 137
Rowlett, Margaret 30
Rowley, Sir Joshua: and Summer Schools 6, 7, 8, 9, 10, 12, 29, 30, (establishment) 1–2, (finances) 14, 15, 16
Rumford, Beatrix 46
Rust, David 22, 59, 63
Ryder, Mrs K. W. 23

Saitas, Stephen 140, 154
Salmons, Carl 166
Samter (Hollenberg), Linda 66
Samuel, Miss W. Graham 4, 4 *facing*
Sanchis, Frank 82
Sander, Penny 108
Sands, Patricia 102
Sargent, William R. 102, 166
Sartor, Caroline 94
Sassoon, Adrian 108, 130
Savage, Charles C. 54, 56, *153*, 154
Savage, J. Thomas 82, 128
Savill, Rosalind 83, 88, *90*, 162; at Summer School 63, 66, 69, 95, 130
Sawyer, Charles 13, 21, 37, 60
Scharmer, Roger 59
Schoeser, Mary 131, 132, 164
Scholle, Hardinge 4, 4 *facing*, 23
Schwartz, Marvin 17
Schwartz (Warren), Arete 66
Scott, Gary 113
Secondo, Joellen 140
Seiden, Melvin 72
Seifertova, Hana 151
Sesoko, Tsune 74
Sewell, Darrel 74
Shackleford, George Green 112
Shadel (Spillman), Jane 33, 46
Sharkey, Anne J. 71; and American Friends 33, 57, 71–2, 73, 85–6; at Summer School 48, 59, 63, 75
Sharmany (Parsons), Ilona 63
Sharples, Joseph 168
Sheeran, John 103, 117
Shellenberger, Barbara 132
Shifrin, Susan 166
Shinn, Deborah 78
Shrigley, Ruth 132
Shropshire County Council 9, 11, 21, 42–3, 44–5; *see also* Attingham Park
Shrub, Derek 30
Simkova, Dr Gabriela 108
Simmons, Lady 29, 34
Simpson, Marc 82
Sisa, Jozsef 103

Skerry, Janine 159
Skjelver, Ruth 59
Slavicek, Lutomiv 94
Slavin, Richard 63
Sly, Elizabeth 30
Smith, Helen 168
Smith, Margaret ('Megan') 166
Smith, Molly K. 119
Smith, Murphy 22
Snow (Delaney), Barbara 4, 4 *facing*, 7, 37
Snyder, Clyde C, Jr. 52, 56, 63, 67, 73
Solomon, Philip 46
Sommer, Prof Frank 4, 4 *facing*
Somorjay, Selesette 132
Spang, J. Peter 158
Special Weeks: setting up 90–2; ('82) 92–3; ('83) 97, 98; ('84) 105; ('85) 108–9, 112; finances 80, 84, 92–3, 96, 97, 99, 105, 110–11, 141
Spencer, Katherine 94
Spitzmüller, Anna 28
Sprigg, June 119
Springer (Roberts), Lynn E. 46, 51, 59, 63
Standen, Edith 99, 109, 128, 156; offices 21, 25, 27, 73; at Summer School 17, 18, 23, 24
Stanicic, Stanislav 33
Stapleton, Ian 108
Stayton, Kevin 98, 115
Stearns, Margaret 22, 24, 59, 63, 73
Stepan, Carl 148, 150
Stevens, Letitia 159
Stevenson, Sylvia 77, 80, 86, 91–3, 97, 105
Stewart, Janet 167
Stirling, Alexander ('Sandy') 88, *89*; apptd Trust Chm 90, 142–3, 144; and American Friends 96, 113, 115, 135, 141; planning reviews 97, 124–5, 141
Stirling, Mary 105, *109*, 111, 113, 122, 128, 143
Stockwell, David and Em. 4, 4 *facing*, 86
Stokes, Jayne 159
Stoklasa, Dr Jarek 88
Stone, May N. 99
Stote, Sally Lawson 51
Stote, Sheila Lawson 29, 32, 34, 51
Stover, Donald 69
Straeten, Judith 140
Strauss, Jane 78
Strauss, Linda 108, 166
Strauss, Monica 108
Stritzer, Nina 131
Strong, Sir Roy 87
Stuart, Carola 78
Stubbs, Jane 140
Stubbs, John 140
Study Day, ('90) 161
Study Weekends, ('89) and ('90) 161
Study Weeks 111; ('86) 110, 113, 114, 115, 122; ('87) 128, 129, 135; ('88) 122, 135–6; ('89) 146–7, 163; ('90) 151–2, 156, *157*, 163; ('91), Paris 134, 163–4; finances 122, 129, 135, 136, 141, 163
Summer Schools: ('52) 1–8; ('53) 8–11; ('54) 11; ('55) 12–14; ('56) 17–18; ('57) 19; ('58) 19; ('59) 19–21;

('60) 21–2; ('61) 23; ('62) 23–4, 48; ('63) 27–8; ('64) 28–9; ('65) 29–30; ('66) 30–1; ('67) 32–3; ('68) 34–5; ('69) 38–40, 47; ('70) 46, 47; ('71) 48–52; ('72) 56; ('73) 57–9; ('74) 60–1; ('75) 63; ('76) 66–7; ('77) 69–70; ('78) 72–6; ('79) 77–9; ('80) 80–3; ('81) 86–8; ('82) 94–5; ('83) 97–8; ('84) 101–3; ('85) 105–9; ('86) 113, 114, 115, 116–22; ('87) 129–32, 164–5, (questionnaire) 132–4; ('88) 137–41, 165; ('89) 147–51, 163, 165; ('90) 154, 156–60, 163, 165; ('91) 165–70
Summerson, Sir John 48, 54, 59, 85; at Summer School 6, 8, 10, 11, 13, 19, 28, 32, 43, 51, 57–8
Swan, Susan 94, 145
Swank, Scott T. 150
Sweeney, John 22, 28, 37
Sydnor, Lucy 39, 86, 99, 103, 111
Sykas, Philip 140
Szabolsci, Dr Hedvig 59

Tabb, Maria 112
Tackett, John 166
Taggart, Ross 56
Terrace (Koch), Lisa 29, 75, 155, 158
Theus, Charlton M, Jr. 33, 86
Third Weeks: ('56) 17; ('58) 19; ('59) 19–20; ('60) 21–2; ('61) 23; ('62) 24; ('63) 27–8; ('64) 28, 29; ('65) 29–30; ('66) 30, 31; ('68) 34–5; ('69) 39–40; ('70) 46; ('71) 48, 51; ('72) 54; ('73) 57; ('74) 60, 62; ('75) 63, 65; ('76) 66–7;. ('78) 73, 75–6; ('80) 80; ('87) 130–1; numbers too great 31, 41, 57, 58, 76, 80; scholarship funded by ('69) 40; value 62, 80; *see also* Special Weeks
Thomen, Lydia 108
Thomerson, Carole 145
Thompson, Eleanor 63
Thompson, Francis 6, 7, 82
Thompson, Glenn 39
Thompson, Nicholas 82, 110
Thornton, Jonathan 66, 98, 106
Thuillier, William 53, 57, 59
Tibbles, Anthony 94
Tichelin, Isabelle van 158
Tickell, Simon 131, 166
Tillotson, John; Chairman of Committee 21, 22, 27, 30, 31, 35, 41; and Trust 43, 47
Tindale, Christine 82
Tomlin, Maurice 28, 30
Toms, Geoffrey 40; Deputy Warden of Attingham 34, 36, 39, 40; Warden 47, 48, 52; Joint Asst Director 48, 59, 63
Toorn, Miss Van Der 11
Townsend, Gretchen 167
Toy, Ann 108
Tracy, Berry 51
Treuherz, Julian 103, 168
Trevelyan, Sir George, Bt. 4 *facing*, 10, 13, *53*, *169*, *171*; career 53–4; and H. Lowenthal's tape 137; on Lady Berwick 56–7; Patron 59; retirement 47, 48, 52, 54; and Summer School 2, 4, 6, 9, 11, 12, 14,

19, 22, 32, 39, 131, *169*, 170; at Thirtieth
Anniversary 86
Trevelyan, Helen, Lady 4, *4 facing*, 6, 14
Trimble, Mildred 34
Truman, Charles 69, 80, 83, 97
Trusted, Marjorie 132
Tschirch, John 159
Tucker, Elizabeth 87
Turner, Louise B. 94
Turner, Prof Suzanne 78

Valk, Margaret S. 22, 30, 34
Van Derpool, James Grote 4, *4 facing*, 7, 8, 21, 37
Van Derpool, Peggy *4 facing*
Van Ingen, Anne 119
Varian, Elayne 23, 25, 26, 33
Varian, John 23, 25, 26, 27, 33, 37, 52
Venable, Charles 159
Verspyck, Rudolph 81, 87
Vibert (Sloane), Jeanne 98
Vickers, Jonathan 69, 81, 87
Vilimkova, Milada 46
Vincent, Clare 28
Vincent, Gilbert 108
Vincent, Giles Newby 119
Vinson, Vicki 140

Wagenvoord, Mrs James 28
Wainwright, Clive 33, 162
Waite, James 46
Walker, Mavis 137
Walker, Stefanie 165
Wall, Charles 11, 21, 37–8
Wall, Christopher 15, 20, 21, 22
Walsh, Breffny 108
Warren, David B. 39, 46
Warren, Phelps 26, 27, *40*; and American National
Trust support 72, 76; Chairman Emeritus 84, 86,
99, 103; death 98, 105, 109; and finance 67; *Irish
Glass* 27, 33; memorials 98, 165, (Lecture) 109,
127–8, 135, 162; Patron, Attingham Trust 84;
retires as President 76–7, 79; and setting up of
Trust 41–2, 43; and slide library 48; 'Some
Historical Notes' 26–7, 76; and Summer School
23, 28, 29, 31, 34, 36, 46, 51, 62–3, 67; tribute to
L. Powel 68
Waterfield, Giles 74–5, 83, 103, 124
Waters, Deborah Dependahl 63
Watland, Gerald R. W. 28, 72
Watson, Sir Francis 6, 10, 11, 19, 23, 28
Weaver, O. J. 14
Wellicome, Lavinia 119–20, 147
Wenger, Mark J. 82, 102, 111

West Dean College, Sussex 2, *70*, 101, 105, 115, 137,
151
Westman, Annabel 85, 86, *106*; on Scholarship
Committee 81, 83; Secretary to Trust 86, 90, 143;
and Summer School 69, 95, 102, 109, 110, 115,
146, 151, 157, 166, (Assistant to the Director) 86,
88, (tutor) 83, 86, 126–7, 130, 137–8; and Winter
Week 145
Westman, Tim 110, 115, 151
Westwood, Rosalind 140–1
Whiffen, Marcus 4, *4 facing*
Whitelaw, Patti Foos 29, 59, 75
Whitman (Kinghorn), Susanna 66, 131, 132
Whitney, William 161
Whitworth, Roger 151
Wilk, Christopher 74, 98, 128, 164
Williams, Helen *24*
Williams, Mrs Earle Kress 22, 29
Williams, Patricia Eileen 66
Wilson, Elizabeth 59
Wilson, Gillian 33, 166
Wilson, John 82
Wilson, Timothy 132
Wilton-Ely, Prof John 101, *107*, 113, 125–6, 162;
Director of Studies 105, 110, 113, 114, 117,
118–19, 122–3
Winslow, Enid 48
Winter Week, ('89) 134, *144*, 145
Wittgenstein, Dr Franz Sayn 14
Wittmann, Otto 22, 28, 73
Wolfe, Kevin 166
Wood, Ann 148
Wood, Charles III and Elizabeth 31
Wood, David 158
Wood, Lucy 141
Wood, Mrs Neal S. (Josephine) 59–60, 63, 101
Wood, Pamela 108
Woodhouse, Dr Anne F. 157
Wragg, Tom 6, 30, 82
Wright, Caroline 72
Wriston, Barbara 9–10, 21, 28, 38, 99, 109
Wyatt, Robin 159

Yetter, George 159
Youngblood, Patrick 87

Zador, Dr Anna 28
Zakariás, János 141
Zelleke, Ghenete 98
Ziegler, Ruth 63
Zikova, Eva 82–3
Zimet, Henry 102
Zimmerman, Philip 69
Zrebiec, Alice 132, 145